Speak for Yourself

Also by Angus Calder

RUSSIA DISCOVERED: NINETEENTH-CENTURY FICTION FROM PUSHKIN TO CHEKHOV

THE PEOPLE'S WAR

REVOLUTIONARY EMPIRE: THE RISE OF THE ENGLISH-SPEAKING EMPIRES FROM THE FIFTEENTH CENTURY TO THE 1780S

Speak for Yourself

A Mass-Observation Anthology, 1937–49

Edited by
ANGUS CALDER & DOROTHY SHERIDAN

JONATHAN CAPE
THIRTY BEDFORD SQUARE LONDON

First published 1984

Jonathan Cape Ltd,
30 Bedford Square, London WC1

British Library Cataloguing in Publication Data
Speak for yourself: a Mass-Observation anthology, 1937–1949.
1. World War, 1939–1945 – Great Britain – Sources
2. Great Britain – Social life and customs — 20th century – Sources
I. Calder, Angus II. Sheridan, Dorothy
941.084′08 DA566.4

ISBN 0-224-02102-8

Typeset by Computape (Pickering) Ltd, North Yorkshire
Printed in Great Britain by Mackays of Chatham Ltd

Contents

Illustrations

PLATES

between pages 52 and 53

between pages 84 and 85

between pages 132 and 133

between pages 180 and 181

FIGURES

Acknowledgments

We owe thanks to more people, ex-Mass-Observers and others, than can be listed here. Angus Calder is very grateful to the Leverhulme Trustees for a Research Award in 1979, and the Arts Faculty of the Open University for its financial assistance thereafter. Amongst several former Observers whom he has interviewed, it seems not invidious to single out Charles Madge, one of the founders, for his courteous help, and Mollie Tarrant, a later full-timer, for her enthusiastic interest – but this does not imply that others have not been helpful and enthusiastic!

Angus Calder and Dorothy Sheridan owe special debts to Nick Stanley, author of an admirable doctoral thesis on M-O, and to Julie Helm. We should also like to thank Professor David Pocock, Director of the Archive and, of course, the Archive's trustees, Professor Lord Asa Briggs, James Fulton, CMG, and Henry Novy.

For permission to reproduce copyright illustrations we are grateful to the following: Godfrey Argent Ltd, no. 12; BBC Hulton Picture Library, no. 11 (e) and (f); the *Daily Mirror*/Syndication International Ltd, no. 11 (a), 'Jane'; the Controller of Her Majesty's Stationery Office (Crown copyright), no. 13; Hutchinson Publishing Group Ltd, *Nude Ego* by Roye, 1955, no. 11 (c); Mary Lou Jennings/British Film Institute, no. 10; the Trustees of the National Gallery, no. 11 (b), by Roger Van Der Weyden; the Estate of Mervyn Peake, no. 8; Humphrey Spender, nos 1, 2, 3, 4, 6, 7 and 9 (nos 1, 2, 3, 4, 6 and 7 are part of his 'Worktown' collection and nos 6 and 7 are taken from *Worktown People*, Falling Wall Press, Bristol); the Tate Gallery, no. 11 (d), 'Bath of Psyche'; Julian Trevelyan, no. 5 and Michael Wickham, no. 15. The remaining photographs are from the collection of the Tom Harrisson Mass-Observation Archive at Sussex University.

For illustrations appearing in the text we would like to thank the following: *Daily Mirror*/Syndication International Ltd, no. 2; Marion Dewhirst/*Everybody*, no. 1; Eric Frazer, F.S.I.A.D./*Radio Times*, no. 3; the Illustrated London News Picture Library, no. 4 and Thomson Organisation Plc/*Sunday Graphic*, no. 5.

Extracts are reproduced by kind permission of: Hutchinson Publishing Group Ltd, 'The Tube Dwellers', from *The Saturday Book*, October 1943, pp. 101–7; Illustrated Newspapers Group, 'Who'll Win?' by Tom Harrisson, *Political Quarterly*, Vol. 15, 1944, pp. 210–19; Penguin Books Ltd, extracts written by Charles Madge and Tom Harrisson taken from *Britain by Mass-Observation* (Penguin Special 1939, pp. 139–84), pp. 65–72; and Syndication International Ltd, 'What is a Pin-Up Girl?', from *Picture Post*, 23rd September 1944, pp. 144–7.

I

Introduction

This anthology is drawn from the Tom Harrisson Mass-Observation Archive at the University of Sussex, which holds an extraordinary range of material collected in the period 1937–49, when Britain underwent war and, as some thought, 'social revolution'. We have tried to represent that range, though to do so fully would require a selection five or ten times as large as this.

The great 'events' of the period – mass unemployment, the blitz, Churchill's defeat in 1945 – were covered by Mass-Observation's social researchers, using a wide variety of methods which we shall explain as we go along. (Again, we have tried to represent that variety.) But a passionate concern for 'trifles' unconsidered by others, for the sights and sounds and smells of ordinary life going on irrespective of politicians and generals, marked Mass-Observation's founders. And so, in about 1938 they came upon the incident captured in the first of our selections, which we introduce to you as 'The Bolton tortoise'.

1. Full-time Observer: The Bolton tortoise, c. 1937

DOG AND PARTRIDGE LOUNGE (BOLTON) THURSDAY, 27 MAY

Three women, seven men: All regulars, speaking to each other, mostly market people.

Large, tough guy with masses of hair held down by a hairnet sits at table with group of four (one woman), puts his head in his hands and complains of being tired. They talk about trade being bad. Hairnet suddenly takes a small live tortoise out of his overcoat pocket and threatens woman with it. She screams a little.

'What do you feed it on?' someone asks.

'Milk.'

'How much?'

A quiet thin man in bowler sitting in another group leans forward and says quickly, 'Quart and a half.'

Hairnet says, 'I give it a saucer full on Sunday.'

Woman asks how old is it.

'Only 36.'

Conversation goes on about how you can't drown tortoises or suffocate them, only way to kill them is to cut off their heads. 'But you can't get at their head.'

That 'observation' was probably the work of John Sommerfield, who led the special investigation into pubs and drinking which was conducted by Mass-Observation's 'Worktown' team in 1937–9. This was part of a would-be comprehensive survey of life in a northern industrial town. Four 'Worktown' books were on the stocks when war began in 1939. *The Pub and the People* was already in proof, and was finally published (by Gollancz) in 1943, reprinted (by Seven Dials Press) in 1970. But only manuscript drafts remain of three other volumes, which were 'more ambitious and extensive' in the opinion of Mass-Observation's founder, Tom Harrisson – these were to cover 'politics and the non-voter', 'the religious life of "Worktown"', and 'that tremendous climax of the industrial year, the week's holiday in Blackpool' (*The Pub and the People*, pp 8–9).

Introducing the book, Harrisson claimed that it 'spoke for itself'. We would like to make the same claim for the material which we have gathered in this book. When we found 'hairnet' and his shell-clad companion lurking in one of the 'Worktown' boxes of raw material now stored in the Mass-Observation Archive at the University of Sussex, we laughed more like scriptwriters hitting on a good gag than like scholar and archivist engaged in research. And there's lots of other material like that – incidents from the everyday life of forty or thirty-odd years ago suddenly pounce from faded manuscript pages, too inconspicuous to have reached the newspapers, more vivid (and vouched for) than memory. John Sommerfield was a novelist, and the vivacity of this item may owe something to his eye for character and his ear for dialogue. Secondly, the way his observation was set out depended on Mass-Observation's serious 'scientific' aims. Even the fact that the 'quiet man' wore a bowler was not irrelevant to these – *The Pub and the People* contains four pages (140–3), decorated with statistical tables, about the clothes which Bolton people wore when they went out to the pubs. (Even in the 'better class' lounge bars, on weekdays, it was averred, only 13 per cent of customers wore bowlers, though this leapt up to 25 per cent on Saturday nights: 'hairnet' would be submerged, in such a table, into the category 'no hats'.)

Our aim in this introductory section is to provide information which readers will need if our book (or rather Mass-Observation's) is to 'speak for itself'. In later sections, we will confine editorial comment to a bare minimum. Here, though, we feel we must give a short outline of Mass-Observation's early history.

It was founded early in 1937 by three young men, all of them remarkable, who met each other in a remarkable way. The crisis of Edward VIII's abdication had brought to the attention of intellectuals the extraordinary hold which the monarchy still had over the British popular imagination. It had also seemed to expose gulfs between the 'Establishment' and the 'people', and between the newspaper press and public opinion. Its broader context, social and international, was such as to worry intelligent people. While the South-East of England prospered, the North, Wales and Scotland still suffered mass unemployment. In Spain, Franco was beating the Republic (for which John Sommerfield fought). Franco's Falange appealed to atavistic loyalties. In Germany, Hitler's rise to power had been a triumph for irrationality. Could anything be done to check the revival, as it seemed, of barbarism, to avert the major war which seemed certain?

Late in 1936, a school teacher named Geoffrey Pyke wrote to the *New Statesman* urging that 'primitive' public reaction to the abdication should be subjected to 'anthropological study'. (12 December 1936). The journal's first issue in the New Year carried a letter in response from Charles Madge, announcing that a group had already been formed for precisely that purpose. He pointed out that 'fieldwork' would have to proceed in a 'far more roundabout way' than in Africa or Australia. 'Clues' might be found 'in the popular phenomenon of the coincidence' – in fact, British society was so 'ultra-repressed', in a Freudian sense, that perhaps 'clues' could only be hit upon 'in this form'. He called for 'mass observations' to create 'mass science' (2 January 1937).

Coincidence struck at once. Tom Harrisson published only one poem in his life. This appeared in the *New Statesman* next to Madge's letter. Harrisson was then in Bolton, conducting 'anthropological' fieldwork into industrial life. He wrote to Madge and, within a month, Mass-Observation was founded. Madge, Harrisson and a third man, Humphrey Jennings, published yet another *New Statesman* letter calling for '5000 observers'. Their approach must be as objective as possible, but at this stage the triumvirate were expecting that their collaborators would investigate above all the outward signs of subjective phenomena, for instance:

Behaviour of people at war memorials,
Shouts and gestures of motorists,
The aspidistra cult,
Anthropology of football pools,
Bathroom behaviour,
Beards, armpits, eyebrows,
Anti-semitism,
Distribution, diffusion and significance of the dirty joke,
Funerals and undertakers,
Female taboos about eating,
The private lives of midwives.
(30 January 1937)

This catalogue of projects now seems bizarre (though, truth being stranger than imagination, it did not anticipate the Bolton tortoise, nor the Welsh tapioca bomb which will explode later in this anthology). But Mass-Observation's founders were not advertising a game, a stunt. They could justify their strange preoccupations intellectually, and politically.

Madge was a poet, born in 1912, who had already been accorded the accolade of selection by W. B. Yeats for the *Oxford Book of Modern Verse*. He had read science at Cambridge, had 'dropped out' with no degree and, at the suggestion of T. S. Eliot, had gone to Fleet Street as a *Daily Mirror* journalist. He knew Jennings (1907–50) well from student days, and the latter was working for John Grierson's famous GPO Film Unit, based close to Madge's home in Blackheath. They shared an interest in Surrealism, a continental movement in poetry, art and ideas which aimed to apply the insights of psychoanalysis while not ignoring those of Marxism (Madge was at this time a rather inactive Communist). It is easy now not to notice the common ground between the documentary movement in film and in literature (where George Orwell was a current exponent) and the small group of British Surrealists. Both emphasised the primacy of reality. The camera showed what was 'really there' in the texture of everyday life, disregarded by previous art but, for democrats, significant. The Surrealist insisted that images from the subconscious, triggered there by things seen in the streets, or perhaps by press headlines, must be given unmediated expression. In both cases, one aim was a kind of social therapy; in either case, a further aim might be social transformation.

Harrisson's career had already been stranger than fiction; indeed, Mass-Observation seems almost the least unusual of his manifold activities, between his birth (in 1911) as the son of a military hero who ran the railways of Argentina, and his death in 1976 in a road accident in Thailand. While a schoolboy at Harrow he had published his first book, a guide to the birds of the area. Like Madge, he 'dropped out' from Cambridge, where his best friend was the dipsomaniac novelist-to-be Malcolm Lowry, but he continued his career as self-taught naturalist, organising an important ornithological survey. He also made himself an anthropologist, going in 1933 to the New Hebrides with a scientific expedition from Oxford and staying on to live with cannibals on the island of Malekula. Typically, he was taken back to civilisation by none other than Douglas Fairbanks (Sr) who called with a yacht and signed him up as adviser for a Hollywood movie (never made). Back in Britain, penniless, cut out of his angry father's will, he 'went native' in Bolton, working in manual jobs, and studying the customs of Lancashire.

He, Madge and, briefly, Jennings, operated Mass-Observation from two distinct bases. In Bolton – 'Worktown' – Harrisson gathered together a shifting body of fellow Observers. Some, the core of the 'Team', were paid a pittance whenever Harrisson had some money. (Local industrialists gave him help; Gollancz, the publisher, provided advances.) Others were volunteers – local people, such as Bill Naughton, then a coalman, later famous as a novelist; social scientists such as Dr Gertrude Wagner; eager undergraduates; and London artists and intellectuals. The Worktown team had distinguished friends. Humphrey Spender came up to take photographs which are now famous. His brother Stephen took an interest, and so did Tom Driberg, then 'William Hickey' of the *Express*. William Empson, poet and critic, investigated the contents of sweet-shop windows; the painter Julian Trevelyan memorialised the famous Bolton mill chimneys.

Meanwhile, in Blackheath, Madge and Jennings organised the 'National Panel' of volunteers. By the end of 1937, over 500 people had been recruited as unpaid Observers, through appeals in the press. Their main task had been to keep a detailed account of everything they did from waking until sleeping on the twelfth day of each month throughout the year. Mass-Observation saw these one-day diaries, which were called 'Day Surveys', as an experimental method of collecting information about people's lives and as a way of training Observers in the art of 'continuous observation'. In an early publication, *First Year's Work*, Tom Harrisson and Charles Madge wrote: 'The original purpose of the Day Surveys was to collect a mass of data without any selective principle, as a preliminary to detailed studies of carefully chosen topics.' After January 1938, Mass-Observation's interest shifted to the recording of activities on special days such as Easter Day and August Bank Holiday, and then to more specific topics. The diary form was resumed in September 1939 when full personal diaries were requested from the Panel of volunteers. From the start, Mass-Observation stressed the value of using amateurs – 'Mass-Observation has always assumed that its untrained Observers would be *subjective* cameras, each with his or her own distortion. They tell us not what society is like but what it looks like to them' (*First Year's Work*, p. 66).

The two examples which follow have been selected from about 300 Day Surveys which were written for 12 September 1937. The first is written by a housewife in Kent, married to a farm labourer and with three young children. The second is written by a young middle-class man, single and living with his brother in Cheshire. In contrast to the domestic immediacy of the first Day Survey, the second one has a self-consciousness and an air of composition which suggest it might be more fictional than actual.

Material was sent to Mass-Observation on the understanding that the organisers might make free use of it, but would not disclose the names of volunteers. We have maintained, in this anthology, the principle of confidentiality – 'Phyllis Walden' and 'William Bradley' are fictitious names. Otherwise, we have edited our chosen extracts as lightly as possible, given pressure of space. We have made cuts, but not changes. Mass-Observation 'jargon' will be explained as necessary.

2. (a) *Phyllis Walden of Keston: Day Survey, 12 September 1937*

7.15 a.m. I rouse to find myself chuckling at the remembrance of the droll description of various scenes from the film and show *Okay for Sound*. This was by two fellows in the little beer house where my husband and self have made a habit of meeting on Saturday evenings on his way home from B. to which he cycles every Sat afternoon to see his people. For the first time I am moved to want to see a Talkie film. If it could reduce me to such a state of helpless laughter at a second-hand description I feel sure it would be a tonic.
7.30 I go down, make tea – take up tray – we both have tea and digestive biscuits in bed. I enjoy this immensely as every week day have to get up at six o/c to get himself off to work by 6.45 a.m. The children start to yap – He shouts at them to 'Shut up, it's Sunday.' Smothered laughter from the boys' room as they endeavour to carry on the morning 'strafe' without enough noise to bring him in there. A plaintive voice from Jay, 'Can I have a cup of tea Mum?' Tell her, 'Yes, if you go downstairs and get a cup.' I have everything on tray. She does so and brings up paper which has just come. I decide I don't want any skim milk and it's too late to rush and wash and dress now anyway. Must get there before eight o/c when dairymaid goes to breakfast. Very weak this decision, feel very lazy.

8.30 He asks, 'What's for breakfast?' I say, 'bacon fried potatoes and fried bread'. Says he'll have his in bed. Very glad about this, as table very small when we all meal together and he does find fault with the children's table manners so. He says, 'Come on I'm hungry. Won't breakfast be late?' and
9 o/c I get up, wash, make more tea, cook breakfast and feed everybody. He says he'll help with the housework, as Jay has contracted a skin complaint and I have to dress her 'bad places'. This takes half an hour. Clear away wash up. We both tidy dining room. He helps me upstairs too. Then at
10.30 I start to prepare dinner. This consists of roast beef, potatoes, beans and marrow all from own garden. Apple pie and custard to follow.
11.30 Stop to make coffee – beg children not to run in and out of the garden they do hinder one so. He comes in from garden for lunch. I have a feeling dinner is going to be late. Serve me right shouldn't have been so late getting up.
2.15 Dinner on the table at last. I am surprised I've not had a 'wigging' from himself at it being so long after one o/c our usual time. But I just couldn't hurry today. We all enjoy meal. I think of all those visiting his niece in a big London hospital. Hope her foot is not too painful. Eldest boy finishes his dinner in a hurry and cycles off to B. saying he will bring the latest news of her, when they get home from visiting – Glad Mick's tonsils are out – A fortnight ago I was rushing off to visit him at District Hospital. Feel it's a good job done before the winter sets in.
3.30 Clear away we wash up together. Children out in garden. I make scones for tea.
4.45 Sit down. Look at wireless programme – Decide to tune in at 5 o/c.
6 o/c Rouse to the tune of crockery being put on the table Himself getting tea ready. Good gracious! I've been asleep an hour. Rush to wash and change. Looks very dull going to rain I think. Wonder if Jim took his mac on the back of bike – I'll bet he's forgotten it. We have tea. Wash up together.
7.30 Put children to bed. Himself sits nursing cat. I curl up in a low armchair. Listening to wireless. Going to get dark early tonight. Raining. We sit in the twilight.
8.15 Listening to service from St Martin's. Most unusual thing for us to do. Looking back, I never remember having done this before. Neither of us are church goers. Still have not lit up. The fire glows more and more redly. Quite dark now except for the lights of passing

coaches and buses flashing by. So peaceful – where is the usual restlessness and sense of shut-inness (I know no other way of describing it) that drives me out even on wet murky evenings to the top of the hill to breathe and 'sort things out' and get the fret of the day out of my mind? All gone – everything so utterly at one that I could wish for many more days such as this.

9 o/c We stir to get supper. Light up. Wonder why the boy is so late.

9.15 Jim comes in. Says he borrowed a mac from his Uncle and then didn't need it as rain held off while he cycled home. His cousin is better may be home in a week with leg in plaster. Glad of that.

10.5 We all go up to bed. A most restful day in mind. Know that the usual rush and bustle of every working day will start tomorrow but have enough courage to face it with equanimity. Why can't *every* week-end be like this? . . .

No notes made. Report written partly Sept 19th and partly Sept 24th. Have found it possible to *re-live* days marked for day-surveys even after so long a period as ten days. In the past have been able to do this for own pleasure – now find it a very helpful accomplishment to writing up these reports.

2. (b) *William Bradley of Bebington: Day Survey, 12 September 1937*

[. . .] I live with my brother in the top-rooms of tall old-fashioned house which the owner has converted into flats.

The district is quiet and away from the main roads and traffic, but once very select and residential is now gradually declining through the encroachment of Council property. A good many of the residents still remain, however, and despite the proximity of the council houses and the conversion of some of the old houses into flats the district is far from being what one usually calls working-class. There are plenty of trees, orchards and gardens about and the open country is less than fifteen minutes' walk away.

The rooms occupied by my brother and I are sparsely but for our needs, quite adequately furnished. Though attic rooms they are quite big and are well lighted by window and skylight. The kitchenette which was originally a landing contains sink, stove and two tables.

Introduction

SATURDAY MIDNIGHT

Heard grandfather clock next door strike the hour, was sitting in armchair, legs up against the fireplace, book in my lap. Looked up at alarm clock on mantelpiece and watched minute hand edging away from the twelve. Thought of course of 'Mass-Observation'.

My brother, who works late on Saturdays and had only been home about an hour, lay dozing stretched out on the couch. His pipe was out and had fallen on his chest. His arms were folded. Two cats lay across his legs. A newspaper he had been reading stood crumpled on the floor. He breathes heavy and would likely be snoring soon. The fire was low and another cat sat in front of it his nose almost touching the bars of the little grate. But the room was warm – stuffy probably to anybody coming into it from the fresh air.

I was depressed. My girl was ill in bed and this had been the first Saturday we had not been out together. It hadn't seemed like a Saturday at all. Also one team had let me down on my football coupon. Had they won I'd have been quids in this weekend. I felt heavy and restless, supposed it was because I hadn't been out with the girl. Different to other Saturday nights – usually felt light and cheery and at ease in every way. But didn't seem so welcome this night. If Grimsby hadn't drawn I'd have won a packet. The fire stirred and a cinder fell into the ash pan. The cat, startled, leapt on to the arm of my chair. I swore and pushed it off roughly. Sparks flew from my cigarette and when I put it to my mouth again it wouldn't draw. Thoroughly bad-tempered now I got up, went into the kitchenette, opened the window and leaned out. The house next door was in darkness except for one window, and that was the window of my girl's bedroom. The curtains were drawn apart, though a fair distance away I could see half of the bed the shape of her head on the pillows. I lit the gas so that she could see me and then waved to her. We did this every night but tonight it didn't give me so much pleasure. I put on a glowering expression and hoped she could see how miserable I looked. I waved only half-heartedly too for I wanted her to see that I was sulking. She threw me kisses but she got none in return.

Then in a desperate desire to hurt her I pulled the window down, making as much noise as I could and turned out the gas. In the darkness I stood and watched her. I'd never acted like this before, usually lingering over this peculiar 'good night' ritual and I knew she'd wonder what on earth was wrong with me and probably fret the whole night over it. She waited a few minutes and then I saw her hand move. She disappeared from my view and next moment had switched out the light. Now that she was gone I became filled with remorse. I struck a match, lit the gas and opened the window again. I made as much noise as I could, was pretending to call one of the cats, but though she must have heard me her room remained in darkness.

Disgusted with myself, everybody and everything began to prepare supper. I put the water on for the coffee and made some cheese and onion sandwiches. We sandwich most things; it saves a lot of bother.

My brother came into the kitchenette and began cutting up meat for the cats. Their food is kept in the oven and the moment they hear the door being opened they dash into the kitchenette, tails up, and begin crying impatiently for their supper. I tripped over one and in a fit of anger grabbed the three of them and bundled them into the bedroom, 'Stay there until your supper's ready,' I said.

I made the coffee and took it and the sandwiches into the room. My brother fed the cats, gave them a basin of milk and then came and sat down by the fire again. The fire was almost out but I poked it into a little life. After supper I lit a cigarette and settled down with my book again. A cigarette tasted good after coffee. The book I was reading was called 'All the Fields Were Green' by Michael Harrison. I was liking it better than any book I'd read for a long time.

My brother was getting ready for bed but I went on reading until I'd finished my cigarette. It was nearly one o'clock. I closed my book and threw the stub of cigarette in the fire, then I went down to the middle-flat, which is un-occupied, and closed the windows – a precaution against tramps climbing up the wall and spending the night there.

When I went into the bedroom my brother was sitting up reading. I got into bed and smoked my last cigarette of the day. It was about twenty past one when I switched the light out.

The alarm awakened me at half past seven. I switched it off and wondered whether I should get up now or lie in for a while. Then remembered we hadn't much coal so decided to lie in.

I turned over and tried to go to sleep again, but sleep had left me. I began thinking about my girl. I tossed and heaved about and strove desperately to think of something else. But it was no good. God, for a pure mind! I cursed – to hell with this for a bloody life, I'm getting up!

I threw off my pyjama jacket, went into the kitchenette and swilled my head and shoulders under the cold tap. After rubbing myself down with the towel I felt better. I looked out of the window at the house next door and grimaced at her window – woman, I said, you're a bugger!

I went into the bedroom again and dressed myself then after going to the bathroom went downstairs and collected the Sunday papers. 'Reynolds' and 'The Referee'. Then I lit the fire, made myself a cup of tea, pulled my armchair up to the fire and settled down to the papers. At nine o'clock I began cleaning and tidying the room and kitchenette. This occupied my time until about quarter past ten. Then I called my brother and began preparing breakfast. Our breakfast was rather a mixture. It consisted of fried egg, bacon, sausage, tomato, black pudding and potato cake. But it tasted good. Afterwards we had a cup of tea and some bread and marmalade to freshen the palate. When breakfast was finished I washed up while my brother fed the cats. It was nearly half past eleven when we settled down for a read – I to my book and my brother to the Sunday papers.

At twelve-thirty listened in to Haydn Wood's 'A Manx Overture'. Turned the wireless off when this was finished.

Between then and two o'clock we either dozed, read, or played with the cats. At two o'clock listened in to a silly story written and well told by Algernon Blackwood.

It was then time to think of preparing dinner – it was to be rabbit stew. I went into the kitchenette, cleaned the rabbit and left it to soak in salt water while I peeled the vegetables. This is a tedious job and I usually listen in while I'm doing it, but there was nothing decent on the wireless at the moment so I played my Gramophone Society records of Dvorak's pianoforte quintet in A Major. When this was finished I still had some carrots to peel so began Brahms Sextet in B Major, was not in the mood for him and put the record back after playing one side of the first. Frederic Hammond playing the 'Waldstein' carried me through to the end of my chores. At half past three I had the stew going nicely and I sat down with my brother again, but he got up then and went into the kitchenette to shave. When he had finished I made some tea and we had that and a few biscuits to put us on until dinner was ready. At four o'clock we listened in to a recital by Laelia Finneberg.

From then until about half past five we either read, dozed or played with the cats. We were in no hurry for dinner and I had a very low gas under the stew. But at half past five we thought we might as well have it. We did and by six o'clock we had.

Then we listened in to William Farr talking on the cinema and we both decided that his was the best talk since Alistair Cooke left the

BBC. At six fifteen we listened in to Dolman playing the 'Waldstein' and a nocturne and three studies by Chopin. Enjoyed the recital immensely.

All through the day I had kept an eye on the house next door for signs of my girl, but I'd seen nothing of her. Evidently she was still in bed. It was now seven o'clock, an hour since dinner, so we had some coffee and biscuits. At seven thirty listened to last act of 'Wind and the Rain' played by Sheffield Rep. Company. Thought it insufferable. Church service followed so we didn't listen in again until the news. I listen to the Sunday news with the expectation of some famous man having died over the weekend. They usually do. 'We regret to announce the death of – '. I'm always disappointed if the announcer hasn't that little bit to say. The twenty-five minutes of Franz Lehár music which followed the news was we thought the best thing the BBC had given us for many a long Sunday. At nine thirty we had tea – cold ham, salad, stewed damson and custard and cakes. While preparing this I saw that there was a light in the girl's window. The curtains were only half drawn apart and I couldn't see the bed. This angered me – most likely she was sulking because of my behaviour last night. Damn her then!

After tea I decided to go out for a walk. I didn't bother to change into my best clothes, or even to wash and shave. It was a drizzly night and there wouldn't be many people about. I put on my raincoat and an old trilby and telling my brother I wouldn't be long went out of the house and headed for the country. I had only been walking about five minutes and was still within the lamps when I saw a girl I used to know, years ago when I was in my teens. She was by herself. At first I was delighted to see her but then I remembered my day's beard, the old coat and hat and felt I must look a pretty disreputable sight so I hung my head and pretended to wipe some dirt out of my eye thinking I might pass her unrecognised. But she had spotted me. She herself was fashionably and expensively dressed – I wondered whom she had married. She stood in my path and held out her hand. 'Bill my darling how are you?' she said, I looked at her then, pretending just to have seen her. 'Why Marie,' I cried. 'Fancy seeing you!' Soon I forgot all about my untidy appearance, it was so good to be in her company. She was a dark pretty girl, rather foreign looking, high cheek-bones, slanting pencilled eyebrows and very attractive eyes. But her mouth excited me the most, it was red, loose and shapeless. I longed to kiss it. I asked her was she married and she laughed and said no bloody fear – I like to be independent. She told me she had a hairdressing business in Liverpool and was doing very well for herself. I congratulated her and jokingly asked her if she could give me a job. 'A receptionist in a ladies' hairdressing establishment would suit me down to the ground,' I said. She laughed at that but expressed surprise at my need of a job. 'The last I heard of you,' she said, 'you were in Ireland, doing fine, and married and everything.' I told her that was years ago, though they were wrong about me being married. 'It was a close shave all the same,' I added. She asked me where I was living and I told her 'not far from here, just round that corner in fact.' So she said, 'Would you think of inviting a body to supper?' I jibed a bit at this. 'Sweetheart,' I said, 'I've come down in the world a lot, I now live in an attic.' I felt I couldn't for shame's sake invite her there. But she laughed, 'How thrilling, do take me there, I'd love to see it. It sounds so romantic, what do you do, paint, write poetry or compose music.' I took her arm, 'Come on then,' I said, and then, 'No, I do none of those things. I clean up, wash up, make beds and cook for my brother; I let flats and I collect rents from, listen to complaints of and give notice to tenants. I'm neither artist, poet nor musician, I'm just a poor bloody housekeeper and janitor.' She said I had the soul of a louse, but as we walked along she pressed my arm close to her body. I said, 'Marie, I couldn't have met you at a better time, my girl's ill in bed I haven't been out with her for over a week.' I wonder if she'll understand. After all she invited herself to my flat. She said I also had the mind of a louse. We bantered with each other like this until we reached the house. The front room of the bottom flat was lit up but the rest of the house was in darkness. I opened the door and as we went along the passage to the stairs I heard my brother's voice in the front room. I went in and told him I had a friend and would he not disturb us for an hour or so. It was then nearly a quarter to eleven. My brother understood and smiled in good humoured disapproval. I joined Marie again and struck a match to show her the way up the stairs. I felt glad I'd cleaned our rooms out this morning. We got to the top and I switched on the light in the sitting room. 'Take off your coat,' I said, 'while I make some coffee – or perhaps you'd rather have tea or cocoa', no, coffee would do, and please don't forget to salt it. I busied myself in the kitchenette while she had a look through my record albums. She called to me, 'You seem to be hellishly fond of Italian opera singers.' I said, 'I was once but I grew out of it. Those records,' I said, 'belong to my first gramophone phase. I graduated to symphonies and now I prefer chamber music best of any.' Then added, 'that is, as regards gramophone music.' She said I was a bloody highbrow and hadn't I any dance records. I said there were a few on one of the ten inch albums, 'but they're very old,' I said, 'I only got them for sentimental reasons – they were the favourite lines of a girl I used to know.' 'And love,' she finished for me. I said I didn't think I knew what love was. 'Not now anyway,' I said, 'I thought I did once – when I was about twenty-one.' I made the coffee, set the things on the tray, found some biscuits and cake, and went into the sitting room. 'Supper is served madam,' I said, setting the tray on the table. She had taken her hat and coat off and in the electric light she looked adorable. I went and sat down beside her. 'A kiss first, love, just to give me an appetite for supper.' I was a bit nervous for I didn't know how she would take it. It was ten years since we'd seen each other and though we had been very friendly and gone about a great deal together we had never been sweethearts, had, in fact never even kissed. But we were young then. However I needn't have had any qualms, she'd apparently learnt a bit since those days, and was now as ready with her lips as I was with mine. 'Thanks, Darling,' I said getting my breath. 'That'll do me nicely for now.'

She asked me did I ever go to dances and I said no I couldn't dance. She offered to teach me. 'You'd be surprised,' I said, 'at the number of girls who have tried to teach me, but it's no good. I don't like it it makes me feel foolish.' Nevertheless after supper I turned the wireless on to Luxemburg and we danced. I was wearing flannels and a light sports shirt, Marie who was [also] very lightly dressed. The touch of her was very exciting. She said, 'You're quite right you're a rotten dancer – but I don't mind. I like your grip.' We didn't dance for long. I turned the wireless off. 'Lets sit out for a while,' I said.

We sat down on the couch. I took out my cigarette case and offered her one. She didn't smoke. I lit one for myself. I was feeling rather nervous, this girl may not be as sophisticated as she seemed. I asked her had she ever been with a man. She shut her lips tight and nodded her head up and down, 'often?' I asked. She pursed her lips and said hesitatingly, 'Well, not often' and then 'I don't go with *any* man.' She too seemed slightly nervous. I wondered if I was running myself into any danger. But after we'd talked about it for a while I decided she had all her wits about her and was quite capable of looking after herself.

I got up to go into the bedroom but passing through the kitchenette I looked through the window and saw that there was a light in my girl's window. I lit the gas and waved to her, then I called into the sitting room, 'Marie do you want to see my girl?' She came out to me, 'Yes, where is she?' I pointed out of the window. She had come out probably thinking I was joking or had a photograph to show her. She couldn't understand what I was pointing at at first. Then I put my arm round her and kissed her. I did this knowing full well that my girl could see us. I made a big show of kissing her. I kissed her again and again and again. But Marie had now seen the lighted window next door and began pushing me away from her. 'Is that her in that room,' she asked, and when I said it was she ran into the room again. 'That was a filthy trick,' she said when I joined her. 'What on earth did you want to do that for?' I felt ashamed of myself. It *was* a rotten thing to do. I'd done it deliberately, knowing well how much it could hurt my girl. I suppose it was vanity made me do it. It pleased me to let her see I could do without her, also I'd wanted to hurt her for letting me down yesterday. For my own comfort I tried to explain my action to Marie. I was afraid it was going to spoil the night. 'You're rather a despicable blighter Bill,' she said. I agreed with her. 'I do lots of things for which I absolutely despise myself,' I said. We talked for a while until I felt everything was alright once again and then began to make love to her. I suggested the bedroom and Marie agreed. We got up and were making towards the door when I suddenly remembered something. I looked back at the clock and began chuckling. 'Let's wait another five minutes,' I said. It was five minutes to twelve. She looked puzzled. 'I'm an observer,' I said. She asked me what I was talking about. I explained as best I could. 'And today,' I said, 'is my very first day survey.' She laughed. 'But why wait,' she said, 'and lose what would probably be the best part of your report?' 'There's a limit to everything,' I said, pushing her in front of me as the clock next door chimed twelve.

I made no notes for this report and wrote it Tuesday, September 14th . . .

II

Worktown, Blackpool and London, 1937–1939

In this and later sections we are aiming to provide, not only interesting reading, but also a sample of the various types of Mass-Observation material.

Harrisson and Madge were both very lively writers, and encouraged others to write as vividly as possible. In early days, Madge and Jennings claimed that Mass-Observation was creating a new kind of literature, and some National Panel volunteers certainly signed up because they wished to see their own writing in print. Straightforward self-expression was possible in 'Day Surveys' and in reply to 'Directives' (questionnaires sent out to the National Panel). But when paid fieldworkers engaged in particular projects sent in reports – brief or long – the third person was normally employed. 'Inv.' stands for 'investigator' – a locution which fitted in with the view, taken by some sections of the popular press, that Mass-Observers were like 'private eyes', or spies. 'Inv.' refers to paid workers; 'Obs.' ('Observer') may refer to either a full- or part-time employee, or to a volunteer. Reports were signed with initials only, as a rule.

'E.L.', the author of the 1937 pub observations which follow, was a local Bolton man. Though he entered fully into the 'scientific' aims of Mass-Observation – zealously counting, for instance, how many matches, 'spits' and cigarette ends landed in the spittoons in the Crofter's Hotel Vault one night in May, and trying to render Lancashire speech as directly as possible – his accounts are sometimes highly personal. One night he consumed, between 7.45 and 9.30, fourteen half pints of seven different beers in fourteen different hostelries before meeting Tom Harrisson in the Man and Scythe; that report ends rather proudly, 'Total Beer Drunk 8½ Pints'. He uses the notations ♂ for 'male' and ♀ for 'female'.

'J.S.', John Sommerfield, so roundly abused in our first sample from 'E.L.', uses a more impersonal style, as befits a full-time paid 'Obs.'

THEY MAY BE WATCHING *YOU*

By MARION DEWHIRST

HAVE you ever been for the day to the seaside, or strolled on Hampstead Heath, or merely talked to a friend in a 'bus or tram, and suddenly realised that someone was recording your conversation in a little note book?

The chances are that the scribe was neither a plain-clothes detective, nor a lunatic, but merely a Mass-Observer. The chances are, also, that—if you hadn't a guilty conscience, in which case, doubtless, you melted unobtrusively away, fearing the worst—you turned on the recording angel, and said indignantly: "Here, what do you mean by eavesdropping like that? You ought to be ashamed of yourself," or words to that effect.

How We Behave

THEN, again, the chances are that you have been Mass-Observed and *don't know it....*

Mass Observation sets out to be a new science; or, rather, a new method of finding out scientific truths.

The originators of it reasoned that if a body of information were available as to **why we do and say certain things, how we behave in special sets of circumstances, this would help us to know ourselves and other people better.**

So they issued an appeal for helpers—people who would be willing to keep their eyes and ears open, and write down exactly what they saw or heard.

The first big thing they attempted was a survey of Coronation Day. Every Mass-Observer wrote down everything that happened to him or her on that day, down to the smallest detail. The published results made a most interesting record of just what the popular reaction is to this sort of ceremony.

Another survey—recorded in the recently published report of the first year's work in Mass-Observation (Lindsay Drummond, 3s. 6d.)—dealt with not one particular day, but a particular habit—cigarette-smoking.

Tappers or Non-Tappers

It was found that about 17 per cent. of smokers feel definite hostility to non-smokers, because a non-smoker does not seem "one of them"; that 44 per cent. of men and 64 per cent. of women smokers began to smoke purely because other people do.

Various smokers' habits were recorded. Fifty-four per cent. of smokers tap their cigarette before placing it in their mouths, 52 per cent. of "tappers" place the tapped end in their mouths, and 21 per cent. the untapped end—but hardy any of them can give a reason for their tapping!

At present the Mass-Observers are working on a Northern industrial town—Bolton. Public houses, football pools, the newspapers people read, the things they laugh at—all the details making up everyday life are being examined and tabulated.

Suddenly realized that someone was recording your conversation.

Its Use?

THE use of it all? The machinery for an analysis of motives, feelings and behaviour, may become of inestimable service to us, living as we do in an age when, while the mechanical sciences have advanced tremendously, the social sciences have lagged far behind.

1 'They may be watching you', *Everybody*, 18 June 1938

3. (a) *E.L.: Pubs, 7 July 1937*

PUB OBSERVERS PLEASE NOTE, DRY ROT HAS NOW SET IN UNTIL AFTER HOLIDAYS

I entered the Saddle Hotel at 7.5 p.m. New barmaid being taught to pump beer and check sales. The landlady Mrs Smith was not too keen when the new ♀ was pumping the beer, but every time the ♀ went to the till Mrs ♀ was all eyes down look in. Mrs ♀ was then asked to have a game of dominoes so she called the other barmaid and warned her to look after new ♀ every time she went to the till. There was only 7 ♂ in Vault I watched a group of 3 ♂ have a round of drinks taking 7-7-9 minutes respectively. I then followed them out at 7.30 p.m. as far as Great Moor St where they caught a tram to the Greyhound Track Manchester Rd. One of the three ♂ was telling a story about D[uke] of Windsor but owing to his voice being low all that I could hear was something about the place where they have gone for their honeymoon being called Jubilee Fucking corner. One ♂ also commented on new ♀ he said, 'Somebody'll open her legs for her before she's been here long.'

Grapes Vault 8.0 p.m. 7 ♂ in Vault 3 PTS. Two drunks were very talkative, had been having a good day drinking champagne, whiskey, sherry, and beer, the elder ♂ says, 'Your not driving that bloody car to-night or you'll get pinched,' the other ♂ replied by singing 'When the moon says something to the mountain' the other ♂ kept interrupting about him driving the bloody car, and went on to say, 'I can lend anybody a bloody fiver' one sober ♂ in vault says, 'If you can put your bloody hand on fivepence', 'I'll have a pint' and then said, 'What am I having Tom' the drunk replied, 'They can have nowt wi me Walt' Walt replied, 'Thanks' (5) in Vault when I left at 8.10 p.m. Nags Vault 8.15 17 ♂ present two fours of dominoes after one game finished one ♂ that was watching game was asked to get 4 beers in and one ♂ was handing him his glass he said, 'Stick it up your Flaps' I followed two young ♂ from here and they went to the grand after having one drink.

Saddle Vault 9.30 16 ♂ present.

I followed two ♂ after having two drinks and they decided to mash Bradshawgate. During my second stay Landlord Mr Smith had arrived and I noticed a ♂ near the side door with no beer. Mrs S. said to Mr S., 'There a gentleman here to see you,' he replied, 'I've no time to bother with him' but afterwards went and had a word with him and choked him off. Turning to the customers in the Vault J.R.

says, 'He thinks because I'm a Scotsman and he's a native I should help him, but if I helped all the Scotsmen that come here for help in a week's time there'd be nowt left in the till. In the meantime Mrs S. had slipped through the door and I'm positively certain that she gave the native something. When I was leaving and coming along Bradshawgate about 9.40 p.m. I passed Observers J.S. and Warbrick near Rimmers Outfitters. I shouted twice to J.S. and nearly all Bradshawgate heard me, but because he was with a new observer he didn't want anything to do with me (The Cunt) and in future I do all my own observing on my (Tod Sloane).

3. (b) *John Sommerfield, 25 January 1938*

Caledonian club has Burns Night Dinner upstairs at Packhorse. Obs. sits in lobby, by foot of stairs. From 7.30, when dinner has already started, until 9.30, the following are ALL the drinks ordered.

1 lemonade
6 lemonades
2 bottles hock
2 beers and 1 bottle hock
1 small whiskey
2 bottles graves
2 Crowns
2 sherries
½ bot. graves
2 beers
2 tawny port
Ginger ale
Pint of mild
1 lemonade
1 bottle graves
1 lemonade
2 small whiskies and 1 Crown

Making 8 lemonades, 6½ bottles wine, 4½ pints of beer, 2 sherries, 2 ports, a ginger ale and 3 small whiskies. This is for 75 people.

Barman talks to [illegible] and man in Vault. 'This is a big dinner meeting on account of it being Burns's night.'

'They've got a haggis, pipes, kilts, everything.'

'They'll pipe the haggis in with whiskey.'

'No, whuskey!' (Big scotch accent.) Both laugh.

Man in vault says to them, 'He was just a filthy poet.'

2 men in dinner jackets stop and have milds before going up. The first orders are for lemonades. The waiter keeps repeating, 'There's a lot o' teetotalers up there.' And the head barman sneers visibly, repeats after him 'teetotallers.'

At 7.50 there is the sound of bagpipes. It lasts for less than 1 minute, and is not heard again.

'D'you hear that bloody row up there,' says bowler hat in lobby. All the drinks have to be paid for, for upstairs, but some are booked, and there is an argument between the barmen. The head barman uncorks a bottle of graves 'for Mrs Telfer', sticks his forefinger down the neck, and then wipes it wetly round the outside of the neck.

The landlord comes down from the dinner at 7.56, and sighs heavily, says, 'I'll have a gill of the best.' 'They'll not drink so much now, not until later,' he says to head barman. (In fact, Obs. notes, nearly all the drinks that were ordered have been ordered already.) Landlord says, 'I've a bloody good mind to walk out and leave them to it. There's 75 of them up there. They come and told me this morning there was 73. Then they ring up and book 95. Now there's only 75.' He says he's ordered 20 lbs of haggis for them, though later, in talking to someone else he remarks that it's so rich that no one eats more than a tablespoonful. He complains that they should have piped the haggis out as well as in, and that no one should have had a drink before it was brought in. He says they are doing it all wrong, and complains some more about them having made a mess up with the tickets for the dinner. When the waiter comes down and orders 'Dry ginger and a pint of beer' the landlord exclaims 'A shipping order!'

'Last year it was 40,' he says. 'This time it's 78. I put my Gordon tie on specially.' He seems pretty disgusted about the whole thing. Man in lobby raises glass of mild and says 'Heres to Bobbie Burns anyway'. But this is sarcastic. Another man in lobby, who has a hell of a scotch accent and says he comes from Kircudbright, sits quietly sipping slow milds.

At 8.30 they sing God Save the King upstairs. There are only three more orders for drink after this. And a redhaired schoolgirl of about 15, wearing a dull green school tunic and brown cotton stockings comes down to the bar and asks, 'Can I have two glasses please.'

Humphrey Spender was in Bolton primarily as a photographer. In general, Bolton people (who knew about Mass-Observation's presence from the press) seem to have regarded 'Obs.' and 'Inv.' impassively, if they noticed them at all. Our next selections, however, show that not everyone accepted the role of anthropological specimen.

4. Humphrey Spender: Tribulations of a photographer, 1938

SADDLE HOTEL. 10.15, JAN. 22

I was standing at a counter which gave a view onto a long row of drinkers standing at an opposite counter. The pub was very crowded and those serving drinks were sufficiently busy to keep them from paying much attention to what their customers were doing. My viewfinder was suddenly blocked by a large blue waistcoat and an aggressive voice said, 'What do you think you're doing. My customers don't want any photographs taken in here, nor do I. Its usual to ask the manager's permission.' 'I'm very sorry, may I have your permission?' 'No, certainly not', and he was interrupted by having to serve some more drinks.

Shortly afterwards he came back and I said, 'Now that I know you are the manager, can I have your permission to take a picture of the barman there, waiting with the tray – I shan't include any of your customers.'

'I've said before I won't have any photographs taken in here; my customers don't want it. What's more, before you leave you're going to destroy the films you've already taken.'

I put a protective hand over my camera and said, 'Its a pity I'll have to go without buying another drink.' 'I wouldn't serve you. Come on, destroy those films or I'll fetch a policeman.'

'Oh, is there any law in England which prevents me taking photographs in public houses?'

'You neednt talk in that semi-educated way you won't go until I've fetched a policeman,' and he walked with me to the door, which he blocked, saying, 'destroy those films'.

'Well, let's fetch a policeman and see what the English law has to say about it.'

'Anyway,' said Frank, 'if you go on blocking that exit we can summon you for assault.'

The manager then went out and started beckoning for a policeman, who arrived in about 3 minutes. A sympathetic longfaced man who was completely dazed by the complaint and obviously didn't know the answer to my question – does the English law forbid me to take photographs inside a public house. The manager blustered and talked about forcing me to destroy the films, called me again semi-educated, to which I said my education on English law seemed sounder than his. Included in a mass of personal insults I remember saying I certainly hadn't wanted a photograph of him and he said he wouldn't allow me in the place again. The manager kept on emphasising the point that his customers didn't want it known that they were in there. So I asked him if the place was so shady that they should be so nervous about exposing their presence. The policeman asked me why I was photographing, implying that the manager had a right to forbid publication. I said I had no intention of publishing anything and anyhow probably only had a picture of the manager's stomach which I didn't very much care about; that I was photographing entirely for my own pleasure, life in an industrial town.

The manager then realised he was losing valuable time and went back to scenes of righteous indignation inside his pub.

The policeman laughed and jerked his thumb into the pub, saying the manager was a queer customer.

CONSERVATIVE CLUB ROOMS, FARNWORTH, MONDAY, JAN. 24

One of the women asks another where she comes from. Reply Lowestoft. Ah, then you know all about the fish. (There has been reference to fishing industry before.) That's right.

The woman from Lowestoft is definitely 'refined' to a point of being almost arty. Long yellow straight hair, to an unbecoming length, neat dress, patronising air: slightly embarrassed by my presence. Eventually a Miss Johnson, overbearing, efficient and baggy-faced, for whose permission I have been waiting, comes in and after fixing up the elderly canvasser, turns her attention on me.

She is worried at the idea that photos are being taken while there are no Farnworth people actually at work in the room (all the workers seem to be outsiders) and wants me to wait, but is satisfied when I tell her that the photographs are not likely to be seen by anyone in Bolton, and are only for a pictorial reportage of electioneering irrespective of any specific election.

Joe Willcock became a stalwart of Mass-Observation's 'Worktown' team. From what follows, it seems that he came to Bolton seeking work, and there met Harrisson, perhaps through Albert Smith of the WEA. It is not clear whether, when he wrote these reports, he was already receiving pay as a full-time Mass-Observer. Even if he was, his indignation at the humiliations imposed on himself and others seeking work seems to be both sincere and justified. He writes as if under severe strain. We have preserved his eccentric punctuation, except where we have reordered speech marks, or added them. The spelling remains Willcock's own.

Willcock had been a tramp preacher, known as 'Brother Joe', and warden of a hostel in London's East End. After the 'Worktown' survey ran down, in 1939, he ceased to be a Mass-Observer. But if he had done nothing else for Mass-Observation, these remarkable war reports from the Labour Exchange battlefield would have given him a special place in the organisation's history. A young colleague in the 'Worktown' team described him thus: 'No intellectual and no writer, and certainly no social scientist, his main asset was that he was able to talk to people in such a way as to gain their confidence.'

5. *Joe Willcock: Aggravation at the Labour Exchange, 2 April 1937*

I appeared as usual at 11.15 a.m. today at the Exchange to sign on, and to draw my allowance. The clerk, who has been courteous and helpful to all who appear at his box, and to myself in particular, told me to see the supervisor, I moved over to the place marked 'Supervisor' and waited my turn. I asked why I had to do this for the 3rd time in one week, and all about the same issue. He replied, '*because you haven't been supporting your wife*', I asked what he meant, and he said 'there was some question about it', 'Is there an office, Mr Willcock, in Hornsea?' I replied 'you ought to be able to know better than I, surely there was a list available in your office.' He replied he 'could'nt find one for Hornsea', I then asked him why there was any question about my being paid that which I was by Statuatory conditions entitled to.

I pointed out that I had in 3 *weeks* sent 3 *forms*, at their request, to my wife, and that in each she had deffinately stated that she was married to myself, was not employed anywhere, and had received support from me previous to unemployment; and had received from me 10/- per week since my leaving her, I have told 2 *supervizors* at this exchange that I have moved twice in the attempt to contact with employment, and in the instance of Hitchin, and Bolton the question and remark was the same, '*Why have you come here, we can do little for you.*'

This information, received and docketed on 3 forms in about 20 days at Bolton exchange placed in my Exchange book, and on 3 *visits* to the super. was there for his inspection, and yet the 1st Friday after the receipt of the compleated form from my wife, there is no payment authorized for me, and in the end he goes to the 'phone and returning tells me to come again at 2 p.m. to see the investigation officer.

I went back at 2 p.m. was handed over the 'Investigation office' and led up a palatial set of stairs, courteously asked to sit in a waiting room for the 'Court of Referees' in which there could be seen 3 men with papers in hands, and looking nervous and restless. It was all very 'marble halls'.

The officer came along, escorted me into a room 4 yds square and barely furnished, oak table and green topped, seated with his back to the window he had me facing the light, a rather cute arrangement for interviewing a claiment who is obviously suspect; or why the term 'Investigation Officer'?

He began in a very level and cautious tone and suggested that was something not clear and the reason for my being '*seperated*' not been made clear on the forms or in my statements to the officials. I pointed out that this term seperated, was a term implying a court order based on a recital of domestic differences, and an order made by a court reffered to as a seperation order, and I wished for the 3rd time that day to make it clear that it was a matter of personal convenience in my search for employment, doubly difficult in my case, for reasons of the obvious nature.

The officer stated he was concerned not with what I wanted it to mean, but what the statutes considered my matrimonial arrangements should be called, and that a Barrister sat in an office somewhere in the building who would call it by no other name but the usual legal one, and that he would have to refer to living apart from my wife in such language required by this misterious and importantly intoned '*Barrister*'.

I spent 1½ hours with this officer, and although a lot of the exchanges could not be termed relevant to the issue, he could not avoid, what seemed obvious to me an attitude of my not having disclosed some material point on my circumstances. His whole attitude was one of asking me to understand his position, his side of the question, and only after several attempts could I point out that the person who ought to receive consideration and who needed this in a patient manner, was the Claiment, in this case myself.

He made an admission that there was no need for the 3 dependants forms going out, I pointed out that he did not understand what the mental condition of the average claiment would be and was in my case with this, on the face of it unusual and suspicous case; and that for him to remark (this was stated also by his colleague), 'to be a mistake'!

I told him that my wife was amazed and worried at this repeated form signing, but he only replied to it by way of 'what the Law required', and 'conditions of Benifit.'

He stated I could not receive my wife's benifit for this week, and enquired what she should do for support, his reply was 'Well, what did she do before, when you didn't send it to her weekly, borrow it? *well she can borrow it again I suppose*!'

He then stated it would be his job to find out if my wife was in receipt of help from her people, and what the family income was, what her mother had in the way of income, what did her sister do! was my wife living as a *lodger*, or as a member of the family, I pointed out that she was living as a lodger her mother not being in a position to help her.

'That would have to be found out,' was the reply.

I have had considerable experience of court proceedure, but in this business of Exchange questioning, there is nothing in it to compare with the fairness of Court questioning, and reference to documents possessed. In a Court, documents are available to both sides, – in exchange questioning the official carefully puts his left hand over the papers, scared lest the applicant will see what they contain! The only time there was any remark touching papers held by him, was by his colleague who said 'why have they sent out these 2 forms in a week' 'its a mistake'! but my questioner when I suggested they had made a *mistake* which had made my wife *unwell*, and the officials reply was 'We admit of no mistake,' if this is not damnable twisting I don't no what is!

When I pressed the official for a statement on wether I should get the allowance this week, his reply was 'I dont think so, it will have to go before the Insurance Officer', I asked him then if it meant that for the present my claim was dissallowed, and he replied 'No'. myself, 'what then is the name of the process stopping my Dependants allowance', he replied 'I am worried about you, your an educated man, and you talk to me like this!' 'but I want a reason and a name for

Allow. being stopped,' 'Well call it being suspended then,' 'but for what reason, since I have *received* it since Jan of this year and the conditions have not changed in a single respect, your people have 3 times admitted the claim, and yet now you say, payment will be suspended.'

'Well, I shall fight it all the way and do everything possible to get it, even if I take it to London', he repeated, 'I am worried about you, you don't seem to appreciate we have to check up and investigate these things, you must see that we get all sorts of conditions among claiments seperated from their wives, if there is a seperation order it is all clear, but yours is one of convenience while seeking employment; and we must investigate it!'

It is interesting to note that if they decide that I am not wholly or mainly maintaining my wife, even when I give 10/- all I can give, and 1/- more than they allow, then she has to have recourse to her loccal P.A.C. [Public Assistance Committee] officer who will relieve her, but only on condition that she sues me for not maintaining her! and I, with my wife dragged through the Hornsea 'Court of Petty Jurisdiction' and the whole thing reported in the local press, and even though I care for my wife more than anything else in this life, and I believe in the sanctity of marriage, I should if this course is pursued, be seperated by *law*, and that of Christian England and its legislators, who constantly maintain that family life is the backbone of English life!

There is no escape from this in point of proper procedure, and if I remain unemployed this is a possible spectacle, that she will be sueing me at the behest of P.A.C. officials, and in the court at which I was *Police Court Missioner*, and this if she conforms to proper proceedure, and yet the last thing she would want to do, and the facing of absolute destitution if she did not sign to the application for a summons – 'For not maintaining my wife'.

This must be known to every Investigating officer, and it will be interesting to note what it will be, as a result of his investigations, if they say she is only maintained '*in part*' by me, although I send her 10/- per week, then they will discontinue paying me my wife's allowance. It then follows that she will have to go to the P.A.C., sign the summons, prosecute me, note my income, by now reduced to 17/-, the man's allowance, and they will have to make an order of an amount leaving me sufficient to live on, probably 2/- per week!

Having thus legally forced us apart, they will 'relieve her' and set to work to find out how much her own relations can contribute towards it!

Is this a rational process, to wreck and destroy any hopes of mine to get my wife with me, and if I can't get work, they will force us apart! Give publicity to it, newspapers will see to that. There is one known case in this area like the one I see for myself; but fortunately the clerk of the Court saw the scandal that would arise and pulled strings to stop it.

The official, after about 1½ hours of his valuable time, probably paid in the region of £250–£300 per annum, began to be more friendly and said 'Ill see if we can't get your allowance paid to-day', he went to another room for 5 minutes and returned saying 'Now Mr Willcock here is a copy of the regulations and you can read them for yourself, if you will come downstairs you will be paid'. I went out of the door, and he went into a room marked 'Private' and I saw a few yards from me a Woman (30) official chatting and going over some papers with a young woman of about 25, and the whole was being easily and pleasantly carried on.

In another room off this magnificantly broad corridor, I saw about 12 women sitting there and they could be seen quite at ease and in no way apprehensive as the men I had seen earlier on, all by the way on the same errand, Investigation Officers, or Court of Referees.

I mentioned to the officer that the manner in which the building had been built, indicated that Unemployment was now a thriving and solid Industry, if that could be judged from the Balustrade and staircase. One door facing the top of these wide stairs, cold, cold stone! there is a door marked 'Board Room' Social Service? Industry!! gigantic and solid, Grills and wide counters 33 worried and harrassed looking Clerks, doing 2 claims a minute but more pleasant to the women, small and pompous, small and large Supervisors, pointing to this, pencilling that.

Can anyone wonder at, or see how the claimants can be anything else but nervous as I have seen them this last 3 weeks. When these men are being spoken to by the supervisor, you can see the claimants go red and flustered, I saw 2 out of 3 (at 11.15 a.m. 2-3-U 7) with shaking hands, these men have been sent for by letter, or told by the clerks at the various signing boxes.

You hear the Super say 'Can't you read what does it say there', pointing to a footnote on a form presented by the claimants. Another is sent to the Super. because he has lost his card, 'Have you anything to prove your identity?' This man in a flustered manner, looked over all his pockets and said, 'Eh I've got a gas bill here, but it's not for my present address'. Super. 'let's see it alright, go up to your box.'

Though his almost illegible handwriting is seen in marginal comments on many reports by others, observations by Tom Harrisson are rarely found in the Archive. This adds special interest to his straightforward account of Armistice Day in Bolton, 1937, part of a nationwide study for which Panel volunteers were also mobilised.

The National Unemployed Workers' Movement, founded in 1921, was led by a Communist, Wal Hannington. In the late thirties, it was well past its peak (50,000 paid up members in 1932), and it is interesting that, even so, it could attract the large crowd noted by Harrisson.

6. Tom Harrisson: Remembrance Day in Bolton, 7 November 1937

At 7.57 Observer is passing Victoria Hall. The crowd outside swells on to the tram lines. Men's class leader Binks can be seen holding a wreath of artificial laurel and poppy high above his head as he pushes through the crowd. In less than a minute a procession of some 300 closely packed fours and sixes forms up outside the Market Hall. It walks briskly, nearly as fast as the Observer's normal pace. It is led by a front rank, slightly ahead of the others with man in trilby on left, then Hannah in ordinary parson's clothes with broad dark hat, then Binks with wreath held over chest, then policeman sergeant with stick. Police sergeant and Hannah get into conversation and Binks moves over to Hannah's left. Most of the procession are women, but men are mixed up indiscriminately among them. There is another 200 around the cenotaph. A policeman clears a lane through them, 'Keep back there, please. Keep back', and Hannah walks briskly up to it, taking wreath briskly from Binks and without ceremony places wreath at foot of it. With hat off he stands on the step and says 'Let us sing a brief couple of verses of a well-known hymn that we all know'. Policeman (there are 7 in sight) says to two women who are standing on plinth of cenotaph at library end, in loud voice 'Just stop that, will you – don't desecrate the thing', and Hannah turns to see what is happening before announcing that the hymn is to be 'Abide with Me'. In his broad Scottish accent he proclaims the first verse and all sing it. On the Town Hall steps at Library end another Scotch voice has been talking about the workers in Spain under the red banner of the NUWM [National Unemployed Workers' Movement]. It stops. During the singing of the first verse everyone is still except two tram men talking to a policeman all with hats on. Hannah now proclaims the second verse which is then sung. Then he gives a brief prayer, including 'And those gallant men (died) to make possible a dream that men have dreamt through the ages – the dream of universal peace – . . . On this sacred spot help us to jump back, blessed God, to our sacred selves, to turn the sword into a ploughshare and the spear into a pruning hook.' (Obs. is particularly struck by the use of the phrase 'jump back', a realist metaphor of the sort not heard in any church, though the indoor element is reproduced by the sword and ploughshare.)

There are now about 700 people present so that the buses are going round the back of the Cenotaph. About 150 on the Town Hall steps, several men with their hats on. Now Hannah asks for another verse of a hymn, 'Oh God our Help in Ages Past'. Then Hannah gives the blessing, which culminates in 'Till his second Coming'. Then Hannah says 'shall we disperse as quickly as we can and help the Officers.'

Three lads walk away, saying 'Hello – lets go and listen to these now'. And many apparently think the same for the NUWM has the largest audience yet seen. The Scot there who looks a foot shorter than Hannah, is five steps higher. He is saying as Obs. passes on his way to an appointment with a Unitarian, that the workers who have died in Spain died for a real ideal. Those who died in the Great War, not so real. 'We believe also that a million British working people were deluded by the British . . . class, were deluded into doing so. There can be no question whatever but that they went to France believing that they were helping to bring an end to militarism, to bring an end to Imperialistic wars, on the part of the Kayser'. At 8.10 the area is nearly back to Sunday normal.

Mass-Observation in Bolton aimed to give all aspects of life their due – sport as well as politics, religion as well as sex and holidays. Hence Observers were deputed to attend every kind of religious service. Besides the major denominations, and well known sects such as the Pentecostalists, they encountered the little known phenomenon of Mazdaznan, a body so obscure that even its cognomen cannot be found in standard encyclopaedias and dictionaries.

As our first report, by Joe Willcock, makes clear, Mazdaznan had arrived in Lancashire from America, was reminiscent of Christian Science, and combined the attractions of church and health club. It seems to have been supported financially by the import and marketing to members of health foods.

Next year, an Observer, up briefly from London, a young woman, 'B.P.', infiltrated the sect. The second report is by her. Not willing to be identified as an 'anthropologist', she ran, as will be seen, into personal embarrassment – such as many other Observers risked. Unusually, she employs 'O' rather than 'Obs.' as an abbreviation.

7. *Worktown Team members: The Lancashire Mazdaznans, 12 April 1937; 9 March 1938*

'THE SCIENCE OF LIFE'

12 APRIL 1937, THE CO-OP CAFÉ, BURY, 7.30

I attended this meeting at the invitation and in the company of a Miss Scroggs, a Bolton Theosophist.

These people have a meeting place in Bolton over Bestwick's Boot Shop in Churchgate, and meet on Monday evenings at 7.30 p.m.

This group is growing in Bolton and is attracting members of the Theosophists.

It has for its audience 5=♂=2 young
=3 middle
40=♀= 20 grey
♀= 15 middle age
♀= 5 young

And of these about 6 are school teachers of whom 2 come from Bolton.
Miss Simons of Rochdale in the Chair.
Dr Jessie Anthony of San Francisco and Manchester who is a Dr of Medicine and a 'Dietician'.

This lady is an amazing person in stature, she is about 5′.10″ in height and a perfect figure that is the comment of all present. She is dressed in a dark purple evening gown, covering in Skin Tight fashion her bosum and posterior; long flowing sleeves and all the seams of the gown go in a V shape to the 'vagina' this is obvious to any one.

She is Eton Cropped and the Hair in front comes down over the forehead, flat. An oval face slightly powdered, and a long mouth uncoloured giving the impression of an Egyptian Priestess Re-incarnated. She wears silver evening shoes. She sits there pleasant faced, but stiff and straight, hand laid across her solar plexus, palms upward, when she rises you fear that her gown may split at the thigh seams, but no it only sweeps the floor.

The chairwoman is an erotic and sexy ♀ of about 35, full lips and an adoring smile for Dr Jessie; sometimes for me! a fact!

They open the meeting with a piece of classical music.

Then Miss Simons rises to announce that they will sing the hymn or song on the sheet 1st. To this do add an exercise of circular motion by the finger tips on the hollow below the centre of the ribs.

'To Vibrate below the Sternum bone'

'and sing Let not your Heart be troubled'

Then Dr Jessie Rises figure erect and hands, palms upwards laid across upper part of her stomach and except for about 10 seconds they remain there for all her lecture.

'How to be happier than we are'

'There is a ways and means to this end, and we have come here to tell you how it is attained. Happiness is a state to be attained by only the individual. And can only be got by the freedom of all that is confined within the heart. To do this you must vibrate the gland in the centre of your Plexus; and these vibrations carry all over the body, also making a contact with a certain part of the brain: it then releases the mind, and where is the mind you will ask, in the penial gland in the brain.

By these vibrations you release fine Etherreal substances ever to be renewed, developing a mind state.

Then we can call on that mind to do our bidding, the Saviors Bidding! it will have a force to uplift one. And in releasing those forces you are swept out of despondance into happiness. You will have the confidence of, and Assurance of some thing unseen.

Faith is confidence of and assurance of something unseen.

The vibrations of proper breathing and exercise touches the brain cells, and this helps us to have faith, and when there is faith there is *no doubt*.

You can then not know what it is to be superstitious, everything you think and do is positive.

A child may suffer from certain difficulties they are the result of Pre-Natal Breathing and Vibrations on the gestating embryo.

We hold in Mazdaznan that if the Individual will learn to breathe properly that he or she will overcome any and all imperfections.

We must learn to establish rythem in the body cells.

Go to bed and lie on your back, and breathe naturally, and as you inhale, 1 second to each count you will find that you can hasten or shorten the breathing, the average is 3 seconds to the complete breath rythem.

You see the Mother strikes this breath Rythem into the Embryo.

With the establishment of the proper rhthem you can create the perfect child.

Anything you can think, you can do. Establish in your minds the thoughts of Plenty and enough to spare. For instance that if everyone only having to labour 2 hours per day as their share of life's labour.

And God speed the day when the creative thought is an established fact.

Benjamen Franklin released this thought in 1760 in 'Poor Richard's Almanack'.

Children

'You can see children being turned out of school at the age of 14, and this at a time when they are passing through the most difficult period of their life.

You see their smiling faces, but they have sad eyes.

You see a man is not matured till he is 40, and these children have responsibility thrust on them beyond their years and Physique.

You must hold the thought that they shall not be turned out into the world, but kept at school till they reach the proper age, *18*.

To elevate our thoughts is to begin the building of a paradise on this earth. It is impossible for the Lord God Almighty to hold an imperfect thought.

He is not responsible for the Armaments that destroy man.

Only the truth can make man free.

But the truth is inexplicable. The manner of Jesus to Pilate is that truth reveals itself to the individual in the depths of his heart, and where it touches it reveals the truth.

We are taught that we are concieved in original Sin, it is true of the world that we are born in Sin, but it never should be!

We taboo all the eugenical Laws, but we do apply them to Cattle, Horse and dog breeding, we know that there is a certain time for them to be mated, and yet we taboo to this for our own lives and matings.

Present day attitude is that of the 'Machinary of the Uncultured'

Break down the Barriers of your slavery due to the Bad breathing of man to-day.

This fetish of English *tea* at every hour of the day, tea, tea, 50 times a day. (Dr Johnson)

Seek ye 1st the Kingdom of God and its Righteousness it is written you; and you will achieve a state of serenity and certainty.

Mothers, do awaken to a sense of your responsibilities to the embryo within you.

Never forget that the body is the Temple of the living God!

Get into the proper breathing rythem. The rythem of this world is the 7 second rythem.

Mothers note that life should be a glad sweet song mid Soul-Body spirit.

In Russia, if you do not work, you do not eat, I hope you don't have to come to that here. (♀ of 50, 'hear, hear')

9/10th of the world's productivity is going to waste, we hear of people starving, and 98 per cent of all talent is going to waste.

It is possible to change our environment, animals do so, it will make us stand stronger and on our own feet.

Our breathing exercises are based on those used for thousands of years.

The breath goes into the lungs, and mixes with the Galamic Substance, bringing life to the body.

Concentrate every 3 hours on breathing and for 3 minutes, and then you will see the vastness of life.

During the singing of the hyms they go through several exercises.

1 is breathing and at the same time massaging the gland under the centre of the Ribs, near the Solar Plexus.
2 Taking deep breaths, (and to music) on release of breath, you hum the music played.
3 Singing of hyms and banging knees with the flat of the palms.
4 The raising of hands and arms in various circular movements, (you imagine they are going to shout 'Allah').
5 The rolling of the head in circular movements; going fast and then slow to the music.

Most of the people present did the exercises but you noticed the smiles on some of the faces, some gave it up after a time not being able to keep it up.

An old ♀ of 58–60, said, 'I have faith in this new movement, if it can do so much for Dr Jessie Anthony, then I want it for myself.' ♀ was grey and suffering from muscular trouble, probably Rheumatism, stiff in the neck.

Another ♀, had been a member of Bolton Parish Church, a theosophist, a 'Rosacrucian', and now a 'Mazdaznanite', and said she, 'I know now that I have found the truth, I knew it as soon as the bill announcing the meeting, and when it came under the Door, I said this is what I have been waiting for!'

'Isn't she a marvellous ♀!' (Dr Jessie Anthony).

5 ♀ present had the 'Eton Crop' and all of those about 40–45 age.

Collection was taken in a bag, and taken back to the table at the door entrance.

WEDNESDAY 9 MARCH 1938. WEATHER, DRIZZLING

General information

O. was invited to tea with Mrs Bridges, of 135 Bradford Street, before the service.

O. arrived at 6.10 p.m., as the week previously, arriving at that time, she had found the family at tea. On this day, however, she was greeted with the remark, 'Ah thowt yer weren't comin'. Ah 'ope yer'll excuse us, we've 'ad oor tay.'

O. was shown into the kitchen, at the back, where tea was ready. Mrs Bridges, junior, and an elderly lady, friend of Mrs Bridges senior, acted as hostesses in place of Mrs B. senior, who was spending the day with friends from Wigan.

The tea was according to Mazdaznan Lenten diet, with exceptions for the visitor, which will be enumerated.

Items eaten, in order.

1. A slice of herb and nut cake, made by the hostess. Greenish in colour baked in a pie dish, and turned out like a mould. Cut with a knife, like a pie.
2. A dish of green salad, with spring onions, lettuce, endive, watercress, radishes, tomato.
3. A trifle, made of tinned strawberries, jelly, some sort of thickening such as sponge-cake, and cream on top.
4. Bread and butter.
5. A plate of cakes, fairly plain.
6. A pot of tea. Two jugs of milk, one ordinary milk, the other Libby's unsweetened condensed milk.

Remarks

O. Is this Mazdaznan diet?

H. Yes. We don't eat any meat in this house.

O. It is nice to have salad . . . this is the first I have had since I came to Bolton.

H. Oh, you'll always find salad on Mrs Bridges's table . . .

O. Will you have ordinary milk or Libby's cream in your tea? We have Libby's, instead of ordinary milk in Lent, because we aren't supposed to have no dairy produce, it's mucus forming, Miss Dempster says. But she says Libby's don't matter.

O. Do you find you get very hungry?

H. No . . . we can eat pulses, you know, peas and beans. This is the first Lent we've kept strictly to the diet . . . though we've belonged three years. Harry, he don't like it so much . . . he says when supper time comes, he wants his supper. We don't have no supper, in Lent. But he don't ever eat meat, we don't have no meat in this house.

Note. Mrs Bridges, junior, a girl of about 24 years, looks remarkably healthy, with a rosy complexion. She is not plump, but not thin. Mrs Bridges, senior, is a very thin, frail, white-faced little woman.

As O. had nearly finished tea, there was a knock at the door, and in came a woman with a basket of eggs . . . She travels in her car, apparently, selling eggs from some farm. Mrs Bridges, jr. bought a dozen eggs. As she put them on the sideboard, she said, apologetically . . . .

'We have eggs for when visitors come. We don't like to have nothing to offer them except Mazdaznan diet, in case they don't fancy it.' The old lady, who had been in the scullery, came back at this point, and on seeing the eggs, said . . .

' 'As she gone? . . . There now, Ah usually take 'alf a doozen eggs . . . an' she's gone now. Why didn't yer call me?'

Mrs Bridges, jr. was rather anxious to be gone to a special class that was meeting today for the first time, at 6.30 p.m., and O., who felt that she was responsible for the lateness of the tea, begged her to go, and she would follow later with the old lady, to the ordinary meeting at 7.30. But Mrs B. said she 'wasn't so keen . . . they was only practising exercises.'

At 7 o'clock, we all set off together, after a great argument about washing the dishes. O. was not allowed to help. The old lady and Mrs B. jr. did them together. At first, Mrs B. jr. was about to go to the early meeting, and O. was going with the old lady, but then the old lady went into the scullery and began washing up, whereupon O. went to help her dry up, and at that, young Mrs B. became annoyed, and said she didn't like going and leaving the dishes to someone else, and if the old lady wouldn't leave them she wouldn't go. So it fell out as described.

O., knowing from the Mazdaznan Magazine that Dr Hanish did

not approve of girls smoking, did not offer cigarettes. She did not see any signs of smoking, except a pipe on the mantelpiece.

On arriving at the Women Citizens' Hall, Somerset House, in Churchgate, it was only 7.15, and the caretaker asked us to wait in the sitting room, the door on the right at the head of the stairs, and next door to the hall in which the meeting was taking place. Singing could be heard, without a piano accompaniment, in the next room. The old lady went up to the cloakroom on the floor above, and came down without her hat. O. took the opportunity to examine the book shelves. There were about twelve shelves, i.e., two sets of shelves with six rows of books in each . . . but there were no religious books at all. (This library, of course, belongs to the Women Citizens.) The books were nearly all lives of great women, and feminist movement books.

Several other women came in to wait, Young Mrs Bridges had gone in to the remains of the exercise meeting. The women were all very friendly, smiling and saying 'Good evening' to O., even before the old lady returned. They talked among themselves.

After the meeting, a woman came up to O., whom O. had had a short conversation with in the tram on the previous Sunday evening O. had been returning from the Unitarian Church in Halliwell Road, when the woman sitting opposite had leaned forward and said. 'I'd like to speak to you, if I may. Weren't you at the meeting of Mazdaznan last Wednesday?'

O. 'Yes, I was.'
W. 'Did you enjoy it?'
O. 'Yes, it was very interesting.'
W. 'I'm so glad you enjoyed it. Are you coming again?'
O. 'Yes, I'm coming to the meeting next Wednesday.'

After the meeting, O., and the woman whom she had seen in the tram, had some conversation, in the course of which she asked the woman if the wooden plaque on the mantelpiece was the Mazdaznan Symbol. The woman said it was, and gave O. the information set forth on another page . . . about the meaning of the colours, and the fact that Queen Victoria had been interested in it, and that the device was on the florins of her reign. The woman showed O. a florin to substantiate this story. She made the remark about symbolism in other religions.

Young Mrs Bridges then came and talked to O. and told her about the Sunday service in Manchester, and how they wore white. 'We all wear white,' she explained, 'when we go. Mazdaznan don't approve of black, and dark colours.'

The first woman also told O., in talking about Mrs Bridges, that she was a wonderful person ... It was she who helped to organise Mazdaznan in Bolton. She had been many things ... She had been a Christian Scientist, and a Rosicrucian, before she became a Mazdaznanite. She liked trying things.

Young Mrs Bridges told O. at tea, that Miss Dempster was known as Mother May, and she believed she was a district nurse by profession ... at any rate, she was some kind of a nurse. She had a sister, too, who was a nurse.

O. 'I saw in the magazine, that there used to be someone called Sister Jessie, at Bolton.'

H. 'Dr Jessie. Yes ... she is a real doctor ... or used to be ... but of course, Mazdaznan don't really believe in doctors.'

O. 'Did you know Dr Hanish?'

Young Mrs Bridges. 'Oh, no ... we've only been joined three years. He was still alive when we joined, but we never saw him. He passed over in America.'

After the meeting, O. told young Mrs Bridges that she was sorry she had not been able to follow the exercises, but she had written them all down, and would practise them. They then went out, together with the old lady, and two or three other people. Outside, they waited about, as if loath to say good night, and Mrs B. asked O. which way she was going. As last week, O. had taken the tram to Davenport Street [where Mass-Observation had its headquarters] with the story that she was staying with friends in Powell Street ... and as this time she wanted to catch a number ten bus ... it was a rather awkward question. Last week, young Mrs B. and Harry, her husband, had insisted on seeing O. on to her tram.

O. said vaguely that she thought a ten bus would do for her. 'Why, where do ee want to get to then?' asked a small thin man of about 45.

'St George's Road,' said O. cautiously.

'Ee, a noomber ten boos won't du. Yer want ter tek a N tram, or an O tram,' said the old lady.

It seemed that the small man unfortunately lived that way himself, and would show O. how to get home. O. said vaguely that she always got lost in Bolton ... which was more or less true.

Goodbyes were said. The old lady said, 'Well, goodbah. Ah dorn't soopause Ah shall see yer agen.'

Young Mrs Bridges hesitated, and said, 'I hope I shall see you again some time, before you leave.'

O. said, 'Yes!' and later on, 'I'll see you again.'

The small man then escorted O. to the tram stop, remarking that either an O or a N tram did for him. As only the former was at all good for O., she sincerely hoped that it would come first. Actually they got on to an N tram. Conversation was about Mazdaznan most of the way. The small man thought it was a very wonderful thing, because it told you how to live all the time, and most religions did not bother about your health. It was so practical.

O. 'Did you know Dr Hanish?'

M. 'No, no . . . I joined through Mrs Bridges. No . . . The Master passed on three years ago.'

O. 'Wasn't it in 1936?'

M. 'Oh, no, I think it was in 1935.'

O. 'I thought I had seen it in the Mazdaznan Magazine . . . Mrs Bridges lent me the numbers for 1936, and there was an announcement of his death in one of the numbers, I thought.'

M. 'Oh, I think that was the anniversary of his death. No, I am nearly sure he passed on in 1935.'

Conversation was also about Mrs Bridges. O. said she thought she was American. M. said No, she was a Boltonian born and bred. One of the nicest ladies he had ever met.

At the Crofters, the man got up to get out. O. said she thought the next stop was hers. To her horror, the man sat down again and said it would do for him, too. So they got out at the next stop. He then asked where O. lived. O. thought any more lying would get her into trouble, so she said Bertrand Road. Oh, yes, he knew it well. He lived just along on the other side. She ought to have gone on several stops further. O. said feebly, how stupid of her, but then, she wasn't used to Bolton, and always lost her way.

The man said that he had to get his supper. He lived all alone since his Mother passed over, two years ago. When he got opposite his house, he said that he would just run in and put his bag away (one supposed it contained his supper . . .) and then would walk home with O. O. protested, that he would be taken too much out of his way, and he would be so late for his supper. But he insisted.

On the way to Bertrand Road, he told her about the way he lived, and did for himself, and how he loved cooking and washing up, and did not have a housekeeper, because he really loved to do housework. He worked in the town, and got up and did all his housework before he went, and his exercises, and he could not bear a mess. If a friend came to see him, and did not lend a hand, he did not get asked again. But then, he always made his friends lend a hand, and if they did not like it, they could stay away. It was raining pretty smartly now, but he said he liked to feel the rain in his face.

He asked no questions about what O. was doing in Bolton, but was interested to hear she came from London. He said he knew all about London, they lived in restaurants, and never did any housework. He loved it himself.

At the end of Bertrand Road, O. was afraid he would want to come in, and as she had given the Bridgeses to understand she was staying with friends, she thought this would be rather difficult. But though he lingered talking for ten minutes, he did not come any nearer to the house, so at last she said goodbye safely.

Walter Hood was one of the full-time team. Reminiscing in a recording made in 1972, he recalled how it was his job, when funds ran out, to approach Tom Harrisson for cash so that the team could buy fish and chips. He was in his early thirties, brought up in a North-Eastern mining community, which clubbed together to buy him further education at Fircroft College, then at Ruskin. But he was unemployed, down and out in London, when by chance he met Tom Harrisson. He was an ardent socialist, and was an active and popular member of the Bolton Labour Party, which gave a supper in his honour when he left the town in 1938. He soon went to Australia and New Zealand on a TUC scholarship, and ended his life as a long-serving and distinguished functionary of the Congress.

One of his most interesting reports now follows. It shows that Mass-Observation was not always grinding hard work.

8. Walter Hood: Outing with a girl stranger, 19 April 1938

I passed the girl in Knowsley Street – she looked at me hard so I turned back and made her acquaintance . . . She must have walked by slowly because she was only about 3 yards ahead of me . . .

I asked her where she was going in the rain – 'Oh! just taking a stroll', then she suggested we might go to the pictures.

She was about 20, dressed in cloche hat and a brown tweed coat, brown high-heel shoes. At first when I met her she carried her umbrella in her left hand – but when we turned to walk in the town – and cross the road to the left hand side she moved it into her right so that I was partly covered *when walking on* the *outside* of the pavement.

We went to the 'Embassy' . . . estimated 250 ♀ at 9.30 p.m.

Re-actions of the *crowd* –

The picture was about 2 girls – who for publicity's sake went and spent 10 days in a forest – it was a comic . . . Everyone roared at the dress of the 2 ♀ when they entered . . . One was dressed in a tiger's skin – and the other an exaggerated Indian squaw dress . . . Also it caused lots of amusement when the blonde in the tiger's dress thumped her chest like 'Tarzan' She did this 3 times and there was loud laughter each time.

There was much amusement when the girl had a terrified look on her face because she had seen a cub tiger.

When a mad-man comes onto the scene with an imaginary horse and makes the girls get onto [it] there was lots of laughter during the whole of scene . . . especially when the chap says – 'your standen' on its tail' – (loud laughter)

Also when the girls came out of the wood – each 'crackers' with an imaginary horse –

The big picture was George Raft in 8 o'clock . . . George Raft in this was a band conductor – I asked the girl if she liked this picture Yes. 'But it's not a good part for George Raft – he's a tough guy.'

The laughter was caused in this by one of the 3 ♀ who sang together, who along with George Raft struggled to find fame on Broadway. – But the girls didn't find happiness because Geo. was a stern manager and task-master and made the girls go to bed early. They accepted one invitation and found that society frowned on them so they came back to George and the Radio.

Laughter . . . *When* the girls wanted to go to Egypt to ride on camels, and jogged around the room.

When they were telling the Boss off, and he was standing behind them –

Their antics when they were well-to-do. One had 3 dogs – which caused a laugh.

The other having her toe-nails manicured. And asking for things in French.

The theme song 'I'm in the mood for love' (The girl hummed it twice afterwards).

Girl – V. Keen about the picture, her favourite film-star John Loder. The Best Film which she had really enjoyed 'The Ghost Goes West' – She does not like thrillers – but good singing and something to laugh at – or a good story (love) – She knew lots of film stars that I had never heard about . . .

I asked about capes . . . She said that they were not in fashion, were really in fashion a year ago – and now were just being worn out. No one would buy one – it's all raincoats

On Veils: When I asked her about veils she said that some are started to be worn at the back now. She said that they come and they go, but thought that they started in the Spring with the winds.

When we went inside she went into back seat . . . (In this picture place the seats at the back are for two.) Naturally I followed . . .

She placed her umbrella under the seat – and asked me to remind her of it when the show was over.

She sat quiet, for ten minutes, then I offered her a cigarette – She took off her hat . . . loosened her coat . . . took off her gloves – and took the cigarette. It was when the wild-looking man came on the screen that gave her an opportunity to appear afraid. She got hold of my hand – as she leaned slightly forward. I put my left arm around her – She slightly lifted her right arm – so I put my hand around her breast – I 'messed around' – All that picture – During the Raft picture when the singing of sentimental love songs – she left go of my hand and started to rub her hand up and down my thigh –

I then began to feel the breasts of the girl with my now disengaged hand . . . she stopped my hand straying too far. We also did some kissing.

After the show we took a Gt. Lever Bus 15. It was still raining – we got out before the terminus. She took me to a shop-door-way – with a street-lamp shining in . . .

I tried to persuade her to move along to her home. 'No' – she said, 'I always stay here with a chap, at least for the first time.' She wanted to see me again . . . I got the Bus – She was a pretty girl too.

Which brings us to Blackpool. Mass-Observation's Blackpool survey of August to October 1937 was a high point. Some eighty Observers descended on the resort, which was where 'Worktowners' from Bolton tended to take their holidays. In Bolton, Observers had operated undercover. Here Mass-Observation, Harrisson thought, could function openly, even seeking publicity – it would seem to the town like more holiday fun, another stunt.

Brian Barefoot recalls: 'We all went to Blackpool by different means of transport . . . and once we were all there, each member of the team was put up at a different category of hotel, guest house or boarding house, so as to cover as wide a range of visitor as possible. I was in a clean and comfortable small hotel, frequented by "lower-middle" or "middle-middle" class visitors. Walter was in a more proletarian establishment; Joe Willcock was, as far as I can remember, inevitably in the doss house. Tom's headquarters was at 61 Shetland Road, the front room of which resembled a press room, with four typewriters in constant use, press cuttings and notices pinned all over the walls, and a constant flow of telegraph boys to the house. Tom Harrisson at that time was conducting almost all his correspondence by telegram, which in itself was a very charismatic thing to do ...'

His landlord or landlady 'Observed' the Observers. Her or his account reintroduces many observers previously mentioned, though the list is certainly not exhaustive (Brian Barefoot, for instance, does not appear). Certain persons described as coming from 'Bolton' had been there as members of the Team, but were not residents of that town. Reynold Bray was an explorer friend of Harrisson's soon to die horrifically in the Arctic. 'Zita' was the second Mrs Crossman, wife of the rising Labour politician, and was in fact one of the many who came from Oxford. Some persons noted, including the Swede and the Burmese, have left no other traces yet discovered in the Archive.

9. Blackpool resident: Mass-Observation in Blackpool, 1937

Thursday Aug. 12th 1937, a young man and a maid came to Shetland Road, looking for a room to rent, which they required for meetings or local office, to which Observers could meet at any hour to write up their notes on the day's work. No 61 Shetland Road was chosen as a suitable place and terms were fixed up, after a little bargaining on the part of the lady.

The Lady and Gent arrived in a sports car which gave the appearance of a couple on holiday.

Sheila [Fox] was the lady's name and she was dressed in a grey tweed costume and a wee green beret, perched on the rear of her head. Her age about 25 years. Herbert [Howarth] was dressed in blue sports shirt and grey slacks. Time about 2.30 p.m.

A week's rent was paid in advance and on Friday the 13th Mass-Observers entered with type-writers and usual office equipment, work commenced at once. Each day brought fresh and enthusiastic observers who had been out, gathering data.

Amongst the early ones, being Dicky and Ivan who are local young men. Letters and grams were continually arriving and the post and messenger boy were kept busy. The neighbours were amazed at the comings and goings of these young people, who were in and out continuous.

After a couple of weeks' activity, the Director of Mass-O. came over from Bolton, the northern headquarters. He was pleased with the accommodation and the work being carried on in Blackpool.

During, Aug., Sept. and Oct., there was a stream of Observers arriving from Bolton and London. The Bolton people came over for a week-end rest from their labours in the industrial towns. During the Illuminations we had officials from London office who took photos of the various and interesting side lines, of which B'pool leads other seaside resorts.

The office was soon turned, from a respectable front sitting room, into a cross between a drawing office with its charts and diagrams pinned on the wall and a novelty or gift shop and a toffee shop with its sweets in cellophane wrappers. Picture post-cards and trick novelties all over the mantelpiece and the mantelpiece figures, were decorated with a string of coral beads and a monkey on elastic. Blackpool Rock and a trick bottle of Bass completed the set. Newspaper and cuttings were scattered all over the table, chairs and the floor. The reports made by Observers covered every kind of topic and were interesting as well as humourous, of the 1000+1 details of a popular seaside.

OBSERVERS

Observers who were here, were delightful company and very interesting to us.

1. A young student from Oxford who was the leader of the local party, was quiet, a little shy and reserved. 2. Sheila was full of life and first impression was to me, imperious and upish, but after short acquaintance was unaffected and free. A tendency for the company of men. 3. Ralph was from London, a keen worker and a neat appearance. He was from the literary world and whilst here, wrote articles for the newspapers. 4 and 5. Dicky and Ivan came in during the evenings after their everyday work and spent much time here at weekends. 6. Joe [Willcock] was an Observer from Bolton. His home town in East Yorks. He had two interests in Mass-O.: church and pubs. 7. Walter [Hood], also from Bolton, home place, Durham. His work, was Labour and its kindred subjects. These two Observers came here for a rest and relax from industrial Bolton.
Now I come to the figurehead of the movement in these northern spheres:

TOM HARRISSON

A young man, who on first acquaintance, impressed me as a keen student of any subject he was interested in. He had a tired look in his eyes, but after staying here for a few days, he benefited in health.

He, like all Bolton Obs, needed a rest and as no restrictions were placed, on going to bed or getting up, he retired about midnight and rose again at any time between 9 a.m. and 3.30 p.m. Sleep he wanted and he got it.

First impression was, of the strong silent man of the films. A worker who shows the example, to all who labour with him.

Time, place or money, also personal appearance, of no account, if object attained. Shows his appreciation of small kindnesses given him.

8. Martin, A Student from Cambridge and interested in a lighter vein of Mass-O. His interests, while here were the cinemas and entertainment. Hobbies, motor cycles, camera and lady. Also a good linguist. 9. Zita [Crossman] was also from Bolton and her interests were mediums, the Tower, Gardens and Olympia. Charles Madge, Humphrey Spender, Mr Trevelyan, Bunny Mellor, Mr Yong and several others have visited here. Humphrey Spender, I believe was official photographer. 10. Barbara was also from Oxford, home town nr *Stoke*. A good worker and set an example to men Observers, by commencing early in the morning. During her duties as Observer, she attended a fashion parade at Cleveleys, on behalf of Sally Mays Frock Shop as Compère on the microphone. 11. Dorogen or pet name Dodo. Another good worker with early habits. Lovely disposition and always sociable and home London. 12. Bruce was from Oxford also home town. The neatest observer yet. A pleasure to meet him. 13. Steve: from Oxford, home town Worcester. He was tall and very boyish, perhaps I should say, Mother's boy. He was good company and a keen worker. 14. Patrick. Another from Oxford, also neat and tidy. His interests were boarding houses of small size. 15. Ruth. Oxford, home town – Todmorden, Yorks. Early riser and early to bed. Chief food. Nuts and fruit, drink, water. 16. Freda. Oxford, home town – Bedford. A nice young lady, but no forecasts on points pool. 17. Margaret. Oxford, home town – unknown. Another nice girl. 18. Mr Yonker. Sweden. Pleasant and interesting and keen on Mass-Ob. 19. Pamela. A quiet girl of brilliant education, from Oxford. A pleasant little lady. 20. Barbara P. London. Young lady keenly interested in Mass-O. 21. Reynold B[ray] from Bolton. Exploration of the cold storage (icebergs, etc). 22 and 23. Misses K. and T. School teachers. London. 24. Humphrey Spender. London. Films. 25. Dr Oser. St Andrew's University. 26. E. Letchford. Bolton. Unemployed. 27. Dr James. Lecturer. M/c University. 28. Mr Moore. Sycology. 29. Ivan Lockwood. Lib-

rarian. 30. Jim Tomlinson. 31. and 32. Ursula and Julian Trevelyan. London. 33. and 34. Charles and Kathleen Madge. London. 35. Francis Flaherty. London. 36. Miss Goulton. London. 37. Miss Stooke. London. 38. Tom Hannaford. Bolton. Publican and music. 39. Tom Binks. Side piecer. Bolton. 40. and 41. Eric and Alice Bennett. 42. John Summerfield. Writer. London. 43. George Howarth. Blackpool. Coop. 44. Clara Briggs. Blackpool. 45. Doris Boothman. Blackpool. Typist to Mass-O. 46. Neo. Burma. Rango.

Joe Willcock, typically, made contact with Blackpool's seamy underside.

10. Joe Willcock: Making and selling Blackpool Rock

ROCK-MAKING. JUNE 8

X-L. Rock Company of Blundell St. Near the Central Beach. This firm are to be found at the back of one of the side streets 100 yards from the Front, they occupy old premises, at the rear of boarding houses, they have as neighbours in the same premises bedding makers.

There are only 2 men and 3 girls work here, all their stuff is made for the trade on the Front.

There is one long table, a piece of it is of metal, this is heated to allow of the Rock to be worked, on the right are 2 boilers, these have dripping down the sides after the boilings.

Sacks of sugar in the same room, the air conditioning is by keeping the doors open, from appearances these might have been stables at one time.

These people at the time of the visit are making the 'Lolly-Pops', The plasticy green stuff is cut into lumps, the man then presses it into the iron 5″ dia. circle, then passed on to the other man, then puts a stick into it, turns it over and smooths it on the Terazzo topped table, this is then passed on to the girls, they turn the hoops over and smooth them on the marble-like table.

When they are cool they are taken out, covered in cellophane-type paper, these are sold on the Front at 6*d*. each, they are sold wholesale at 4/- the Doz. 50 per cent profit.

These same people make rock, this is sold at 30/- to 36/- per cwt.

Asking the man who made it, this man was said to be 'That chap knows more about it than anybody else', this was told to Obs. at the Lab. Exchange.

'You can't say exactly what they make selling on the Front (he said) they make what they can get, but they never make less than 5/- on the 28 lb box, if the pay 36/- for the cwt. they can make easily 20/- for the cwt., and they might sell anything from 1 cwt. to 3 and 4 cwt., it depends on where they are selling, there are spots better than others, in the Illuminations they sell most near the Amusements on the Central Beach.

They lots of times are selling without paying for the stands, then they get the police on them, they're always in court in the Season, you'll see them, when they see the police, pick up their boxes and beat it, I know some of them are chaps on the dole, they don't always pay their fines, you never hear of them getting sent down for not paying their fines though.

There's chaps as owe £2 and much more, they still keep at it.

The reason why there are those who sell rock to the dealers so cheap is because they won't pay the Board of Trade wages, there's men as will work for £2 a week, that's how they get it so cheap, take it out of the chaps' guts, and put cheap stuff in it.

Theres people making rock as the authorities don't know about.

We get £3.10s a week and lots of overtime in the Summer, we do well in the season, then go up to the 'big House in the Winter', there's no work in Blackpool then.

That's when people should come to see this place. Nobody knows the number of them as sells rock here, they get it from so many places and theres no register of them.'

He told the Obs. that nearly all of the people who made rock on a small scale were sugar-boilers, those who had worked for the bigger firms, then saved some money and set up on their own.

Nearly all the chaps who work on the sweet trade have scalds from time to time and show on their arms.

ROCK-SELLING. JUNE 9

Obs. met a Burnley youth of 22, this fellow was in St Chris. Hostel in London some 6 years ago, he was now hanging about the Station (Central), waiting to carry bags for the visitors, shoes through at the soles, shirt worn thin and dirty white, tall and lean-jawed with skin dried by the Blackpool sun.

'Theres nowt here in Winter, you have to fiddle best you can, on the U.A.B. [Unemployment Assistance Board] or the P.A.C. [Public Assistance Committee], they give you about 15/-, then you got to wait for the Season opening to get owt, in the Season I try and sell Rock, but it's for the other chaps, I can make about £2 to 50/- a week if you don't get caught, the older cops don't run you in the same, it's them young uns as can run what catch you, you put your swag down, and get going, then you keep your eyes open for the cops, you can't be in one place for long though before they are after you, I owe about £7 in fines to the court, they don't send you down for it, but if they get you for being drunk then they tell the magistrates that you owe it, then they give you Hell for it.

You can't make a living in this place unless you fiddle for it, you've got to be bloody cute to get owt, it's easy come when you have and let it go, there's more Cissy's here than in London though.

One way of picking things up is when it's warm at night in the Season, then you get the couples lying out on the sands, they're too bloody keen on what they are doing, then you walk on the sands, see their hand bags and snaffle 'em, they never tell the police 'cause they don't like their folks knowing where they were at that time.

I've been here now for 18 months, and believe me you can always get a drink where you can't get anything else, some times in the Winter you can pick up something at the football matches. But you've got to be careful, because there's always the tecs from the Lab. Exchange on the watch.'

He told the Obs. that some of his pals waited at the stations, sometimes at night they got drunks and then got pally with them, and lifted what they could from the victim.

'The idea in the rock-selling, more so in the Illuminations, is to offer more than the others, so the chaps get rock made that's a bit thinner, so they can offer more bars to the bob, there's more rock sold then than in the Season, folks seem to want to take summat back with them to the kids, and towards the end of the Lights you'll get more for your money off the makers, they want to get shut.'

One of the main preoccupations of Mass-Observers in Blackpool was, of course, sex. Twenty-three Observers, as individuals or in groups, collected information about it. A fascinating and rather imposing chapter in the draft book on Blackpool resulted. We have room only for extracts from this.

Harrisson began his scientific career as an ornithologist, and some of his methodological quirks followed from that. He demanded from his Worktown team observation of many behavioural trivia which could hardly be analysed or used in any significant way. But sex was rather well-suited to his 'bird-watching' approach.

It also offered, as will be seen, alluring opportunities for 'participant observation'. These extracts are included, not only because sex in Blackpool is interesting, but because of the light they shed on the methods and attitudes of the Observers themselves.

11. Mass-Observation: Sex in Blackpool

Blackpool has its sexual legend. We have already noted the way that the Camp and Hydro are misrepresented as sexual blackspots. The same is true of Blackpool as a whole, when you get some way away from it. In the south Blackpool has widely the reputation of being an immoral town, and in Worktown this is so among people who have never been there, or who go there seldom. An observer (SW) who lives in Worcester told people there that he was coming up to Blackpool, was warned 'against observing too many Blackpool females – excessively fast'. Was told 'in Blackpool hotels and boarding-houses all bedrooms communicate with each other by doors'. Compare:

> Unemployed man, Worktown. Himself, did not like Blackpool at all, unless it was just to sit on the Promenade and look at the sea or to go to the Pleasure Beach and watch the expressions on people's faces. Had not been to Blackpool since 1921 ... Believed that Blackpool was no good for young people since they were unused to that sort of freedom for 51 weeks of the year, and went wild in their one week in Blackpool.

What actually happens – 11.30 p.m., a fine evening on the Prom:

> The sea is rough, the sand covered.
>
> 2 men, 2 women. One of girls lies on a form, knees pointing up; boy stands gazing down on her.
>
> 2 men walk slowly south, larger with left arm round other's neck.
>
> 1 man, 1 woman. Kiss, arms clasped round shoulders, 35 secs.
>
> 1 man, 1 woman. He fondles her breasts.
>
> 2 men, 2 women. Separate into couples. Kiss, standing.
>
> 1 man, 1 woman. He gazes into her eyes. Kisses her neck, rubs her nose with his moustache. They peck. She looks up. They talk. She clasps handbag. They cuddle. She tries to press him to her

lips. He kisses her neck. She rises from form, tightens her girdle. He presses her breast, drawing her down. They cuddle. He does not kiss her. They both get up, he towards station.

2 men, 2 women. One man presses girl under him, on railings. Look at waves. Straighten to look at two people. Man eases position. Sticks out backside. Leaves girl, goes to left, blows nose and wipes mouth. Takes hanky out of right trouser pocket, puts it in left.

At a glance Blackpool shows such scenes without restraint. In Worktown we must walk along the back streets at night, after 11.15 when lights are all put out. There, at scattered intervals along the walls, will be closely-linked couples, standing, one or two in each back. Sexual intercourse enjoyed in this way (as common in winter as summer) is generally known as 'having a knee-trembler'. It is the pre-marital or extra-marital method of all those Worktowners who have only the darkened back streets and who often cannot marry for simple economic reasons. It is easy to get a girl-friend in Worktown, if you can show yourself sensible, and have some money, and like cinemas or dancing or (less often) drinking. It takes some time to do anything you like with the girl, if it is possible at all – which it generally is. But this type of sex, backwall and knee-tremble, is only a fraction of the indoor married intercourse. In both there is a marked tendency to concentrate on the week-end, on Saturday night and Sunday early afternoon. The Saturday night out, at cinema or central pub (see *The Pub and the People*) is partially preparation for this. Again on Sunday afternoon when the children, whatever parental views, are sent out to Sunday school you have time to 'forget about work', sex can be fully enjoyed, and intercourse is often downstairs on the sofa, called 'A soffey ender', such afternoon intercourse being termed 'mattinay'. Unemployed are widely supposed to have intercourse more frequently, and our data indicates that this is true, as it is that they go to bed later, sleep longer. Shop assistants who have Thursday afternoon off often have their mattinays then. And if a chap wants 'a shot' during the week, O.K. 'if the wife is willing'. Decent men 'won't take advantage' of their wives, and this is a frequently-expressed point of view in Worktown's morals. Within this framework there is much sexual freedom: adultery, exchange of wives, and 'Living tally', though little promiscuity.

Bearing these points in mind, we may expect and understand a wide range of sexuality in Blackpool, where a position parallel to that of unemployment is created. Certainly the Blackpool backset is strongly sexual . . .

HOLIDAY SEX

It is now possible to examine holiday sex in its own right, without the complications of resident sex and the organised public pro- and anti-sex manifestations. Now we can go out, with a definite objective, on to the dunes and into the alleyways.

As people came out of the Tower and ballrooms many were in mixed couples, having met for the first time that evening. The mechanism of contact and pick-up is the essential start. It has various forms other than the dance, and its simplicity is best illustrated from the holiday diary of a mill-girl:

Friday: Arrive at Blackpool. Staying at Hull Road. Visit the Tower, met 2 young men from Sheffield, went into the Bar and had a few drinks afterwards danced, then on the promenade strolled on the sands. Had supper at Café (Chips and Coffee) arrived back at digs 12 o'clock.

Saturday: Morning went for a drive to Fleetwood, got back for 12.0 dinner. Afternoon went to Pleasure Beach, picked up with 4 young men from Wakefield, had a good lot of amusement, enjoyed the Grand National best, went for a drink to the Huntsman. Evening went to the Tower dancing, from there to the Gardens and then back to the Tower, which we like best. Visit the Café garden for an ice. Listen to the Ladies Band which was playing the Blue Danube.

Sunday: Went to the Huntsman in the morning with four Scotch boys, stayed till dinner and then met them afterwards and went to the Pleasure Beach. Went for a ride in a car to St Anne's with four more boys. Arrived back at digs with boy friend 11.30.

Monday: Strolled on the prom with friends and met 4 Scotch boys, went dancing on the pier and drinks in the bar, enjoyed watching the Tight Rope Walkers and then went and had photo taken. Back to digs.

Tuesday: Went on the pier dancing, came off at 11.30, went up the Prom, went in Doctor Q was very interesting show . . . (No mention of being picked up Tuesday and Wednesday.)

Thursday: Went to visit a friend's then had a stroll on the Pleasure Beach on my own then on prom. After tea went to

Tower dancing with the lady friend, came out, went home down the Prom, picked up with two young men from Preston.
Friday: Didn't go out while afternoon, went down to Pleasure Beach again on my own and then from there back up the prom. in the rain, it was throwing down and there was not a person to be seen. Night went to Winter Gardens, picked up with a sailor from New Zealand. Went and had a look round the amusement penny machines, he won me two bracelets and a powder box. We danced and then home.
Saturday: Morning went with him to Pleasure Beach, and had a good round of amusements. He left at noon for Liverpool to catch his boat. I am leaving Blackpool today.

Though the males are supposed to do the picking-up, the females make their opinion sufficiently clear in behaviour:

Two girls walking towards the Manchester Hotel, about 18 years old. Both smile luringly at three boys passing in the opposite direction. No effect. Two more boys come up. They smile again. All stop and talk. The girls stand arm-in-arm, and the boys with their hands in their pockets. After about 10 minutes talk they walk on in the opposite direction. Running across the road out of the way of a bus, they bump into four boys whom apparently they know. They all stop, talking and laughing, for two minutes. They then walk on again still laughing, the boys once more going in the opposite direction. They occasionally glance at busy stalls but never stop to buy anything.

So that, as so often, George Formby is not imaginative but observational when, in his 1939 Opera House show, he gives Beryl the part of forceful young lady who vainly tries to pick up himself as shy boy. In 65 per cent of recorded cases the girls took the initiative in this way. Popular is the lounge-about approach:

Two girls, 19, come and sit by the railings. One rubs her backside up and down and eventually seats herself on the top rung facing the Promenade. The other stands leaning on the rails, looking at her friend and talking to her. She gets down and both lean seawards. Two youths, 20, come up and get on with them, taking the same stance on their south. Both youths cross their legs.

Impressions of a young local male (JB), August Bank Holiday night:

One line of girls walking along, with two separate groups of men following them. They walked very slowly and turned round at every provocation. Both groups of men following were evidently wanting to pick them up. Both were between 20 and 30. One group was more or less reserved and comparatively well-dressed. The other, a crowd of complete toughs, very poorly-dressed, shouted to the girls and made loud jokes among themselves. It was this group that had most success with the girls. These seemed quite fascinated with the wildness and loudness of one group of followers, while they paid hardly any attention to the other group, who continued eyeing them all the time.

Watched a group playing a sort of rugger-touch, the boys against the girls. The game became very rough, and was punctuated by short struggles between a boy and a girl. The girl nearly always dropped to her knees and then onto the sand. The struggle always ended up in a deadlock, and they stayed clasped together on the sand till one of the girl friends rebuked her. Then they would get up and laugh.

In one group one of the young men began betting one of the girls that she could not stand having smoke blown down her throat. She said she could, and knelt on the sand while he put his mouth over to hers and blew some smoke into her face. She giggled and slithered down full length. This may have been accidental. The youth then held her down though she had made no attempt to rise, and continued to blow smoke in her face. Then he gave this up, and merely lay against her, and both became motionless. Then the friends who had been playing about on the sands came back. They did not seem surprised at seeing them sprawled on the sand, but as soon as they approached, the couple on the sand got up laughing and chaffing, and began dusting themselves. Then the girl's friends told the boy he was a bully to rough-house with girls. The latter replied to this that if she didn't keep quiet he would do the same to her. Then a short scrap ensued in which all joined, the girls were easily overcome, and all ended up by more or less lying on each other in order to keep each other down. It ended by one of them getting up and proceeding to dress. Then they all got up and went off in macs, one with his arm round the shoulder of one of the girls.

In passing we may note that the faint note of Puritan indignation in this account is typical of one reaction of the young local intellectual to his native backset.

Unaccompanied females will have difficulty in staying so, as a tall

1 Entrance to fortune-teller's booth, Blackpool, 1938

2 Tom Harrisson, Bolton, 1937, by Humphrey Spender

3 A meal at 85 Davenport Street, Bolton: Harrisson (standing), Walter Hood (left) and two Mass-Observers, 1937

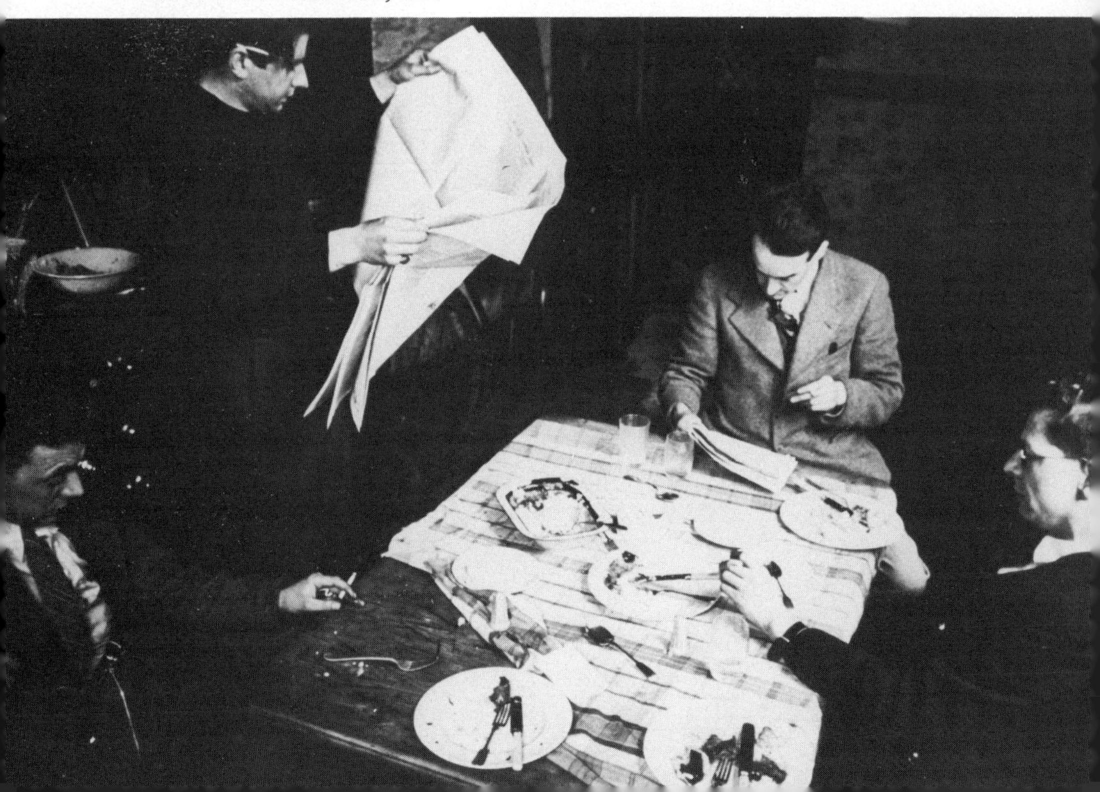

dark one of 24, standing on the prom. at dusk, found (SF); man of 28 comes up:

He: Are you lonely?
Obs. Not particularly.
He: Are you dancing?
Obs. Here?
He: Come dancing with me.
Obs. No.
He: We can go to a show or anywhere you like.
Obs. No.
He: Well, we'll kill time till my car's ready. Are you coming with me, sweetheart?
Obs. I'm busy.
He: Alright. I'll meet you afterwards.
Obs. No.
He: Well, will you kiss me goodnight?
Obs. No.
He: Would you if it was dark? (Pinches observer's cheek.)
Obs. No.
He: So you won't come then?
Obs. No.

He goes. Next comer is a 'Jew boy':

He: What are you writing down?
Obs. Oh, I'm interested in gulls.
He: Is it the laundry?
Obs. No.
He: I should think you'd get a shirt for it if you sent it to the laundry. Had a good time last night.
Obs. Oh, where did you go?
He: I didn't get in till half past two.
Obs. Well, where did you go?
He: I went to a strip tease show.
Obs. Where was it at?
He: Why, are you interested in people getting undressed?
Obs. No, I'm interested in shows in Blackpool.
He: Well, if I told you you'd know as much as I do. Are you coming out with me tonight?
Obs. No.
He: You're a funny girl. (Pinches observer's cheek.) Well, I'll be going now.

Another female observer, blonde, 35, wife of an Oxford don-Labourite, stood outside the Tower and received five invitations in rapid succession:

1. Middle-aged man in bowler and mackintosh: 'Will yer come to bed with me, love? 'Ave yer done it before?'
2. Very tall middle-aged man fairly well-dressed: 'Are you all alone, sweetie? Come along with me and I'll give you a real good time. Come on, now, don't be shy. You don't want to be alone tonight, do you?'
3. Man, 30, wearing mackintosh and cap: 'Come to show with me, lass? I'll pay for you but you'll have to give me a cuddle. What about it lass, come on.'

Obs. 'No, thank you, I'm just meeting a friend.'
He: 'Oh, come on now, 'e isn't as grand as all that, 'e's probably got another girl by now.'

4. Little Scotchman in charge of slot-machine, age 30.

He: Well, how's life treating you?
Obs. I'm enjoying myself, thanks.
He: Where are you staying?
Obs. Along the front.
He: Are you here long?
Obs. No.
He: Where do you come from?
Obs. Down South.
He: I wish I'd met you yesterday when we were closed. I'd liked to have taken you to the pictures. I could see you Monday night. How about it?

5. Man, age 45, brown suit and cap: 'Are you alone? Come and have some supper with me? I know a real good place. Do you live here? Oh, come, I'll show you the sights. You're too pretty to be all alone.'

This simple contact en passant is replaced at the expensive hotels by a more elaborate system. Paying more than 15/- a day you are in a place large enough to enable bedroom manoeuvres, and free of direct landlord or landlady censorship. In one of the most expensive and supposedly 'loosest' (stories of bell rung at 8 so that people can get back to their own rooms, etc.) an Observer, during a week's stay, scored:

1. Outside a bedroom. He: 'Norah, Norah.' Laugh from within.

He: 'You must come and see my friends Mutt and Jeff. They're bright lads. Come and have a drink.'

2. Man says good morning to girl at desk. She says if he says good morning again she'll begin to think it's she that's tight, not him.

3. At dinner on Monday man at table to girl at table: 'I'm sure I've met you before here.' Girl does not recognise him but says that his face does seem familiar. This seems to be an accepted formula for introduction, used six times; in no case was it followed up, and in no case were names exchanged.

On one occasion one girl stopped another in a passage and said: 'Oh, don't you remember me?' The other replied: 'Well, you see, I lost my memory this winter and I can't remember anybody before then.' They talk for a minute and then part, giving each other room numbers but not names.

4. Woman writing in hall, time 12.30. Young man approaches.

Man: Good morning.
Girl: You've said that before.
Man: Have I? Well, it's afternoon now.
Girl: Well, if it's afternoon, why do you say good morning?
Both laugh loudly at this.
Girl: This is the place I was staying at.
Man: (Looking at postcard) Why did you leave it for Blackpool?
Girl: We were driven here by the weather.
Man and girl continue to talk about Scotland, Ireland, weather.
He: Well, I must be going. Be good.
Girl: I always am.
He: No, really?
Girl: Well, my only fault is smoking too much.
He: I've only one vice.
She mistakes this for *voice*, as he is Irish and broadens the I. It takes a short explanation before he really makes his meaning clear to her. Then there is nothing to be said about it.
He: Well, as I said before, be good.
Girl: I always am.

With these special intricacies of middle-class behaviour; back in the streets and pubs where the workers are, less inclined to roundabout:

Manchester Hotel. Three men.
1st Man: White Bud won the Lincolnshire Handicap in 1918.

2nd Man: Eh Jim! you'll have to get me out of this bloody mess. I'm sure that tart's in the family way.
3rd Man: If you were all spawn you couldn't make a child.
4th Man: Come on, let's have another drink.

Two men of 35 approach two women of 30 on the end of the Tower Bar; they speak to the women, who reply. 'No, you've got it wrong, she's not Slackie, go on where's your wife, we're waiting for our husbands.'

Two boys and two girls.
1st Girl: Eh, come on Maude, you don't want owt tonight, let him have it tomorrow. (Laughs.)
1st Boy: She's coming wi' me, arn't ta lass, if tha doesn't tha can go to hell.
2nd Girl: I'm going wi' Jean, I'll see thee tomorrow, don't forget.
1st Boy: Aw don't be so bloody ready to go, I'll take thee.

Victoria Street. 4 youths, 1 girl (23).
1st Man (to girl): Yes, so long.
2nd Man (to girl): Bugger off.
1st Man: Come on.

2 men, 2 women (45), working class, drunk.
Woman: I'm not going on t' sands with thee. Tha can take 'im on t' sands with thee, but I'm not going on sands with thee.

All this culminates, along a small strip of promenade and sand at 11.30 p.m. (24/8), in:

Man leaning against bathing van. Girl in white swagger coat up against him, embracing.
Lying on ground, man trying to get hand up girl's dress. She has left leg pointing into air balanced on right knee, as if trying to prevent him.
Couple sitting above hulkings.
Two couples in shelter, embracing.
Couple under hulkings, lying embracing.
Man feeling girl under hulkings.
Couple kissing in shelter.
Two men leaning over hulkings to peer at couple, who get up, girl arranging her dress. Then watchers go away, grinning.

Barracking young men are common; thus:

Youth and girl lying embraced on sands, in such a manner that man's right arm could not be seen. Much amusement among group of young men, who stood watching, cat-calling and proffering such advice as 'let him have it'. Couple ignored them for a while, then looked out to sea.

Watchers are not youths only. For older men of scoptophilic tendencies the sands at night are a happy hunting-ground. Whenever a couple gets down on the sands, they very quickly have a ring of silent, staring, immobile individuals round them. This is particularly the case in the dark shadows of the Central Pier. Apparently immune from rebuke verbal or physical, silent circles surround each couple, observing their manoeuvres from a range of less than two yards.

This tolerance naturally helped Observers in their study of sex activities; all the same a certain toughness was required to get a report such as:

Two couples on seat opposite the Palatine Hotel, facing the sea. We sat on seat adjacent, twenty yards south. TH commentated, RP screened him, HH wrote from the dictation, RG screened him, TIR pretended to be sick over the railings.

Breakdown. She looked at the wrist watch on the inner side of her left hand. Her left hand then goes onto her head. She is passing her fingers over her eyebrows. The man's hand is locked on her left hip. Shows a slightly frayed cuff. The girl got her left hand up over his arm, then further, onto her eyebrows, onto her eyes. She holds her hat from her fork. Then her hat goes over her bosom. Her hand twiddles the hat. She feels her head again. She turns and laughs. Looks at RG with disfavour. Her hand goes to the inside of her hat and passes round inside. Her head lies back on the seat, she is laughing, she wants him to kiss her and he does not. He snuggles up against her, she up to him, he down to her, her head goes away, his head follows, she accepts, they give one another the works. Time of kiss – 33 seconds. His head is up against her cheek, he is looking into her eyes. Her head goes right away. He scratches his nose with his right hand. He nuzzles into her, her head lies back. Time – 17 seconds.

Now a new position. They are looking out to sea, cheek to cheek. She looks at her watch. She moves. He puts his hand under her left breast and pulls her down. She titivates her hat. In the original position, except that his right hand is further down near her thighs, they kiss. Time – 28 seconds. As he comes out of the

> kiss he slips his hand further down. They are cheek to cheek. People come and sit by them. They sit upright. They are looking out to sea, not holding at all. Then she has her head right up, looking left, he is looking at her cheek. She titivates her hat on her left breast, touches her head. She gets up. He pulls her down. Screws himself up against the back of her neck. They kiss. Time – 26 seconds. Barracking from crowd passing. Then in again, boring right in. Time – 22 seconds [. . .]

We have already said that the back street is the *locus classicus* of unmarried love in Worktown; here [are] the results of turning car headlights on back streets in the central Blackpool area:

> In the back street behind Vance Road seven couples necking against the wall and in the corners of doorways. In the other back street on the other side of Vance Road five couples. In a gate near where the back street comes out on to Coronation Street a man alone. His girl standing in Coronation Street looking down the back after him. As we come out one of the couples emerges behind us: 'Ooh, come on now, it's five to twelve.' Another couple comes out behind them. Back of Vance Road one couple necking. Also, back of Albert Road, leaning a foot apart in one corner of the gateway, cigarettes in hands.

None of the vigorous activity that Worktown backs would show at the same hour.

Sample counts of couples under 50 during daylight gave 49 per cent no contact, 1 per cent handclasp, 47 per cent arm-in-arm, 3 per cent arm round waist. A non-comparable sample of couples 11.30 to midnight (232 cases):

Sitting down and embracing	120
Standing up embracing	42
Lying on sand embracing	46
Sitting kissing	25
Necking in cars	9
Standing kissing	3
Girl sitting on man's knee	7

At 10.15 p.m. of 82 groups on a strip of promenade 54 were couples, and of these 50 were seaters, 26 embracing, 8 loungers, 9 kissing, 5 talking, 1 looking at the sea, 1 eating chips.

So far we have seen only kissing, petting, necking. It will be noticed that the above table has no category for 'Copulating'. There is a simple reason for this: none of these couples were copulating. When we began work in Blackpool we expected to see copulation everywhere. What we found was petting, feeling, masturbating one another. Observer units combed the sands at all hours, crawled around under the piers and hulkings, pretended to be drunk and fell in heaps on located sand-couples to feel what they were doing exactly, while others hung over the sea-wall and railings for hours watching couples in their hollowed-out sandpits below. Lines of observers systematically beat the notorious sand dunes, with results such as these:

> HH nothing, in 300 yards. RG stalked one shadow – Observer's. RP saw a man and woman (40) plump, unattractive, middle-aged, walk slightly apart. Then she took the man's arm. He follows their footsteps backwards; they had apparently been sitting in the sand. A car comes from Blackpool direction. Apparently two men and two women inside. Drives alongside convalescent home up to dunes. One man sitting on seat alone at side of road. Man and woman coming off dunes (inland side of road), arms round each other's necks. Between convalescent home and three hundred yards north HH and TR saw nothing. As they came towards the car which had just been parked there the two couples went from the sands back to their car and drove at speed towards Blackpool. Heavy wind this night. Sand blowing. Strip of sand hills quarter of a mile alongside the railway, RP came across only one sign of life, a squawk; could not find the girl who had uttered it because of the dimness and the wind. Later RG reported that he almost stepped on a couple in the same spot, heard girl's voice sobbing, 'Oh, Ted, Ted. Oh, what are you doing?'

All the alleged sex-areas were covered in this way, including four miles of prom, two miles of artificial cliff, six miles of sand, acres of dune and park . . .

Typical of the difference between truth and legend was an incident at 1 a.m. when a band of weary Observers – weary from working the sands and dunes – stopped for coffee at an open-all-night stall on the prom. The stall-holder, an old hand in Blackpool, in conversation said that it was disgusting the way some of the young people went on, that right now there were thousands on the sands, and the large part of them they'd stay there right through the night. In fact, there were three couples.

Altogether, as a result of exhaustive research and many pick-ups by Observers themselves, we scored four records of copulation. One of these was by an Observer (it should be added that several of these Observers were picked for their experience and skill in this kind of work in Worktown, Oxford, and other M-O surveys):

> Observer then gets talking to group of five people, 3 women and 2 men. One of the women said her name was . . . and resided at Leeds but used to live at Worktown, been married 8 years and had a boy aged 8. I asked her was her husband with her she replied 'No'. Observer bought her a drink (gin) and she told me that her hubby was a neurasthenic and said she had come to Blackpool for some fun. I said 'that's what I'm here for too.' We had another drink and I asked her where she was staying and she replied 'up North'. I asked her if it would be alright if I took her home and she agreed. So after closing time we came out and with her being a married woman the arrangement was that I should follow behind her. I followed quite a good way along the Prom until we got to North Pier. Then she turned round and said, 'I'm sorry, Jack, it is Jack, isn't it?' Observer replied, 'Yes, Jack Longford.' 'I live down Central, Charnley Road', so we cut through into Central Drive and dived down several poorly lit streets until we came to back Charnley Road. Observer got her to lean against a wall so that he would not dirty his clothes. She is about 5ft 8 inches in height, well developed, brunette dressed in blue costume, white tammy and sandal type of shoes with no stockings on. She was quite gushing when I kissed her and after several more Observer began to play near the thighs and felt a pair of artificial knickers, pulling these down, at the same time kissing her . . .

Observer proceeded in a normal fashion, but was not allowed full satisfaction as she kept on saying 'Oh, don't, Jack, you might get into trouble' and 'No, no more, Jack, I'm afraid'.

Second case was with middle-aged couple, who performed a public act on South Shore cliffs. Third under Central Pier. Fourth, and doubtful:

> About 8 p.m. on aerodrome saw couple (18 she, 21 he) on aerodrome grounds, man with his hand up girl. Man turned away at his appearance, girl tried to pull her clothes down but only managed to get her underskirt down.

It is the considered opinion, based on detailed study and continually negative results, that in relation to the number of persons on holiday in Blackpool, the amount of extra-marital actual sexual intercourse is negligible, less than on a Saturday night in Worktown.

In fact, if there is a slot-machine whose readings truly reflect the Blackpool scene it is the new 1939 *Love Meter*, to be found in Luna Park, and costing ½d, not the usual penny. Under the slogan 'Measure your Sex-Appeal on this Love Tester', the following varieties of temperament, in this order and arrangement, appear:

Bashful	Uncontrollable
Shy	Furious
Modest	Flirtatious
Indifferent	Lovable
Cold	Jealous
Harmless	Careful

Against flirtatious a green electric bulb, against furious a red one, against each of the rest a white one. 'Drop Coin in Slot. Squeeze Handle for Answer.' A continuous sample produced the following results:

Cold
Modest
No result at all
Careful
Flirtatious
Lovable
Bashful
No result at all
Jealous
Flirtatious
Cold
Lovable
Bashful
No result at all
Cold
Shy
No result at all
Careful
Lovable
Jealous
No result at all
Careful
Cold

You are never indifferent, never harmless, never furious, never uncontrollable. Apparently, you can never be an extreme case. Blackpool unexpectedly counsels (and creates) a golden mean between indifferent and uncontrollable.

Sometimes persistent reporters made us say something and we generally said that 'Blackpool was the most moral town in England'. This always got headlines, and several times seemed positively to annoy the municipal authorities, so that both the Mayor and the Chairman of the Publicity Committee made public press statements of hostility to M-O. For it is probably important that the myth and its correlated holiday dream shall be kept up; though the imputations of brassiered belle on postcard and publicity brochure bear little relation to the real thing, they are nevertheless true, true in the minds of innumerable Worktowners.

Mass-Observation's first book, *May 12*, a study of George VI's Coronation Day, had not been a success – it seems to have sold a bare 800 copies. Humphrey Jennings had been the main compiler – his methods were odd, amusing, infuriating, and only a few critics, Evelyn Waugh being one, were really appreciative of them. This was Jennings' first and last major job for M-O – thereafter he dropped out from the organisation, though he remained in touch with Madge and Harrisson and carried Mass-Observation's broad aims forward in the remarkable documentary films which he directed during the war.

A second book, *First Year's Work* (1938) drew on material sent in by the Panel of volunteer Observers. During the second half of 1937, they received questionnaires (known as 'Directives') asking them about their social lives, their smoking and drinking habits, their reading preferences and – rather obscurely – what they kept on their mantelpieces. By 1938, Mass-Observation had come to regard the panel as a useful source of information on a wide range of issues and relied heavily upon it to monitor public response to the political events of that year – the year of the Munich Crisis. Their material was often combined with more directly obtained data which was gathered by full-time Observers based in London.

By mid-1938, the Worktown operation was losing impetus. Harrisson's interest largely shifted to London. Mass-Observation studied the important by-election at Fulham West in April 1938, which Edith Summerskill won for Labour from the Conservatives. (In effect, the Observers, 'participating', helped her win it, as she acknowledged.) Harrisson recognised that this by-election provided a localised setting for the study of reactions to the international and national crisis which was ultimately to lead to war.

In November, Harrisson and Trevelyan attracted much publicity with an

Page 14 THE DAILY MIRROR Tuesday, December 6, 1938

He and his thousand followers are giving their services to the "DAILY MIRROR"

Public Busybody No. 1

By TOM HARRISSON

For two years TOM HARRISSON has been working on a NEW IDEA. . .

This young scientist has gathered round him a corps of men and women in different jobs, living in different parts of England. Their job is called MASS OBSERVATION. They note YOUR BEHAVIOUR in a certain set of circumstances, and make reports on it.

During the past weeks Harrisson's men focused on Halifax during the recent outbreak of razor-slashing in that town.

Here he tells some of the incredible findings of his observers.

SLASH! . . . a shadow in the darkness of an alley . . . the sweep of an arm . . a girl screams.

The Slasher. . .

Does he really exist?

Is he real?

Or is he a fake?

To try to get at the truth of the whole affair, a Mass Observation unit have been spying in Halifax.

They have been listening to conversations in public-houses and tea shops.

They have even canvassed for opinions from door to door.

This page will tell you what they have found out.

Before we turn to Halifax, let's look at a little "attack" incident at Walworth, London, S.E.

It actually happened a fortnight before the Halifax ripper broke into the news.

✦ ✦ ✦

On November 25 it was reported that young girls in Walworth were being accosted by a man who asked them if they had dropped a comb. He then followed them and attacked just as they were about to enter their homes.

Mass observers went to Walworth, and these were some of the findings.

Notice them closely, because they have a strong bearing on the slashings which subsequently took place in Halifax.

There was no scare among residents.

Six out of twenty-five women interviewed in the district neither knew nor cared anything about the attacks.

Fifteen of the twenty-five had only read about them in newspapers—proof that there was little "scare" talk about the incidents.

Moreover, observers counted the women who continued to walk through the "attacker" streets alone after the incidents.

Twenty-six per cent. of the total number of women were unaccompanied. Not mtch sign of a local scare here.

In fact, in streets only a few hundred yards from that in which the attacker operated it was found that residents and passers-by actually knew nothing of the incidents.

Now, these facts had been noted during the days immediately before the Halifax slasher struck for the first time.

With the findings of Walworth, mass observers focused their attentions on the Halifax rippings.

First let's find out what the "slasher" looked like according to what people in Halifax told observers.

These are the compiled descriptions of the slasher.

He is made out to be rather like the average thug of detective fiction:—

"Flat, boxer-like face . . . few teeth. Wearing a dirty-coloured raincoat and a grey trilby. . . . Moving in stockinged feet."

"He has bright buckles on his shoes."

"Black teeth."

. . . enters all conversations, mainly humorously When spoken of seriously, most people think it is not one man.

"Ever since the Phyllis Hirst child murder in Bradford a few weeks ago, there have been isolated attacks on young women, and now the slasher.

"There is the certainty here that the person responsible will slip up by being too bold."

Another observer in a textile mill writes:—

"One man told me that his wife visited a woman who lives on a main street, yet who had the door chained, despite the fact that her husband, heavy and 6ft. tall, was in the house.

"A carrier from Halifax told me that a man hurrying down a hill to catch a bus had been

2 *Daily Mirror* feature, 6 December 1938

exhibition called 'Unprofessional Painting' at the Peckham Health Centre (London). Much of the show was provided by the 'Ashington Group' of self-taught miners and artisans in Northumberland, who had been 'taken up' by Mass-Observation. Other exhibitors included lower-class Londoners and Czech peasants. Trevelyan called for a 'national movement' to bring painting and people together. Harrisson's statements produced the ineffable headline, in a local paper, 'Anyone Can Paint a Good Picture – says Scientist' (*South London Press*, 11.11.38).

Harrisson stood forth as a populist – and was more and more a successful publicist, whose articles were sought by editors. While Madge continued the Bolton survey, directed towards the study of the 'economics of everyday life', Harrisson took charge of a survey of anti-semitism in London's East End. The fieldwork seems to have been primarily carried out by one full-time Observer, a working-class man originally from the North of England, who lived in Whitechapel, just off Commercial Road. Most of the reports deal with the Jewish community in the East End and it may seem, therefore, that the choice of the following extract is unfair, being brief and not at all connected to anti-semitism. Nevertheless, it is an irresistible example of the extremes of absurdity to which Observers were prepared to go in pursuit of the 'facts' – 'Even the drab and sordid features of industrial life will take on new interest when they become the subject of scientific observation. Squalid boarding houses will become for the Observer what the entrails of the dogfish are to the zoologist . . . In the detection which we intend to practise, there is no criminal and all human beings are of equal interest. We do not intend to intrude on the private life of the individual. Collective habits and social behaviour are our field of enquiry' (*Mass-Observation*, pp. 29–30). Presumably, with this exalted purpose in mind, the Observer was able to record the following incident immune from any suggestion of voyeurism!

12. Leslie Taylor: Undressing in the East End, 5 February 1939

Description of male 25 cockney (Irish) undressing for bed. Time 11.40 to 11.48.40 p.m. Light was originally switched on in room.

Male came into bedroom dressed in blue shirt, dark suit, only. He undid the front of his braces and slung them over his shoulder, sat down on bed, immediately got up and lit a cigarette stood facing bed smoking his cigarette, 20 secs. Talking and motioning with his arms to someone already in bed, 10 secs. Sits down on bed again and strokes his chin with his right hand, 5 secs. Pulls off his tie without undoing the knot, throws it over bed rail. Bends down and takes off his shoes, throws them to other side of room away from bed. Holds his head in his hands, 25 secs. Rolls up his shirt sleeves, picks his nose with his left hand, and rubs it on his shirt. Throws cigarette into fireplace (not visible), scratches back of his head with right hand. Motions to person in bed and shows the motions of a boxer an exhibition lasting 15 secs, scratches his back with right hand, pulls off his trousers, sits on bed and rubs his hand round his balls. Gets up and rubs his legs from ankles to knees. Stands up erect and goes over to fireplace, folds his trousers and goes over to bottom of bed putting them carefully over the rail. Sits down on bed, picks up newspaper from floor, looks casually at front page, stands up, climbs on bed, throws back clothes and slides slowly into bed and pulls clothes over him. Time taken 8 mins. 40 secs.

In January 1939, *Britain by Mass-Observation* was published as one of the red-and-white series of Penguin Specials. Its bold account of public opinion during the Munich Crisis gave it acute topical appeal. It was widely and well reviewed and was reported to have sold 100,000 copies in ten days. We have extracted material from a chapter on the current dance craze, the Lambeth Walk.

It contains material which was gathered between 1938 and 1939 in the course of an investigation into the dance music industry partly financed by Mecca. One Observer was mainly responsible for the work, which included not only descriptions of people at dances but also interviews with musicians and band leaders, dance hall proprietors, entertainers, dance instructors and sheet music publishers. No full account of the investigation has ever been written.

Mass-Observation's interest in the origins and evolution of dance patterns extended beyond the purely observational; in the development of mass public dancing and the trend away from couple-based dance routines, Mass-Observation glimpsed what it felt to be a political expression in cultural form.

In an article for *Picture Post*, 7 January 1939, Tom Harrisson describes how a popular dance, the Chestnut Tree, was assiduously promoted by C. L. Heimann, head of the Locarno Dance Circuit, who had previously popularised the Lambeth Walk in dance halls. He claimed that the Lambeth Walk was 'the first British dance to challenge American supremacy' because it could be enjoyed by people with no formal dance training and because it was 'typically English'.

13. Mass-Observation: Doing the Lambeth Walk, 1939

Any time you're Lambeth way
Any evening, any day
You'll find us all doin' the Lambeth walk.

This is the song that half the world started singing in 1938. To the song a dance was added, a dance that was half a walk, and it caught on as no new dance has done for years. You could, and can, find them doing the Lambeth Walk in Mayfair ball-rooms, suburban dance halls, cockney parties and village hops. Scotland and the industrial north took it up as keenly as the south. From all sorts of out-of-the-way places came news of its penetration. An observer who visited the far-away isle of Arran reported that the 'natives' were doing it there. It spread to New York and thence right across America; to Paris and thence to Prague – Geoffrey Cox reported in the *Daily Express*, September 6, 1938: 'Czechoslovakia's Little Man is keeping his head . . . Over the week-end his thoughts turned to . . . a strange new English dance, the Lambeth Walk, which has just hit the dance- halls of Prague.' While a leader-page in the same paper, crisis-day, September 19, said:

> 'Paris was herself last night, the restaurants were filled, and they were all doing the Lambeth Walk, and when a Frenchman does it, it looks like drill in a gymnasium.
>
> They love the song, and think it is a sort of national anthem. When everyone toasted "M. Shamberlaing" in the café last night, they sang the "Lambeth Walk" at attention.'

If you are prepared to be scientific about society, you must be prepared for surprises and forget your pre-conceived ideas. What people feel about the war danger is an obviously serious subject, but it is less obvious why the popularity of a dance is of anything more than a frivolous interest. But if we can get at the reason for the fashion, and see it in its setting, it may help us to understand the way in which the mass is tending. We may learn something about the future of democracy if we take a closer look at the Lambeth Walk [. . .]

Lambeth Walk is a working-class shopping street, just off the arterial Lambeth Road and the Kennington Road with tributaries of Lollard Street, Jaxon Street, Old Paradise Street, much condemned housing; street market; a cinema also used as chapel. It continues into Tyers Street, flanked on both sides by huge blocks of working-class flats. The people who live in these flats have mainly come from other parts of London and this is changing the character of the district. There are many factors which are tending to destroy the native cockney culture, but you don't have to look far to find it still vigorously existing [. . .]

A spontaneous talent for dancing and song is a Lambeth tradition, having its connection with music-hall tradition but also having a life of its own. It has many features in common with primitive dancing. Men dress up as women or pretend to be animals. Beer plays its part, but observation showed that those who take part may be *half* drunk, but are certainly not whole drunk. It certainly is true of Lambethians having a bit of fun that:

> 'Everything's free and easy,
> Do as you darn well pleasey . . .'

On August Bank Holiday night, an Observer was asked along to one of the parties. It was the end of the holiday, most of them had 'been to Hampstead and got all boozed up'. On the Sunday there had been a big wedding party which some of them attended and at which the bride had broken her arm. Most would have to be starting work at 6 or 7 next morning. After closing time the whole party proceeded from the —— —— to a house nearby, carrying crates of beer, each holding four quart-bottles. Already at the —— —— they had started swaying into the dance, and on the pavement outside two of the women were dancing with linked arms.

The party was held in an upstairs sitting-room, about 14 by 12 feet, with a piano, two settees and chairs round the wall, and an elegant blue-tiled fireplace – the tiles came unstuck later in the evening. Men and women were there in equal numbers, and including one or two who came in and went out, there were 24 all told – and 28 quart bottles of beer. The party lasted from 11.30 to 1.30 a.m. Four performers took turns at the piano; they all played by ear, and they all played very well. Three others took turns with the accordion. Dances alternated with songs – there were solos by a woman, a young man, and an old man of 83. He was the best singer and his age didn't in the least prevent him from having a good time with the rest. His songs included 'Up Goes the Price of Meat, Ta Ra Ra' and 'My Bradshaw Guide'. All joined in the choruses of these and others, such as 'Lily of Laguna', 'The Lambeth Walk', and 'What does it Feel Like to be Poor?'. The songs they enjoyed most were the ones that were nearest to their own lives, with economics well to the fore. (But the people who go to the Dorchester don't listen to songs about dividends.)

The first time the observer's glass was filled he emptied it. Then he noticed that the others after taking a swig from theirs, handed it on. Perhaps on the same analogy, when one man's nice-looking wife came in half way through, another man, friend of the first, gave her a good kiss. It was all free and easy and went with a terrific swing, but order was kept and there were certain rules, like keeping silence during the solos. Mostly the women asked the men to dance. Everyone danced, old, middle-aged and young.

The striking feature of the dancing was the rolling tempo, less nerve-taut than American swing and hot rhythm, somewhat less martial than the tune Noel Gay wrote for the 'Lambeth Walk' (he also wrote 'Round the Marble Arch' and 'The King's Horses and the King's Men'). This tempo the pianists and dancers managed to introduce into waltzes and fox-trots, but it was most obvious when they danced their 'own' dances, with improvised steps. The dancers faced each other, by two and two, or by three and three, with linked arms. They did jigging steps with their feet, plus some high kicking, then the two lines crossed over, turned and re-formed. As they crossed, they walked in the half-lilting, half-swaggering way that Lupino Lane [a popular cockney entertainer] used in his Lambeth Walk. For the men it is a swagger, arms out from the sides, like a boxer playing for position, for the women it is more of a lilt, with hips swaying. The two get mixed, though, when the men dress as women and behave like them – which is part of the tradition. Also, men dance with men and women with women quite freely.

Two of the toughest men came in, some time after midnight, made up with red eyebrows and white cheeks, each wearing a woman's hat and dress, and also (under the dress) pyjama trousers. One had false breasts, the other a pregnant belly. A woman came up and kicked the belly, and the man with the false breasts made his wife hold them. One of the men made an appropriately lewd remark and there was some pantomiming of the kind that is usually classed as 'obscene' and which is familiar to anthropologists in many kinds of primitive dance. Later another pair of men dressed as women and behaved in much the same way. Finally the party broke up in the best of good temper, singing:

'We play the Lambeth way,
Not like you but a bit more gay,
And when we have a bit of fun
Oh, Boy ——'

The eldest son of the G.O.M. of the party, a fish-shop owner, mid-aged, told the observer how a song called 'The Lambeth Walk' suddenly became the rage in 1903. He was 11 years old then, and danced it outside the Lyceum with his sister. Then it faded out, but in various forms, always changing, still went on at the Lambeth Walk parties, along with the Cake Walk. Observer: 'Did you dance the Lambeth Walk before Lupino Lane took it up?' He: 'Well we had our own show, it hadn't any name. But we always used to say "Oi!"' [...]

More significant, because its effects were observable on a large scale, was the L.C.C. experiment of having Open Air Dancing in the parks. This was in August 1938, and the parks were in working-class areas: Islington, Wapping, Southwark and Camberwell. The success of the experiment was largely due to the popularity of the Lambeth Walk and its capacity for bringing people on to the floor and making them dance. In each case it was played three or more times in the course of the evening – the band leader announcing it as the 'Wapping Walk', 'Highbury Shuffle', etc., according to the place. The performance ended with a prolonged Lambeth Walk, the climax in which everybody joined.

At Myatts Fields, Camberwell, on August 8, 1938, there were 3,000 dancers and spectators. The band played from a covered bandstand round which the dancers danced on the asphalt. Then came a dense ring of spectators and outside that a circular concrete path with people walking round it. Most of the dancers were young, though there were many elderly spectators. Few of the girls had hats, though nearly all carried bags. About half the men had open shirts. Sample counts of the couples dancing showed that there were about equal numbers of man-and-girl and girl-and-girl couples; one or two man-and-man couples were observed. This was not due to a lack of young men but to their relative shyness about going onto the floor. According to an observer with dancing training, most of those dancing had had no lessons but danced well all the same – if they didn't know the steps they invented them. The first time the Lambeth Walk was played, the floor crowded at once. There were threes and fours as well as couples. No one worried about the exact stage reached in the dance. Everyone shouted 'Oi!' and sang [...]

There was the same enthusiasm at Highbury Fields, Islington, on August 11, but on a far larger scale. There the crowds totalled some 20,000, and the official arrangements broke down under the strain. The inner ring of asphalt meant for the dancers became lined on both sides with onlookers as well, leaving only a narrow lane for dancing. One had to fight to get in or out of this ring. The bulk of the crowd stood round outside watching and listening to the music. Announcements and speeches were drowned by the voice of the crowd, in spite of powerful loudspeakers. This was the second open-air dancing at Islington, and the crowds were more than double what there had been at the first. Here too the Lambeth Walk was the chief excitement, though the dancers in the end just tramped and bounced round in a solid mass, speeding into a blind scrum. At this stage the greatest goodwill was maintained, but there was little chance of dancing in the usual sense. The park-keepers who had to hold the outer ring were sweating and exhausted. An observer's report:

> 'Very dense crowd surging outside the small gate in the railings. Three keepers forcibly controlling influx and efflux. Big one forcing a "Gangway!" through the crowd for people coming out.

Entrance in little spurts of 3 or 4, every few minutes. Enormous pressure, usually towards gate, sometimes a reaction as keeper pushes them back. Impossible to avoid treading on other people's feet. Impossible to raise an arm. Crowd rather annoyed on the whole, especially when people are coming out. Keepers pushing, threatening, reviling, reasoning and making jokes by turns. One, small, worried, standing on a seat immediately inside the gate: "Anybody got a pint?" – laughter from crowd; girls repeat the words. Without any personal effort, Observer was sucked towards and finally injected through the gate. Immediate contrast: no rows of seats at that point, large empty space between railings and outer ring of onlookers, no pressure at all.

To two consecutive dances there was no dancing at all. They went round in arm-linked groups of 4–7 or so. Later there were many couples as well as various kinds of grouping, but on the whole no real dancing. Band played "Daisy Bell", "She was one of the Early Birds" and "Two Lovely Black Eyes" in quick succession. No dancing proper. Crowd sang the words . . . Later, conditions for dancing seemed to be rather better – there were fewer people attempting it. Many young children, in pairs or other groups, trying to dance, unsuccessfully, and barging the adults. Many pairs of youths dancing in unorthodox styles. Band plays "Make a Bonfire of your Troubles". Everyone livens up; dancing stops; they hop round together in close lines. Some merely walk. Five young men form a close-linked circle and go forward, rotating slowly. Two young men do separate eccentric steps side-by-side, next to outer ring, causing much amusement among spectators. At end of "Bonfire of your Troubles", pace increases to about double: everyone gives up dancing and runs round. More like a cattle stampede than a dance.

Loud but unintelligible announcement from loudspeakers. One young man to ditto, ironically, "Garron, clap; that was good, wahnit?"

Final dance – "It's 3 o'clock in the morning". Words sung. Joke made about title. Dance ends. Announcer says, after pause: "Wait a minute: there's one thing more. Can anyone tell me what it is?" Small boy somewhere: "Lambeth Walk!" Others take up the cry. Lambeth Walk begins . . . .'

Interestingly, the Lambeth Walk has become *not* the final dance, but a necessary ritual winding-up of the whole affair. And the other dances are reduced to a form as like as possible to the mass-version of the Lambeth Walk. Among other advantages of the varied grouping which supersedes the conventional male-female couple is that it means the boys don't have to ask girls to dance. In the earlier part of the evening when couple-dancing prevailed, an observer counted in two consecutive dances 30 mixed couples and 74 women – some indication of the shyness between the sexes [. . .]

That this mass-dancing accepts and glorifies the Lambeth Walk is significant of the nature of its social appeal, and makes it much more than a piece of middle-class romanticism about working-class conditions. It proves that if you give the masses something which connects on with their own lives and streets, at the same time breaking down the conventions of shyness and stranger-feeling, they will take to it with far more spontaneous feeling than they have ever shown for the paradise-drug of the American dance-tune. The dream-sex of the dance lyric points away from social feeling and activity and towards a world of personal superstition and magic (see the analysis of the dance by Tom Harrisson, *New Writing*, Winter, 1938). It is no more about reality than Hitler's speeches are. Ballroom dancers sleep-walk to its strains with the same surrender of personal decision as that of uniformed Nazis. These Lambeth Walkers are happy because they find they are free to express *themselves* without the hypnosis of a jazz-moon or a Führer.

The dance, then, was in the first place an out-door thing of the seasons and of communal participation, 'a prayer with the legs'. But it lost all earth and harvest meanings when industrialism submerged the village green in factory and soot. Yet the dance-urge is strong, and stuck. Through the nineteenth century dancing stayed largely social, though more exclusive (big houses) in patterns of Lancers and Waltz, indoors. Jazz scattered that, and, with the war, made dancing a couple affair, the boy and girl, in a restaurant or dancehall. The words still had the pre-industrial angles, heaven, rain, moonshine and corn, thanks to the American Negro and his homeland nostalgias. Co-operating dances faded away, and for the past fifteen years we have been doing steps increasingly stereotyped and repetitive. Last year Big Apple and Shottisch attempted to socialise slightly again. But only the Lambeth Walk succeeded in a big way, because it makes everyone do the same thing at the same time, and express their togetherness with smack and shout. The effect on the private tempo of dancing has been great, may be greater. Partly because one or two people sensed the deficiency in Hollywood jazz, more by chance hit and miss in a situation where many ordinary folk felt that deficiency, the Lambeth Walk has swept the world, is the first contemporary dance from this country that has put the world on its feet, in the same sort of way (but much more so) as its close relative, the Cake Walk, did when taken up by Charlie Chaplin who lived in Lambeth thirty years ago. And the success of the Lambeth Walk has shattered a whole lot of dancehall dogmas, about people's inhibitions, the urge to escape, etc., etc., etc. . . .

III

The Blitz and its Aftermath, 1940–1943

By the late summer of 1939, 'Mass-Observation' had become a household word (see Figure 00). Yet, despite the vast success of *Britain*, the organisation was in trouble. The Bolton books, incessantly advertised as 'appearing shortly', were, in fact, except for *The Pub and the People*, still in an untidy stage of drafting. As for the treasures sent in by the National Panel, the small full-time staff in Blackheath couldn't really cope with them. As an astute journalist had pointed out long before, Madge, after only a year, had found himself buried under an estimated 2,300,000 words of Day Reports, sent in by the Panel, and this represented 'infinite regress', with information constantly outstripping Mass-Observation's capacity to process it (*Reynolds News*, 1.5.38). Nor could Mass-Observation improve its sketchy finances unless it compromised its 'scientific' objectivity by doing market research work. Its founders actively sought such work – with the proviso that Mass-Observation itself must retain possession of its results for the benefit of science and of posterity.

Then and later, Mass-Observation would claim that its National Panel gave it special access to movements of opinion which routine questionnaires could not detect. On page 10 of *Britain*, it stated that there were '1,500 amateur Observers'. This was somewhat disingenuous, though less so than the figure of 2,000 used on the dust jacket of the first edition, then dropped when the book was reprinted. Nick Stanley has established that this latter figure represented all those who wrote in during the first three years of the organisation. But excluding 'once off' replies, a bare 1,095 people joined the Panel between 1937 and 1945. In 1939, the peak year of Panel activity, only five men and one woman actually replied to all the monthly questionnaires, and Dr Stanley shows that 235 men and 114 women formed the 'small select band' who wrote in more than four times (Stanley, 1981, pp. 147–58).

In the summer of that year, just over 400 people replied to the ques-

3 Eric Frazer woodcut to illustrate a programme announcement on Mass-Observation in the *Radio Times*, 1 June 1939

tionnaire sent to the Panel on 'Class'. Men outnumbered women by over two to one. Over a third of the respondents were unmarried men under twenty-five, and though the women were better spread as regards age, three fifths of them were under thirty-five. Nearly three quarters of this Panel were unmarried. A surprising proportion – about one fifth – assigned themselves confidently to the 'upper', 'upper-middle' and 'professional' classes. Seven out of sixteen described themselves as 'middle-class' or 'lower-middle-class'. Many who refused to commit themselves, or nominated unusual categories, would clearly have been judged 'middle-class' by others. Fewer than one in six regarded themselves as 'working-class'.

The 'typical' male Mass-Observer was a young clerk or student, the 'typical' female was a teacher or middle-class housewife. Unrepresentative of Britain's population as to age and sex, the Panel was also 'skewed' geographically, with a very heavy bias towards the South-East of England.

Does all this mean that the Panel was sociologically worthless? Certainly not. It gave Madge and Harrisson access to the private opinions of hundreds of people. The young middle-class men and women who predominated came from a highly significant segment of the population, moving left in opinion, under the impact of world crisis.

The outbreak of war gave Mass-Observation's work a sharpness of focus it had been lacking. All its findings had significance in relation to national

"Excuse me, madam—I am a mass-observer and it may interest you to know that you are the 25th person to use that particular expression when tripping over that sandbag"

4 Cartoon from the *Bystander*, 6 March 1940

morale. Even before the actual declaration of war in September 1939, Harrisson, now in charge of the Panel, called upon volunteers to send in diaries. These would be even more difficult to process than the 'Directive replies' which still came in, but they would provide much fascinating material for later researchers. Madge and Harrisson soon put together a very lively account of the early phases of the 'Phoney War', *War Begins at Home*, published early in 1940, and Mass-Observation acquired a dignified, if secret, role as supplier of reports on morale to the Ministry of Information.

When Mass-Observation published the first issue of its new magazine, *Us*, in February 1940, it could report that the organisation employed, in London and Bolton, 18 full-timers. In war-time, staff were hard to retain or replace, but the organisation, paradoxically, was stronger, its base stabler, than before the war. This was despite the fact that Madge left, in the summer of 1940, to study spending and saving under the National Institute of Economic and Social Research. The surrealist poet had developed an interest in 'hard', positive statistics. In 1950 he would become Professor of Sociology at Birmingham University.

One of Mass-Observation's most important fields of war work was the investigation of human reactions to being bombed. Tom Harrisson told, in his *Living Through the Blitz* (1976) how 'units of trained investigators were sent anonymously to blitz towns to make overall reports, prepared regardless of any official accounts, departmental feelings or published glosses'. Indeed, these reports contrast sharply at many points with the genial image of Britain 'muddling through', propagated by most material published at the time and much of what has appeared since. Meanwhile, Mass-Observation was trawling in scores of diaries in which civilians described their behaviour and feelings from day to day. Unlike most other archive material of this kind, the Observers' 'War Diaries', sent in month by month, are guaranteed free of second thoughts; their writers had no chance to amend them.

One of the most interesting diaries was kept by a woman graduate of Cambridge University, aged 24 in 1940. She came from South-East England but was living in Monmouthshire, where she was employed as a statistician in a works which was helping to make aircraft. She was engaged to a young doctor. They married early in 1941 and she became for a time a cheerful housewife. Then Tom was called up, she went back to work, and the later years of her diary radiate acute unhappiness. But in the summer of 1940 she was buoyant, as the extracts which follow show.

(The 'yellow' warning was a preliminary one, advertising that bombers were about. The 'red' warning meant 'action'; the 'white' message cancelled the warning.)

14. War diarist: The Battle of Britain in Wales, 1940

June 26

We had another air raid soon after twelve. I was barely asleep so it woke me. I drew my curtains over the window as a protection against flying glass, but, since I live in a bungalow, there was no point in getting up, for my bed was as safe a place as any. I heard my landlady get up, and she asked if I were awake. I must have dozed again, for it seemed only a few minutes before the allclear went, and another few minutes before the warning sounded again. After that I slept soundly. My paper did not arrive once again, and I felt that I was very much behind in the news when I got to the office. However there was but little news. One bomb had dropped on a petrol tank in Newport. Many people were feeling tired through having been up half the night. Jill said that she was called each night by the watchman, and had to go and sit on the calorifier steps. She cursed, but felt that she must do it for the sake of the watchman and the boys on the night shift, at any rate until everyone is more used to air raids. My landlady is complaining that she feels sick and ill today, and that the noise of the syrens made her heart bad. I suppose that we shall have another raid tonight and that my paper will not arrive in time for breakfast. That puts me out more than anything. I shall keep my curtains drawn in the future, although I hate sleeping with covered windows, but they will give a certain amount of protection against flying glass. Unless bombs are dropped very near here they will not disturb me.

June 29

We had an air raid 'yellow' message this morning, and the telephone girl had worked the factory warning for a minute before she was told that she ought to do nothing before the 'red' came through. I have been asked to sleep at the works once a week, to take the warnings, and signal the factory if the red comes through. Since we have been yellow every night for a fortnight, and instructions are that I am to get up and dress as soon as the yellow message is given, it seems as though I shall have a sleepless night. I went up to Shrewsbury in the afternoon to meet Tom. We went on the river and then cycled to Church Stetton. The place was filled with soldiers, and no rooms available in the hotels, so we decided to sleep out, and found a favourable spot under pine trees. We put on all the spare clothing we had between us, and if there was an air raid we did not hear it, for we were sound asleep until just before dawn [. . .]

July 15

An air raid warning went just before I was in bed, so I put my light out and was soon asleep. I woke up to find it wet again, and I felt tired and cross. Twice during the day we had warnings and all work was suspended. It made me so cross. We never even heard a plane, and yet all the machines in the works were held up, and goodness knows what such stoppages of production cost us. I see in the paper today that from June 16th (I think) to July 13th we have lost 86 planes to Germany's 119. Germany can better afford to lose hers than we can. Surely invasion will be within the next few days [. . .]

July 17
I've recovered my equanimity, thank goodness. Hitler announces that the attack on Britain will begin on Friday, that will mean Thursday night probably, and I shall be on duty. But I hope that it will begin then. I can't quite imagine his idea in publishing a date, unless it is done in arrogance. We have had no warnings again all day. People are inclined to take the attitude that it is the quiet before the storm, and also that the sooner the storm breaks the better. We have got a dance at the works tonight, and everyone is to be told which air raid shelter they are to go to as they are given their tickets. Already we are taking air raids as a matter of course [. . .]

July 21
Last night we had planes over but no warning, and this morning, just before I got up, we had a warning but no planes. My landlady has ceased to be in the least bit disturbed by warnings. She told me that in the village people were saying 'I used to get scared when a warning went but now I just turn over and go to sleep'. I wish to goodness I knew what logic rules the giving of warnings. Our air raid shelters are finished at the works at any rate, so I suppose that next week we shall have to practise getting to them quickly. I feel that there is slightly more danger at the works because it is an objective [. . .]

Aug. 1
Another warning last night. That's seven nights in succession now. We went to the golf course again in the evening. Tried to pick up the Ls to go with us but Eric was on LDV [Local Defence Volunteers] duty. He cursed it. Soon after eleven we were remarking that it was time we got the yellow, when the telephone went, and at twelve we had just said what a long wait we were getting before the red, when we heard the first syren. The electricity was turned off so we drew back the curtains to see if there were any searchlights. Everything seemed quiet. Jill went to bed, and I to the control room. Soon after that the searchlights got busy, and followed the plane directly over our heads. I then decided that I really had better not continue to look out of the window. Just after the all clear, I heard a shout from Eric in the grounds because Jill's sitting room light was full on. We had forgotten that it had gone out because the power was off and not because we had turned the switch off. I hoped that the police had not

seen. Once again we were never given the white, though all was quiet for the rest of the night [. . .]

Aug. 10
[. . .] I slept through two warnings last night. My landlady always sleeps on the couch in her husband's room until the all clear goes. She says that the warning always make him want to pass water, so he needs her. She worries sometimes because he is so helpless. News that three people have been killed in a raid on a Welsh town concerns her more than anything. If people would bear in mind the number of road deaths there are every day, it would help them to keep a sense of proportion [. . .]

Aug. 16
[. . .] Today it has been decided that we are to work through air raids and are to have our own warning to go to shelter when observers on the roof hear planes or gunfire. All the office is very satisfied with the arrangement [. . .]

Aug. 17
The planes were over a lot last night, but I went to sleep without hearing any firing or bombs. However I heard this morning that five bombs had been dropped quite near, including one whistling bomb . . . Then we had to take Vi to Cardiff. We were caught in a raid half-way there, but they let us go on with only our headlights. I felt rather as though I were living in a film. There was a full moon, which gave the cold light one gets in night drives on the screen. We were stopped six times to show identification cards, and once or twice we saw bursts of anti-aircraft fire. Soon after I got back the planes were very low over us. I stayed awake reading until they had gone.

Aug. 18
[. . .] We were in the middle of a large field when we heard a plane. We located it, and shortly afterwards there was gunfire which was coming in our direction. Our first reaction was to run for the hedge. Then we looked at the plane again and saw that it had turned round, and we were no longer in a position where shrapnel was likely to fall on us, so we watched until it was out of sight and earshot. We could not see if there were any direct hits. In the evening the warning went before 10. That is the earliest yet. I could hear a plane about but everything seemed very quiet so I went to bed [. . .]

Aug. 20
The German planes were up to time last night and our night shift spent five hours in the shelters. My letter from Daddy did not arrive this morning and I was a little concerned since I know that they have had more serious raids there, but it came by the afternoon post, and all is well [. . .] There are a lot of colds about in the works. People blame the air raids at night for they get up and stand about watching, although few people round here have shelters. There will be a lot of colds and influenza this winter unless people are more careful.

Aug. 21
There was a public air raid warning this morning, and the decree went round that we were to draw our curtains as a precautionary measure. Our works warning was never sounded. It was odd working by artificial light on a summer morning [. . .]

Aug. 28
One of our felting shifts ends at 11 o'clock. Lately we have been having warnings before 11, and the felters have gone to shelter as soon as the warning has gone, stayed there until eleven, then clocked out and gone home. Of course they are paid for the time they lose due to an air raid, but if it's safe enough for them to go home at 11 it's safe enough for them to work until 11 . . . There is a German plane circling about overhead and occasional bursts of fire from AA guns. Is the object of the isolated planes that we have over every night, and that circle about for hours, merely to disorganise industry? I've just been told that at one of the works near here, where there are no shelters provided for the men, that when a warning goes, they all run out to between the gasometer and the blast furnace, as a safe place!

Aug. 29
[. . .] After dark the works manager came up and we went round all the windows inspecting the blackout. It's bad in the offices although we had special curtains made last year, and the kitchen is atrocious. We had our usual warning before ten and going on till after three, and there was quite a pretty fireworks display over Newport. I had heard that Lucas brothers in Birmingham had been badly damaged by bombs, but this evening I had a letter from an engineer there, and he said nothing about it, so it's probably rumour . . . The night foreman in the machine shop was fuming this evening. He said,

'Here they make appeals over the wireless asking that production shall not be stopped for air raid warnings, and our men refuse to work.' The only solution is to stop paying them for air raids [...]

Aug. 31

[...] Then in the evening we had a dance in our canteen ... Soon after nine it was announced that the sirens had gone, and that anyone who wished should leave the hall for the shelters, but that the dance would carry on. Not a soul took shelter. I felt furious because some of the men there were those who work in our night shift, and refuse to work during an air raid. There were searchlights out and a faint drone of planes when we walked back to my digs, but it was a quiet evening [...]

Sept. 2

There was a German bomber overhead this morning, and they had us out to the shelters, but not for long ... Our power went off at seven o'clock and was off for over two hours. I wondered if air raids have damaged the grid system, and also what they would do about giving our nightly air raid warnings. However it came on again and all was well. There were bombs dropping in the distance and a fair amount of AA fire, but the first all clear went before midnight, and I slept through the rest of the night.

Sept. 3

[...] I was going to a party at the Smiths tonight but Mrs S rang me up this afternoon to say that she had had to cancel it because all the people who lived further than walking distance away, had dropped out for fear of being held up in air raids. The warning's gone now. I can hear a plane overhead and there have been a few explosions. They're getting a little too fond of this valley.

Sept. 5

[...] At lunch time my landlady told me that a gas bomb had been dropped in Newport. Though she would not swear that her information was correct but I had it confirmed in the evening. People seemed to think that it was merely to cause panic. Hitler's remarks about preparing for a five-year war are rather significant. We had 6½ hours of air raid again, with a plane over most of the time and a great deal of gunfire. Our gun is now popping away every night very happily, and it's difficult to tell whether or not some of the explosions are bombs. I was surprised when the all clear went at 4.15. We had

had short quiet periods and then the plane returning for a long noisy one, so continuously for hours that I was not expecting it really to go away until dawn. I wonder if it's always the same plane that worries this valley. There were other planes about, but it seemed to be just one that was circling round here all night [. . .]

Sept. 9

We had such a short warning and so quiet a night that people were remarking about it [. . .] It's nearly eleven and we've had no warning. Our felters finish their shift at eleven. Perhaps, for the first time for weeks, they will work a full shift. I've just heard that the big fire at Milford Haven, which has been raging for about a fortnight, was caused, not by a bomb, but by an AA gun that misfired. That makes it seem far worse to my mind.

Sept. 10

The sequel to our gas bomb at Newport is that the powder has been analysed and that it was a mixture of rice and tapioca! There is also the story going about that 500 Germans landed near here, 499 of whom were shot in three seconds, and the five hundredth escaped. We had four bombs drop a mile from here last night, killing a few chickens, but doing no other damage. The noise woke me [. . .]

Sept. 13

Miss Jones burst into my room this morning saying 'We've brought a plane down! Isn't it thrilling?' A plane was caught by the Newport balloon barrage last night and crashed in flames. Unfortunately it crashed into the only house I have visited in Newport, killing the two children who were sleeping downstairs. I had a card from my aunt who lives in London saying that she was safe although a bomb has fallen in the front drive of the hotel where she lives. She was thinking of going down to my people in Seaford, and yet a few weeks ago she was offering them a home in London because Seaford was so dangerous!

Sept. 16

[. . .] The number of planes brought down yesterday is grand. Surely Germany must be realising now that she is not having everything her own way [. . .]

Sept. 17

There is a fearful gale today. I hear that Newport has been having fun with its barrage balloons, some of which have got caught by the wind and have dragged their lorries along behind them. We went in to the flicks this evening. It was a bad film, and the warning was sounded half way through. No one moved. When we came out there was a lot of flashing of explosives going on – bombs on the docks I think. It did not look or sound like guns. We were glad to be going away from Newport.

Sept. 18

[. . .] Until six o'clock I could not find out what had been happening in London during the night. Most people had either missed the news, or put it on when it was half way through and heard something about 'heavier casualties than before'. I was pleased to hear that that meant 'heavier than the last few days,' and not 'heavier than ever before'. Newport balloons were not up this morning – after yesterday's gale I suppose. We had two warnings this morning. During the first one the roof watcher gave our warning because a plane appeared. We were all on our way to shelter when it passed over us – a Whitley bomber! – so we turned round and went back to work [. . .]

Sept. 20

[. . .] I knew that we would have a happy weekend as soon as I met Tom [. . .] We came back to my digs, expecting the sirens to go off all the way. None went, and for the first time for weeks we had a quiet night [. . .]

Sept. 25

[. . .] There is a German plane about now. I'd rather it wasn't there, but the wasp which wanted to share my dinner worried me more.

We believe that Kathleen Box was a full-time, paid member of Mass-Observation staff in October 1940, when she wrote the diary entries which follow. She later left Mass-Observation to join the Government's War-time Social Survey. She was in her twenties, could be described as middle-class, and was a member of the Communist Party.

She was lodging in Fulham with 'Mr S', a foreman-builder for the London Passenger Transport Board (LPTB) whose wife and daughter had been evacuated to the West Country. The 'H' family lived in the same house, on the ground floor, and consisted of a mother and two daughters. Kathleen Box spent her nights in the basement, the 'Hs' went to next door's basement, and 'Mr S' went out to an LPTB shelter. Tibbles was a cat. J. B. S. Haldane was the Communist Party's expert on Air Raid Precautions. Abe Lazarus was another CP member. Agitation over ARP was a major

Communist preoccupation at this time, and Kathleen Box's implicit attitude to the blitz seems strongly influenced by her political position. But she was an expert, and reliable, Observer, and certainly would not have invented the conversations described here.

15. Kathleen Box: Blitz in London, 1940

MONDAY, 14.10.40, FULHAM

Slept in basement again last night with Tibbles. Hear a good many bombs which don't sound very far off. After the loudest of these I hear movements next door where they sleep in the basement, their wall being also the wall of this house. I hear someone go to the front door – probably the elder Miss H – and she says to, I suppose, a passing warden – 'Was it a bomb?' I don't hear the reply, but the wardens and men from the fire station next door (the other side) as usual are out in the street, talking, laughing and sometimes whistling tunes. I sleep alright as usual.
5.20 Wakened by the H's coming back from next door. (They generally come back when there is an all clear, whatever time of night it is.) So I take pillow and eiderdown and go to my bed upstairs to finish the night there.

9.0 Miss H calls out good morning from the hall as I go into the bathroom. She says, 'Wasn't it a bad air-raid last night?' I say yes it was noisy and ask if she knows where the loudest crash came from. She says the old lady next door, who sleeps in the back basement room, was looking out of the window as she lay in bed and saw the bomb come down. She said it was glowing red hot and very large. When I ask if it was an incendiary she says no it was too big. She says she thinks it must have landed Parson's Green way, which is just round the back of these houses. I suggest that they are after Fulham Power Station, but she says they have already hit this some time ago and that we are getting our electricity from another power station now. She says it is the gas works (Chelsea way) that they are trying for.

10.40 Tobacconist opposite is in high spirits. He says, 'I was running round putting out fires at half past one in the morning.' He sleeps in the trench shelters near Edith Grove with his brother's family. They looked out and saw an incendiary bomb blazing away within about 5 feet of the trench. So out they went, he said 'Get the

4 Graham Bell (left) and Humphrey Spender on the roof of Bolton Art Gallery, 1937

5 Collage by Julian Trevelyan: 'Bolton Scene'

6 The Vaults, a pub in Bolton, 1937

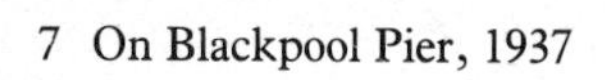

7 On Blackpool Pier, 1937

shovels' and they shovelled on sand from buckets, and when this was all used up they got some cinders from a pile outside a factory near by and threw them on and that put it out. 'My niece was the one. She was running round with a spade. She was as quick as I was. My brother he was asleep, and I didn't think to wake him, of course you don't when you've got something to do, he helped at the finish. We were all running round there. You don't think of the shrapnel falling when you've got something to do, we were working away in it. Then I saw a house blazing over that way (points) and I turned round and saw another house blazing over there (points opposite direction) so I says "Call the fire brigade – sound the fire alarm." So somebody did that and then the one over there went down. Then the fire brigade came and they were putting out the other house when the first one blazed up again. So I said, "Look over there. What about that one." They said "We can't do two things at once, you'll have to get some more help. Ring up the station." And then when we'd done that blowed if another fire didn't start out that way (pointing). Coo it was a night! And they were yelling at the people in the house, "Come out, there's a bloody fire on." Of course I fell over a great block of stone by the factory gate there, getting the cinders and skinned me bloomin' leg all up here. But that didn't matter. After it all we went back to the shelter and had a cup of tea and a fag.' F40 [a woman about 40] comes in whilst he is in the middle of the story and listens to the last part of it. She says, when he has finished, 'Fulham got it badly again last night, didn't it? They say they got it in Delvino Road, and in Munster Road and Horder Road, there's nothing left of it round that corner where the Labour Exchange is.'

I think I will go round to the districts mentioned to do some observation, but am rather discouraged by apathy shown when I ring up 82 [Ladbroke Grove, the Mass-Observation headquarters] so I go and see a friend instead.

Early in the evening go to usual café. Proprietress (F65) looks over headlines of my Evening Standard and says, 'Isn't it dreadful what they're doing everywhere.' I ask her how she slept last night, 'Sleep! You can't sleep. We can't go on like this can we? It can't go on. They'll have to do something about it. I mean he's doing just what he likes now, isn't he. They'll have to do something about it soon or there'll be a revolution. You wouldn't mind if he stuck to military objectives, but it's indiscriminate bombing, isn't it. Oh I think it's dreadful. It can't go on like this.'

6.30 Get home, and go down to take washing off line before it gets darker. Mr S has come in. I ask if he'd like cup of tea and he says he would. So I go up and make one whilst he is doing blackout and washing. He comes up and says, 'It's one thing after another now.' Meaning he never gets time to do anything. He is supposed to be working till 7, but gets off a bit earlier himself. I ask what it's been like in town today, and he says it hasn't been so bad but he heard one bomb come down, and that happened before the spotters where he works gave any alarm. Says that's twice it's happened lately. He tells me more about these spotters. He works in Westminster at the big Transport building with the tower. The spotters are of course at the top of the tower and he works not far below them. They spot primarily for Whitehall and he says that the reason why they cut it so fine is because at first they used not to, but they were told by Whitehall bosses that they were sending people down too soon and wasting time, so now they dare not sound the alarm (claxon) until the very last minute. 'Today before they had sounded the alarm, I hear Whhhizzz over the building. That puts the wind up me. I said come on down, and we dived for the stairs. Not that that's any good because we couldn't get down in time and the stairs are the worst place there. They stop the lift working. The lift has to be at the bottom always when there's a raid on. Now at the underground it has to be at the top!' I say it's a lot of bloody nonsense. And he says 'Of course it is.' When I asked after his son Reg, who lives in Delvino Road where I heard there were bombs, he says he doesn't know but he came over (i.e. whilst Mr S was out) and took some boards, so apparently more windows broken. He's a bit annoyed at Reg taking more boards because he says he's earning good money now and could buy boards for himself, and if the windows are blown out here he won't have any left for himself.

I say I notice it is roped off in Hyde Park near Marble Arch. He tells me the story of this. There was a shelter just underground with about 18 inches of concrete roof. The whole thing was blown to bits. He was superintending the digging out of the bodies. 'I don't want to be on another job like that again. There were heads and arms and legs and feet lying about. The only way you could tell the girls from the men was because of their hair. Their faces were all blown away. There were a lot never identified.' I say it must affect the men who are digging them out badly. He says it doesn't affect you at the time but afterwards. 'It's not the sight of the bodies. I tell you what it is – it's the smell. The smell of human flesh and the blood. It gets you afterwards. Two or three days after that I felt myself heaving.' We talk over the question of shelters again. I remark on the surface shelter with the crater just where it was and blown to bits at Victoria, which I saw from a bus. He says that was only done a few days ago. 'And yet they go on putting them up.' I ask how far underground a shelter ought to be to be safe. He says it depends on all sorts of things, the way it is constructed, and so on. He tells me of an experiment that was made on a shelter somewhere. It was underground and covered over by 24 feet square of concrete. They dropped an aerial torpedo on that to see if it would hold but it went straight through the concrete and blew it all up. '24 feet mind, that's a lot.' I ask him what he thinks about the Haldane type of shelter. He says he has never heard of it. I describe as well as I can from my untechnical mind what it is like, and why it is called by that name. He says it sounds like the tubes with circular steel girders, and says that's as safe as anything could possibly be. In fact absolutely safe. I say I will try and get a pamphlet about it for him, and tell him about the deputation to the Home Office (which I heard of from Abe Lazarus speaking at a very well attended and enthusiastic open air meeting at Bristol). I expect you know the story – but in case not. A deputation of 40 people, representatives of various T.U.s, C.P. and other organisations, went to Sir John Anderson at the Home Office. They were received by a secretary there. Their demand was for underground shelters of the Haldane type to be built in all dangerous areas where there was no adequate protection. Whilst they were talking an air-raid alarm went. They were told they would have to go out in the street and find a public shelter as the shelter at the Home Office could not accommodate 40 extra people. They refused to go and insisted on going down to the Home Office shelter. When they got down there, they found the Home Office had a perfect Haldane shelter of the exact type that they were asking for for the people. Mr S is much interested (and amused) by this. He tells me about the shelter that the L.P.T.B. bosses had built for themselves just when the war was beginning.

I remember when he was on this job he told me something about it then – a year ago. (I can't remember the exact time.) He says this is the second deepest shelter in London, it is at Holborn. They have beds and a canteen and it's all fitted up with beautiful washing places, and there is a dormitory for the women. He says first of all the women clerks, and then corrects himself saying it isn't for the clerks but for the high-up women secretaries. Air conditioning. 'And the stuff that was taken down that place! There were bottles of whisky and wine, and a whole lot of tins of stuff, caviar, and everything else.

I saw it all being taken down. And they went down there all night, but we had to go on working all night. They go down there without any hesitation, they don't wait. But we have to go on just the same after the siren.'

To go back to the Marble Arch shelter, he said he found a girl's diary – he thinks the name was Joan Bennett. It had addresses of various friends and people in it and her own address – he mentioned where but I don't remember. He handed this to the police – 'But I don't suppose they did anything about it. I often think, now suppose I was coming home, no one knows where I am, the raid gets bad and I go into a shelter. Well that shelter is blown up. How is anyone to know I was in it or where I was? Your people don't know what's happened to you.'

Then he tells me a lighter type of story. When he was on a job at Gloucester Road he and some pals used to go to a pub there when they were finished. There were two pubs but one closed down when the sirens went, so the other got all the trade. He wasn't there the night it happened, but one of his pals, an Irishman, was. He was just coming out of the pub when a bomb exploded knocking down houses opposite. All the glass doors of the pub were blown out and all the bottles fell down and there were glasses and bottles floating about the floor in beer and whisky. His friend wasn't hurt but was upset at so much good drink being wasted.

He tells me how a bomb went clean through a signal box on a railway line Hammersmith way. It was an automatic signal so there was no one there to be hurt. And other stories.

There's been a loud raid on all the time I've been writing this – it's now 9 o'clock and I think I shall make some cocoa as my tea is getting a bit low.

One thing I said before is wrong. It isn't the public shelter that Mr S goes to at night but an L.P.T.B. one for the men. They don't get crowded out there, but he says some of the men sleep down the tubes with the other people. Suppose because their wives and children are there.

Our next item is a complete 'File Report', such as Mass-Observation might have sent to the Ministry of Information. Its author, Leonard England, was a young full-time Observer, just short of his twenty-first birthday. He had joined the panel as a volunteer while still a schoolboy at Dulwich College. After service in the army he returned to Mass-Observation full-time after the war, and was head of Mass-Observation Ltd, the company which inherited the name, from 1950 to 1969.

He uses the standard Mass-Observation notations of age, sex and class. 'M45D' means 'man of about 45, looks and/or sounds unskilled working-class'. 'F45D' would be his female equivalent. 'A' stands for 'rich people, the "upper few"', 'B' for the 'middle classes', 'C' for 'artisans and skilled workers'.

Tom Harrisson pointed out, in *Living Through the Blitz* (page 12), that Mass-Observation never signed the Official Secrets Act and, even when working for the Government, retained the right to full post-war use of material, however classified at the time. There are no other contemporary accounts of the blitz as candid as those to be found in the Archive.

16. Leonard England: File Report No. 517, Air raid on Southampton, 4 December 1940

PRELIMINARY

Southampton is a town of some 183,000 people; it has a balloon barrage and a fairly large anti-aircraft barrage.

Periodically, the town has been raided, and these raids have been fairly heavy. The worst raids, however, occurred on last Saturday and Sunday (Nov. 30 and Dec. 1), when 370 casualties were caused and very heavy damage was done. The central and dockyard portion of the town was, in particular, hit, and the High Street has hardly a building standing.

MORALE

People seemed stunned and quiet but, on the whole, not really depressed. One man (45D) who had been in a shelter that had been hit, said to Inv. 'There's no interest left in anything now', but most people seemed to have more hope than this. One woman, for instance, said in a depressed tone of voice, 'I dread the night coming on' and then almost immediately started singing 'Tipperary'. A fireman pointed out to Inv. a notice saying 'Houses Built to Order' and said they'd have their work cut out.

To strangers people were cheerful and civil. But in the hotel, where Inv. stayed and where the residents had spent the two nights of bombing in a shelter together, tempers were more frayed. At dinner one woman (50B) was talking in a loud voice of her fears, her sufferings, and so on; her son wanted to go out in the raid and park the car, and she was sure that he would never be able to get back. Towards the end of the meal, a naval Commander, another guest, said to his wife in what was intended to be an undertone, 'If that woman doesn't stop, I'll . . .' (rest inaudible). Unfortunately the woman heard, and a slanging match went on across the dining room, the woman saying that she thought she was exceptionally brave, after all she had gone through, the Commander saying that it was too much to hear her all day and every day. What the woman had gone through Inv. does not know.

Another case of temper occurred later in the evening. A battery wireless set was working, but only faintly, and everybody was anxious to listen to the 9 o'clock news. At the crucial moment, when the announcer reached news of Southampton, one woman (65B) rattled her beads loudly and prevented another (also 65B) from hearing. Why she did this, Inv. has no idea, she seemed a little senile. At the end of the news, the other woman came up to her, said 'I'd like to murder you', then walked over to her husband and said 'That damned old woman'.

There was not a great deal of interest in bomb damage, except in one large crater near the Green, where a direct hit had been scored on a shelter. There was also some interest in the demolition work which was being undertaken by the army, and when one large wall was dynamited there were laughs and even some isolated cheering. Most interest in individual house damage was at a large departmental store, Jones, which was gutted; men and women were stopping and staring with such exclamations as 'shocking' and 'terrible'. There was very general comparison between damage here and at Coventry, and Inv. felt here a suppressed feeling of pride. On the Monday and early Tuesday people were saying that the damage was as bad as Coventry, but by late on Tuesday this was developing into 'worse than Coventry'; one man (55D) said that it was worse than Pompeii. There was some annoyance at the papers because they had not made so much fuss about the Southampton raid as the Coventry one.

Interest in casualties was low. Inv. heard no talk about friends and relations who had been killed or injured, and round the casualty list, which was posted up outside the police station, there were very few people. Many people did not believe the official figures; they said that there must be many more still in shelters under wrecked buildings, one man (45D) said '3,700 is far more like the right figure'.

There was a fairly general feeling that Southampton was done for.

More than one person expressed the opinion that the Germans would not come back again because there wasn't anything left for them to come back to. One man (55B) said 'We'll have to abandon the whole damn town and build it up again'.

OFFICIAL REACTION, SERVICES, ETC.

Southampton has a large civic centre in which are centralised nearly all public offices, library, and so on. This centre was seriously bombed, and may account for some part of the breakdown.

Gas, light, and water were off in most parts of the town; candles were obtainable in small quantities, so was paraffin oil. But – this was not announced until the Monday afternoon – water was not fit to drink unless boiled. Thus people, getting their water from pumps, taps, and from army water carts which were brought into commission, were then faced with the problem of how to boil it before drinking it.

The offices of the daily paper were hit, and copies were not in circulation again until late on Tuesday. Apparently the authorities had been relying on the paper for announcements; in its place, one loudspeaker van was used. Inv. did not hear this at all, but saw the van twice. There were no notices displayed outside the civic centre beyond a short typewritten announcement about identifying the dead. The news about boiling water, however, did seem to have filtered through to most people.

Many departments had been taken over by the military. The army was demolishing buildings, the RAF and the Army were in charge of evacuation arrangements, which did not begin in earnest until the Tuesday morning. A few naval recruits were engaged in the civic centre. Army was guarding time-bomb areas.

AFS [Auxiliary Fire Service] men had come from as far as Oxford, Northampton, Hove and, Inv. thinks, Cromer; ambulances from Guildford and Farnham; demolition squads, it is said, from London. Police had also been drafted in from other parts, and this caused much confusion, as people were asking the police the way and the police had no idea.

But many borough servants were not being used on important work. Gardeners were clearing up leaves on the tennis courts and on the gardens in the avenue; one whole squad of men on Tuesday afternoon were clearing up mud from the paths on the green by the civic centre. There was very little knowledge of where Rest Centres were situated. Apparently there were 24 in the town – some at least of these had been destroyed – but after asking various policemen and civilians, Inv. could find only two, one of these being the main clearing centre at the Central Hall. Further names were obtained at the Civic Centre, but only with some difficulty. There was a great deal of argument going on there as to whether people were to be allowed in or not, and periodically the doors were shut, and people refused admission; this, despite the fact that police were advising people elsewhere in the town, to apply at the Civic Centre for further particulars. More confusion was caused by the fact that many people were asking for a certain form and the supplies of this form had run out.

The central Post Office was closed but many people were posting letters in the pillar boxes outside. On the Tuesday postmen were going their rounds.

Transport was good. A shuttle train service was being worked between Eversleigh and the Docks station and the time taken by Inv. to get to the town was less than an hour longer than usual (just under three hours). Trams were running on the outskirts of the town, and so were many buses though many of these were apparently starting from unusual places.

EVACUATION

It must be remembered that Southampton had had serious raids before those of the last week. Many women and children had already been evacuated, and more had probably made plans as to what they would do if the occasion arose.

Throughout Monday there was apparently a large unofficial evacuation. Two people (M55B and F65D) spontaneously compared the lines of people leaving the town with bedding and prams full of goods to the pictures they had seen of refugees in Holland and Poland. Some official evacuation took place on the Monday, but at the Avenue Hall rest centre a group of fifty waited all the afternoon for a bus to take them out; the warning went when there were still no buses, and all of them went out to shelters without waiting any longer.

On Monday evening from about 4.30 onwards a stream of people were leaving the town for the night. When Inv. left the train at the docks, he was impressed by the seeming deadness of the town; there were no cars, and hardly any people except those that had left the train with him. But farther out people were moving. The buses were full, men and women were walking with their baggage. Some were going to relations in outlying parts, some to shelters, preceded by their wives who had reserved them places, and some to sleep in the open. 'Anything so as not to spend another night in there.' Many were trying to hitch hike, calling out to every car that passed; very few stopped. This caused considerable annoyance, especially as many coaches completely empty went by.

Trains leaving were full of women and children; many had little baggage, as if they were coming back next day.

The next day many returned after the night, but more were intent on getting out. In some neighbourhoods whole streets had evacuated, most people leaving a note on their doors giving their new address; one such notice read 'Home all day, away all night'. Men as well as women were leaving; one man was going to Northampton to his son's, regretfully, after 26 years in Southampton.

All day people were leaving the town with suitcases and baggage. All of these seemed to set out with a set purpose and aim but all the aims were different. Here and there, for instance, there were streams of people all with baggage. Following these streams, Inv. saw them split up, some going to bus stops, others to trains. Both trains and buses were leaving half empty, there was no great rush. People seemed puzzled by which stations were open, which buses were running, and were moving from one to the other.

The news that anybody could be evacuated by applying at the Central Hall seemed to be leaking out only slowly. One woman midday was telling everybody she met, but another at the same time was telling her friends to go out to Romsey, 'there was still room there'.

The second night there were fewer people trekking out of the town; it was drizzling, and perhaps this deterred some. But there were still a good many and shelters on the outskirts were full. One man, telling Inv. of a friend who had evacuated, said how happy she was, enjoying sleep and good food.

FOOD, SHOPS, ETC.

Outside the damaged area – the damage was confined mainly to the centre of the town and to the docks – shops were nearly all open. Inside the damaged area, a large proportion were still at work; very few shops, still whole, were closed. Nearly all the shops were well stocked, meat, fish, and vegetable shops being practically unvisited by the public. There seemed to be a rush on the bakeries, and, to a lesser extent, the general provision stores, and while there was plenty of bread in the morning this seemed to have run out by the afternoon (Tuesday). Two shops selling hot tea were packed.

One woman, going to her butcher's, found the road blocked. A butcher, hearing what she wanted, said, 'If you can't get through, come back here, we'll serve you.' She was obviously not rationed there.

Tuesday is market day. Very few stallholders appeared . . . none of these went straight back.

There were no communal kitchens, and, though hot food was obtainable at the Rest Centres, there was very general complaint at the lack of hot food. One man (45D) said 'It's getting no hot food that wears you down'. Many people had apparently not had a hot meal for some days. One girl (25C) said 'I feel hungry. I've only had two chocolate biscuits this morning. And tea. But I had to kid myself that it was medicine before drinking it, and it was better. It was made out of my hot water bottle.' One hall, St Michael's, was opening as a canteen Tuesday afternoon.

Inv. saw no canteen at all until 12 noon on Tuesday, when a YMCA tea car was outside the civic centre; tea was provided from thermoses to anybody. Later, WVS canteen took its place nearby and issued free tea and cakes, sausage rolls, etc. to everybody; a great many people wanted to pay for what they bought, and one man expressed a general feeling when he said 'I'm willing to pay for any food, but I can't get it'. During the rest of the day, Inv. saw another YMCA tea car, a Church Army car, a mobile canteen from London, actually serving food, and a few others, including an Australian canteen and an AFS one, moving round. All these, however, were near the centre of the town; in the dock area Inv. saw nothing at all.

A sweet shop said that it had one of the best days for years; was still doing a very good trade shortly before blackout.

RUMOURS

There may have been many rumours about exaggerated bomb damage which Inv. could not check; he certainly found two such stories. His main impression, however, is that there were not a great many rumours about.

Individual examples:

1. From M55B — The AA headquarters down to the ground. (Its top floor burnt out.)
2. From M50B — (naval officer) Ranks, the miller's, is 'no more'. (At least one of its buildings is standing.)
3. From M45D — Haw Haw [German radio propagandist] prophesied that the port would be hit before they attacked and has now given Southampton six days to be evacuated.
4. From M70B — Haw Haw has said that as soon as Southampton is finished with he is going on to Winchester.
5. From 65B — Accounts of air raid damage in this country gets through to Hitler via the Spanish ambassador in London. He is still allowed to send messages in code to Franco who passes them on.
6. From F25C — Many anti-aircraft guns had been taken from Southampton to Birmingham.
7. From M60C — A bomb that fell near the Avenue Hall Rest Centre was aimed at the Centre.
8. From F35C — (Possibly true.) A serious fire was averted at the South Hants hospital by a porter who jumped from one roof to another and put out a fire bomb.

COMPLAINTS

There were very few complaints, beyond a general one at the discomfort caused by lack of services, and consequent inability to cook, shave, and so on. These complaints did not take the form of direct accusation of the borough or anybody, but were more general. The main point was the lack of hot food.

Other complaints:

The sanitary system

The ineffectiveness of the anti-aircraft barrage. (This is not a general complaint, held only by a few people.)

The fact that the papers were not making so much fuss over Southampton as they did over Coventry.

The fact that the papers were making too much of the endurance of Southampton. If the Germans thought that the people were quite unaffected by the bombing, they would come over and give them another dose.

The lack of interest of railway officials, *not* the chaos of the services.

REPRISALS

There was very little reprisal talk, and even when Inv. asked people whether they wanted reprisals, the usual answer was 'What good would that do?' One woman (45D) was heard to say 'We've got to do to them as they do to us, that's the only thing to do'; a man (55B) wanted drastic measures against the actual airmen who did the bombing, 'I'd like to tie them up and put one of their own time bombs round their necks'. On the other hand, a young soldier (25C) said 'There must be thousands on the other side of the Channel feeling like we do every night'.

REACTIONS TO SIRENS AND 'TIME BOMBS'

Monday evening, while Inv. was following the evacuation trek, a gun went off on the Common before the warning had gone. This caused one woman to say 'Good God, they've started already' and men as well as women started running to get to shelter in time. No further noise was heard, however, and people slowed down.

Just before 6, the sirens went and again there was a speeding up among those walking out of the town, this time not so rapid.

At midday on Tuesday, there was another warning. A few women started to run for shelter, but the majority of people took no notice at all. As one man (65D) said to Inv., 'I don't mind at all in the daytime; we know that our men are up after them then.'

All through the day, buildings were being dynamited. At first the sudden explosions caused much alarm among the women, who thought they were all time bombs. After an hour or so, however, people began to get used to the noise and took little notice.

'OFFICIAL SECRETS'

Inv. was asked to show no official permit at all to enter Southampton; he simply showed his ticket at the Docks station, and was allowed through. The same evening, at his hotel, a naval Commander from the docks gave a complete explanation of bomb damage in the dockyard in front of three complete strangers (Inv. and two other visitors who had arrived that night).

MISCELLANEOUS

On the Saturday previous to the serious bombing, a house next door to a pub was demolished by a bomb. The innkeeper was so pleased that he had escaped that he gave a celebration on the following Tuesday with free beer for all. The next Saturday his place also was reduced to ashes.

One man late on Tuesday afternoon tried to walk across an area which the soldiers had roped off because of a time bomb. The soldier shouted at him, the man started to grumble at him. The soldier advanced with fixed bayonet. The man moved off.

This caused much interest. One woman walking with her husband called to him to stop because she wanted to see the fun. Two men (25C) were talking: 'What's that fellow doing with a knife on the end of his rifle?' 'Oh, that's to cut his cheese with'.

Two men are standing in a side street by a damaged building. They are enjoying themselves by trying to throw bricks into a grate that is still standing on the second floor.

A hearse goes through the centre streets with children in, presumably evacuating them. This creates much interest and comment.

One woman who had been evacuated from her house because of a time bomb wanders through the streets aimlessly. She is the only person that Inv. saw doing this.

A tirade against the Americans is the result of a question about the reaction of foreign sailors to the blitz. F65C says that though the Americans call themselves tough, they could never have stood up to what Southampton did. They would have cracked up completely.

In the middle of a damaged street with not more than two or three shops left standing, Woolworth's remains standing without even the glass broken. A man is industriously cleaning the glass.

Two or three cats are to be seen among the ruins in the most unlikely places. These cause much comment from the passers by, men and women. One woman says that they ought not to be destroyed but given milk by the Council; then they would still live to keep the rats down.

Outside a burnt church is a notice indicating that the parish hall is still available for shelter and storage to parishioners. This presumably means that it is undamaged but not being used as a Rest Centre or canteen.

17. Full-time Observer: Post-bombing demolition work in London, 1941

MOTIVES

Not everyone becomes a demolition worker for the same reasons. Some do it because they have always done work of a similar nature – the man who has been a labourer in the building trade all his life. Others are taking the suggestion made by the Government and are doing the work as a temporary measure between jobs of a different nature or while they are waiting to be called up. Some are merely casuals who always have drifted around from job to job and now find the opportunity for doing this greater than ever before. Others come in for loot. A lot has already been said about the laziness of certain workers and as these are nearly always the casuals it is not intended to say any more about them. The true navvy and the looters, however, require more attention than has so far been given them.

(*a*) THE TRUE NAVVY

There is not really much to be said about this class except that they are excellent workers and earn every penny they get. Many of them find it disheartening that the idlers should be paid exactly as much as they are, merely because they are on the site for the same amount of period. This is an occasional source of labour troubles, as will be shown later. As labour becomes more and more scarce more and more old men are coming into demolition. By no means all of these are good workers – some haven't worked for years, some are weak and a danger to themselves. They come from a variety of occupations, including bombed-out shopkeepers. The later ones, of course, are not so good as those who came in early, but they are far more manageable and cooperative than the younger men. Their one object in doing this work is to get a living wage.

Labourers are called unskilled workmen. This is true up to a point, for it does not take years of apprenticeship to learn how to use a pick. But there is a right and a wrong way of using a pick which few of the younger men seem to know. Perhaps the chief skill of the navvy lies in his conservation of energy. He has a long day and if he doesn't keep some control over his movements he will be tired out long before he has finished. This results in the great difference between the two types of worker – the young man, working hard in spasms, then having to rest for a bit while he cools off, and the old navvy, working at the same deliberate pace all through the day and requiring no rests except the official breaks.

(*b*) LOOTERS

Some men come on the jobs in the hope of picking up loot. Even most of those who are not primarily concerned with what they can find are not averse to taking something when it turns up. The press campaign and the heavy sentences for looters don't seem to worry them. In fact, they are stupidly and foolishly open about it, and will often scramble for blooey in full view of passers-by. They value money above everything, and prefer to find a few coppers than something of more value which, however, has no currency value. Their recklessness is apparent in the following extract:

> Joe delightedly told me that someone had driven in his pick and a penny had rolled down. I looked to where he pointed and saw half a dozen men scrabbling in the debris. They continued to poke about for ten minutes, by which time three of them had been successful, to the tune of 9d, 5d and 4d respectively. All the time a woman was watching them from an upper window in the neighbouring house.

Every site has its legend, and these legends do at least serve to make some of the lazier ones work.

> We have been told that some money in a black bag is buried here. Barb was cutting his way through the debris furiously. He looked up and said, 'There's a wallet in here with £65'. Later he said it was £75, and when I reminded him it had gone up, he said, 'I know, I add £10 on every time I speak. There's tons of valuables here'. Others began to speak of finds they had known – £128 saved by a couple engaged to be married, £20 and a gold watch in a house in Harley St.

Looting was one of the things the foreman and ganger had to keep his eyes open for. Not even they could always be trusted, as in the case of Obs's own ganger, who lost his job for looting himself. Another ganger told Obs, when he had drunk too much beer, that he had arranged to take some lead away with one of the drivers. Drivers often work in with the gangers or some of the men in this way, and during the period Obs was with the firm some drivers were sentenced for it at the Old Bailey. On Obs's first day as a labourer he heard the foreman complaining in his characteristic way about the looting:

> Condan found a suitcase and opened it. The foreman pounced on him immediately. He warned us not to open a case if we found it. He picked up a handbag and took out a purse which was empty. Then he turned to us and said, 'It's the funniest bloody bomb I ever came across. I been all through the last war and I done several jobs in this, but I never come across a bomb like it. It's blown every bag open and knocked the money out, it's even knocked the money out of the gas meters, yet it didn't break the electric light bulb in the basement!'

When salvage was taken into the neighbouring house, which was empty, it only meant that the field of available loot had been extended, for the men used to go into the house and scrounge. In the house Obs heard the foreman telling the ganger to keep a lookout for the looters:

> If you see anyone ripping or tearing at a cloth, or picking at a case, send 'im straight up to Barrow Hill. I don't care who he is, send 'im up, even if 'e's your best friend. The Council are very down on that sort of thing. They don't care what damage they do. The people who lived here are ruined, and they want to save what they can. The other day I caught young Condan pulling out some Irish linen shirts and throwing them anyhow on the ground – worth pounds, they were. They're not doin' anything to 'elp the country, they're a fuckin' 'indrance. I'm no angel, meself, but I'm not goin' to 'ave that goin' on.

The Robin Hood attitude to looting has already been mentioned. The ganger, himself a looter on the sly, appealed to the men on the grounds that 'the people hadn't a rag to their back. They're poor people, else it would be different'. One of Obs's mates said the same thing after looking through a case. They both wished that the salvage had belonged to rich people, when they would have felt justified in taking something. One man, a notorious looter, came in for a lot of censure from Obs's mates. They said he was a 'fucking pig – he takes everything he finds and then unloads in the house'.

On the whole, in Obs's gang, it was the done thing to take away anything small enough to be concealed on one's person. The ganger was quite agreeable and even cooperated on occasion. Sometimes someone would smell a rat, and there would be anxious moments, although no one showed his anxiety:

> A woman came to say that only three sacks of coal had been put in her cellar, whereas 5 should have been salvaged from the site. Barb and David, who had been told to take the coal round, looked very virtuous and went across to speak to her. Marsh says he bets they sold the other two, and that David would 'pinch his own fucking mother'. Then he remembered that there was a sackful of coal in the office, which probably accounted for one of them. Then one of the Irishmen found some candles, soap and matches. The ganger said if we want them put them aside now or get them later from the office, because there was a cop across the road.

The gangers, honest and dishonest, take far more caution than the men. The gang is their responsibility and it is a reflection on them if a member of their gang is caught looting. Therefore they have to be very careful who they take on, for it is well known that some men come for the loot only:

> We had a man come round for a job, but Durkin turned him down. Afterwards he told me the man was just out of prison. I said it was rather hard to refuse him work, but Durkin said he had probably been in for looting and we had had enough trouble already. He called me a 'soft-hearted fucker'. Then Sefton, who had been to a foreman's meeting, said a CID man had been working on one of the sites and had just left the job [. . .]

The next item is in form a 'File Report', authorship not known. It was published in 1943 as a chapter in an annual, *The Saturday Book* – 3, edited by Leonard Russell (Hutchinson). It was based on full-time Observers' reports from the London Underground during and after the blitz.

18. Mass-Observation: The tube dwellers, 1943

'But why the devil do they *still* come here?'

The speaker was a middle-aged business man, making his way irritably through the straggling group of shelterers on a North London tube station one evening. The shelter marshal smiled resignedly, and said: 'Oh, I don't know. They get used to it, you know.' And with this seemingly inadequate reply the questioner had to be content.

The problem is one that has puzzled many people. How is it that, nearly two years after the last serious raid, there are still several thousand Londoners who continue to come to the tubes night after night; that there are children nearly three years old who have never spent a night in their own homes?

To solve the problem we must go back to that winter of 1940–41, and consider what were the feelings and motives that first took people to the tubes. For it was not merely a desire for safety, as might at first be imagined. During that winter this country saw the first stages of the formation of a new community; perhaps one of the strangest communities in recorded history. In vast caverns tens and hundreds of feet underground civilised people of all sorts and classes were gathered – not just now and then, as an emergency measure, but for months on end. For the first time in many hundreds of years civilised families conducted the whole of their leisure and domestic lives in full view of each other. To anyone of a sociological turn of mind the situation was full of possibilities – for the first time sociologists could watch the living process of highly civilised individuals adjusting themselves to a pre-civilised, communal form of society.

For this is in fact what it amounted to. Most of these people were not merely sheltering in the tubes; they were living there. The completeness with which their new home filled the time and thoughts of the tube dwellers is well shown by the following description of a Mass-Observation investigator on the spot, during the height of the blitz winter [. . .]

It is against this background that we must think of the tube-shelterers to-day. It must be clear by now that people don't go to the tubes *merely* for extra safety. In the beginning they went mainly for that reason, but they went on going for a thousand social and psychological reasons which have little or nothing to do with air raids. There were some who went for shelter and found there not only shelter but a whole new life in a new society – a society where they could start from scratch and for the first time in their lives make a name for themselves and shine in their social group. Others came from solitary bedsitting rooms with a gas ring, and found they could spend evenings in light and gaiety, surrounded by company. Harassed housewives found that they could halve their housework if the family spent the main part of its leisure time – i.e. the time when it makes the most mess and wants the most food – somewhere other than in the home. The trouble of preparing sandwiches and so forth to take to the shelter was found by many of them to be small compared with the work they would otherwise have to do – make beds, prepare hot meals, wash up, and keep up with the eternal tidying and sweeping that is necessitated by a large family at home. Some found themselves possessed of unsuspected talents for organising, entertaining, or what-not, which for the first time found scope and appreciation.

Can it be wondered at, then, that these people found it hard to leave their new lives when the raids ceased? By leaving the tubes many of them were leaving a life and an environment which suited them much better than 'ordinary' life would ever do. Take the case of 'Auntie Mabel,' from a report by a Mass-Observation investigator in the spring of 1943.

'The family atmosphere, which really did seem to include all the people in the shelter, was probably as much to do with the shelter marshal as anything else. She was a small, spry woman of about 45, who came down every night, and was very proud of the fact that she ran the shelter single-handed. "They all call me Auntie Mabel here," she said. "They all know me. It's real funny sometimes. Up top, sometimes I see them outside, when I'm down in the market say with me 'usband. 'Oh, look, there's Auntie Mabel,' they say; 'Hi, Auntie Mabel!' I should think I'm as well known as anyone in H——. Lovely people they are down 'ere. Never a cross word all the time I been down 'ere. Know everybody, I do."'

Think what it would mean to Auntie Mabel if she had to leave this life of hers, where she is known, respected, and needed, to return once more to being a nonentity of a London side-street, known only to her next-door neighbour.

Investigators studying the tube shelters in April 1943, have found much of this sort of pleasant, social atmosphere that the people find so hard to leave. For instance, this description of a North London tube station:

'I was taken on a conducted tour to see all the young children. They all looked most fresh and healthy. Said the warden: "We've got some marvellous children down here. Never had no trouble with them; no scabies, no skin troubles, nothink. Come an' have a look at our newest baby, he's only three weeks old."

'These young babies were a great source of pride and interest to the women in the shelter, and as I walked round and talked to people

I was several times asked if I had "seen the new baby". Mothers were very anxious to tell exactly how long each child had been in the shelter. Young women went up to each other's bunks to ask how the children were, and the old women would sit and smile round on everybody. The family atmosphere which was apparent in this particular shelter was quite remarkable. Another child in whom the shelterers were interested was George, a plump, dark-eyed, smooth-skinned little boy of five. George specialised in imitations.

'"Do Hitler," said his mother, and George pulled a lock down over his eye, put a finger under his nose and jerkily threw up his arm. "Now Mussolini," and George threw out his chin, curling his lower over his upper lip. "Tojo," and George set his lips, narrowed his eyes, and wrinkled his forehead. A few people standing round laughed a lot, and George greatly enjoyed himself.'

Of course, these tube communities will not last for ever. Like all societies whose *raison d'être* has ceased to exist, they are doomed to disintegrate; but like all societies they cling as long as possible. In many of the tube shelters disintegration has already set in (April 1943). The pleasant co-operative spirit has disappeared and the few remaining shelterers sit about in scattered ones and twos, silent and glum:

'After the M. shelter, the atmosphere here seemed quite inhospitable and grim. People were sitting in isolated groups and often a man or woman would be sitting alone. The shelter marshal was quite a different personality, a woman of about 50, with strained, suffused eyes and a cold suspicious manner ...

'The children were pale and tired, one of them crying intermittently. Other children, poorly dressed and rather dirty, looked more tired and less healthy than in the former stations. In common with the adults with them, they were silent and apathetic.'

If the bombers come again, as they may have come before these words appear in print, new life will have been infused into these moribund communities, and Auntie Mabel may again find herself the centre of tube life, the oldest inhabitant, with a record of three years' continuous residence underground.

Meanwhile the communal atmosphere of 1940 has created something of a new tradition in London's Underground. Wartime relaxation of restraint, plus the presence of members of a multitude of nations whose behaviour is normally less constrained than that of the British, have also helped to make the tube stations a more cheerful place than they were before the war. One hears stories from the suburbs about the behaviour of returning revellers, like this: 'Women drink a fat lot more than they did before the war – even I remember that. You never saw so much of it before the war started. Not that I mind a woman having a drink at a pub. I take no objection to that, not at all. But some of these lasses don't know where to stop. Do you know what I saw only last night? I was coming home by District from Victoria, and there was three American soldiers, young chaps all, with their arms round two ATS. All twined in circles they was, and hardly able to stand, not one among them. One of the girls was sick in the train before we got to South Ken. Sick as a dog she was. The other gal came across to her and took off her cap and tried to comfort her, but she was so drunk she could hardly keep on her feet. Now that's not right to my mind.'

Mass-Observation's investigators, patrolling the tube stations at night in spring 1943, certainly found a great relaxation of restraint in people's behaviour. Piccadilly Circus, while scarcely typical, gives a good picture of the atmosphere which diffuses itself along the line between 10 o'clock and the last train home. Here is an investigator's description of a typical night in April, 1943: 'I arrive just after ten p.m. and see a Canadian officer going off through Shaftesbury Avenue exit accompanied by two policemen and followed by glances from the crowd. "What happened?" says a middle-aged working-class man to a woman. Nobody seems to know. Station is packed, near entrance to trains, and there is a babel of sound. "This place is like a slum," shouts one WREN to another as they go to automatic machine to get tickets. I go into a telephone box. A few drunk soldiers gather in a neighbouring box, and the indistinguishable noise is nearly deafening. Come out again. Young prostitute with angry expression says to naval man with her: "First time I've ever had any trouble." Another angry prostitute passes with man in civilian clothes. "Behavin' like that for no reason at all," she says crossly as she passes me.'

At this point, drowned in the din of voices, the alert sounds outside. A policeman moves on two spectacled youths, and a few minutes later does the same to a group of women. Soon the station is almost cleared: 'A man of thirty, in civilian clothes, is talking earnestly to a young woman by the ticket machines. He has his hands on her shoulders and is looking with apparent sternness into her face as if exacting some sort of vow or declaration. Presently they take tickets and go off together hand in hand. A party is trying to take tenpenny tickets and the machine refuses to work; the three men of the party take turns in kicking it; train official watches but makes no protest. Girl comes from train with American soldier, both seem a little drunk. "Less jus' see whass going on – jus' see whass going on." Another group of three girls and four soldiers arrive. Girls start yelling, "Where we goin', where we goin'?"''

Only at this point does the investigator find out that the alert has sounded, on getting into conversation with a station sweeper. The investigator joins the crowd taking tickets: 'There is no alarm shown. People remark, "Hope we shan't be hung up long," "Wonder how long it will last," "They stop the trains, don't they?" quite calmly.'

A train is standing in the platform, and there is much dispute as to where it is going. A woman porter comes along and announces it is a Stanmore train, and there is a great scramble to get off, most people having decided it was southbound. On the platform again the investigator gets into conversation with a woman of 35: '"Ooh, I wish I was in my bed. I've got to get to the Elephant. I wonder how long this is going on." There is a lot of noise, but nothing can be heard distinctly except the conversation of one's immediate neighbours. "They always put it in reverse when the warning's on," says the woman. "Put what in reverse?" I ask. But the answer is drowned.'

At last a train arrives. There is a terrific scramble to get on board. A man of fifty in imitation Harris tweed coat and with a demoniac expression fights and kicks and elbows his way in. The train moves off: 'It is now as packed as the platform, and people have to fight and batter their way out at Charing Cross, where several people are heard saying that the all-clear has gone. I stand beside two Irishwomen with a coloured man in civilian dress, only about five feet high. One Irishwoman says, "Ah, lovely Pete, he was a nice person, he'd never see an Irish person want." The coloured man says, "When you leave in the morning, you never know if you'll see it again." Presently the other Irishwoman is heard to say, "The Irish people never believe in making a toil of pleasure." "America is the only place you can do as you like in," says the coloured man. Another station. Opposite me is a middle-class woman of 35, and beside her an older man, a hearty business-man type. She looks very attractive in a frosty way. He appears to have picked her up, but is not sure of his ground. He keeps smiling and winking at me all the way home.'

This is London's underground on a typical night on a typical last train home, slightly more crowded, slightly more gay because of the alert, but with a live, unrestrained, cosmopolitan atmosphere. Along the line the thinning communities of tube-dwellers watch this new social life, wonder, perhaps, whether in the winter of 1943 the communal existence which evolved round them two years ago will revive in new blitzes. A certain exclusiveness seems to be developing among the remaining inhabitants of some of the tubes. The bunks, instead of being open to the public gaze, are often shrouded with a blanket slung from the bunk above, cutting solitary sleepers off from the rest of the world. If blitzes start again will the goodwill and communal spirit, the shelter leaders and shelter characters come into their own again, or will the private-booked bunk and potential class-differentiation between the older inhabitants and newer residents of tubedom lead to exclusiveness and cliques? By the time these words are read the answer may be clear to anyone taking the last train home.

Mollie Tarrant, who wrote the next item, was a school teacher before she joined Mass-Observation's full-time team about the beginning of 1941. While at work on a blitz report in Portsmouth, commissioned, ironically, by Naval Intelligence, she was arrested on suspicion of being a Communist spy – she was interviewing a policeman's wife and the policeman overheard her.

As a member of the full-time team, she helped with the twice-weekly morale checks in London, studied drinking and attitudes to Americans, covered by-elections in Scotland and Wales, and so on. She spent about three months in the Welsh coal-mining districts of Blaina and Nantyglo observing the impact of war on what had been a severely depressed area, with three quarters of its people unemployed.

Her account of housing in Blaina seems to follow naturally from the last two items. Blaina was not 'blitzed', and unemployment disappeared, but the housing stock, even so, was poor. Housing became a key issue in the 1945 General Election.

Mollie Tarrant was drafted back into teaching in 1943, at a time when Mass-Observation's team of women full-timers was being squeezed by the Ministry of Labour. She continued to do Mass-Observation work in the school holidays, returned to the organisation after the war, became a director of Mass-Observation Ltd in 1949 and stayed with the firm until 1965.

19. Mollie Tarrant: File Report No. 1498, Homes in Blaina, 1943

Here are some representative homes:

(1) The first house was one of a group of eleven standing back off

the road and opening onto a big muddy forecourt, a short piece of paving running in front of the houses. The water closets stand away across the court and in front of the houses; in the winter the forecourt would probably be squelchy with mud and water. The roofs of the houses looked good, and the outside walls. That was all. Inside, the walls are damp, with damp marks sometimes stretching up nearly the whole of the wall of the downstairs rooms. The front door opens straight into the front room. A second door opposite the front door into the kitchen or living room, a third door into a dirty unpaved backyard. There is thus a through draught. At the back, there is a retaining wall against a pit-tip. The tip is pushing down, and gradually the retaining wall is breaking up, and bricks, stones and pieces of coal used for wedging, lie about near the back doors of the houses.

Inside the houses there is a damp musty smell; the windows are small and space is cramped. People in Blaina spend most of the time in the kitchens where there is always a big range and a good fire. If there is another room, as in the house specially visited in Globe Pit Row, it is apt, as in the parlour already described, to be filled with highly polished, cheap, modern furniture. It is tragic to see this furniture in the houses of younger people set in rooms where the walls are stained by damp, where the floor rises up unevenly and the whole place is rickety and misshapen. There were two miners in the kitchen. One of them said: 'I've been away. You notice things more, coming back. There's only one thing to do with these houses. Pull them all down.'

(2) The second house visited was one which had become a 'back' house, though not originally designed to be. It had once been a four-roomed house with good sized rooms, a staircase rising between the two back and the two front rooms. At present, it is occupied by two families, both using the same stairs and brought into continual contact with each other. There is, naturally, no bathroom, but there is also no indoor lavatory. Lavatories stand across a small backyard and are used by both back and front houses. There are no adequate inside sinks, but the back house has a small tap just behind the back door, and in the living room. The staircase used by the two families was not carpeted and had no banisters. Banisters are not common in the average Blaina houses. The main grievance of a tenant here was: 'No matter what else, every house should have its own lavatory. It's only healthy.' (F45D)

(3) The third house was a cellar dwelling, two rooms only and a pantry which backed against earth. There was no through ventil-

ation and the house was obviously very damp. These low lying dwellings are extraordinary places. Blaina is built on a slope which rises to a flat plain at Nantyglo. One street may, consequently be a lower level than another street, the two connected by steps or steep paths. This has its effect on the type of house built, which may be two storeys on the upper street and three storeys where it backs on to the lower street. This third storey down with a door on to the lower level street is usually occupied by quite a different family from that in the part of the house belonging to the upper level street. The lower house is very obviously unhygienic – has no lavatory or fitted sink inside, no proper garden and small windows only. These cellars were originally meant to be simply kitchens, wash-places, or store houses for the rest of the house and not to be lived in for any length of time. This particular house (under 25 and 28 Church Street) was nicely furnished and obviously a source of pride to its owner. The range was beautifully kept, the brass highly polished, the curtain clean and the floor newly washed. Some of the furniture looked new. The young girl who was tidying the house looked hurt and angry at a comment not intended to be overheard: 'These places aren't fit for anybody to live in.'

(4) The fourth house was a six-roomed house, one of a group belonging to the Blaina Cottage Estate Company. This was a sturdily built house just outside the subsidence area but not unlikely to be some time affected by it. The people living here had been able to spend more money on their houses over a number of years than many other people in Blaina and were fairly well satisfied, both with the house itself and with the repairs which had been done. The big drawback, as with so many hundreds of houses, was the size of the backyard. The housewife was asked if she was satisfied with her treatment by the Company. She replied: 'Oh yes. They treat us very well. There's a man who comes round every so often and you just tell him what's wrong. They get things done quickly too.' (F50C)

(5) Lying well up on the eastern slope, away from the town, is a group of ten bungalows built by the Council for old age pensioners. Like most other council houses, and unlike practically all the remaining houses in Nantyglo and Blaina, they are detached. They are square, sturdy little houses with fair sized gardens, pleasant rooms of average size, big windows and a good view down over the town. They are not particularly beautiful, and have the inevitable made-to-measure appearance of nearly all council houses. A defect is badly fitting doors, but otherwise people have few complaints.

People from some of the slum clearance areas have been put in these nearby council houses.

And here is a similar random sample from Nantyglo:

(1) In Market Road, Nantyglo, there is another block of cellar dwellings. These have long, narrow, often badly cultivated gardens in front of them, and consist of two small dark rooms. These cellar dwellings in this case are simply built in archways which originally were placed to support the two upper storeys of the house. In some cases, the back walls are wet rather than just damp. There are no lavatories or sinks. The house visited in this row had recently been vacated. Overnight, without official permission, another family had moved in and were living there still in extreme poverty. A woman of about 40 and a small boy were in the house at the time of the visit. It was difficult to distinguish anything in the room at first because of the intense gloom: a sack was covering half the window to keep out the draught. There was a bare table in the middle of the living room and one or two wooden chairs. The woman and child were huddled close to the range, but were sitting with the front door open, presumably to let in the light. The living room was separated from the bedroom by a curtain only. There was a stone floor, and the walls were damp and moist.

The child seemed ill and apathetic, and the woman, dirty and in ragged clothes, looked like a wild beast, ready to fight for her right to stay in the house, deprecatory and conciliatory, while we were there, muttering and calling out when we left. This is not an isolated example of 'squatting'. But quite often happens between the time when a tenant leaves a condemned house and the six weeks which must elapse before any further action can be taken.

(2) The second house visited in Nantyglo was in a group of houses, 'one up and one down', some in good repair, usually the property of owner-occupiers, others in appallingly bad repair. Numbers one and two were owned by the same person, who herself lived in No. 1. The second house was occupied by a mother and daughter who were apparently very poor and certainly very slovenly. A narrow, dark, steep staircase led from the single living room to the bedroom. Pails were placed in the bedroom to catch the rain dripping through from the roof.

'When it rains really hard, it all comes through on the bed. But we can't move the bed anywhere else because the room's not high enough. But *she* says she won't do any more for us. *She* says we've got to get out,' said the girl.

The owner of this house was an obstinate, independent old woman of near eighty. Her daughter, a tall erect woman of 45 with a wonderful carriage and thick snow-white hair, lived with her. Both seemed remote from this century. The older woman was using the biggest social insult that she knew when she spoke of her tenant: 'She's a bad, *peasant* woman. She's no use to we. She must go! Her husband have come and banged on the door in the middle of the night and scared we. She must go. We won't do anything for her!'

(3) Another visit was to a council house built under the latest of the Council's housing schemes and completed about twelve months ago. It was a detached house, with three bedrooms, a particularly big kitchen living room, a smaller front room, a bathroom, and a fair-sized garden. There is a big council estate at Brynhyfed standing on the plateau at the top of the hill. It was an enormous improvement on anything else in Blaina, though the rents were correspondingly high (average 12/- to 14/-, instead of 7/6d) and the air and situation wonderfully good.

It was a pity however that some ideas from the older houses had been carried over into the new. The sink intruded into one corner of a very pleasant living room, whereas some of the living room space would have been better converted into a scullery. One thing was noticeable about some of the houses; recently painted doors and windows, polished knockers, clean steps. These better kept houses usually belonged to owner-occupiers.

IV

The Forces, 1940–1945

As conscription extended to cover more and more age groups, Mass-Observation struggled to maintain its full-time male staff, making well-argued representations to various Government departments. But even Tom Harrisson finally joined the Army in 1941 and was sent to Borneo by the Special Operations Executive to mobilise guerrilla warfare against the Japanese in 1944. During the period before he was called up and then for as long as possible during his military training, Harrisson continued to direct the work of Mass-Observation. Ever resourceful, he turned what might have been a serious depletion of his workforce into an asset. Full-time Observers were expected to keep in touch with headquarters; members of the volunteer Panel in the Forces were sent special 'Forces Directives'. Studies of morale, Army education, of leisure and reading habits, of political views and voting intentions were all carried out by Observers within the Armed Forces, sometimes with the knowledge and consent of superiors and sometimes clandestinely.

It has not been possible to include material in this chapter from all the Forces Observers. Valuable material was provided by, for example, Len England, previously Mass-Observation's 'man in the cinema' before he joined the RAOC (he had conducted a number of surveys of audience reaction to wartime films and newsreels); Charles Pepper, who, sadly, died on active service, sent reports from the RAF camp where he was stationed in Iceland; John Sommerfield, veteran of the Worktown Project and main author of *The Pub and the People*, wrote also from the RAF, as did Arthur Calder-Marshall and several others. In return, Tom Harrisson would send them copies of the *New Statesman* or cigarettes – or, occasionally, money.

Most of the Forces work was done in 1940 and 1941. After that, many of the full-time Observers were posted abroad and found it harder to maintain contact. None of the items reproduced in this chapter gives much impression of active service nor of the physical danger which many soldiers faced, but it has to be remembered that the experience of war, at least prior to D-Day, for the vast majority of people in the Forces was a period of waiting, a time of boredom with routine and frustration with authority, a time of separation from loved ones and of the absence of home comforts. No fully comprehensive social history about the men and women who joined the Armed Forces during the Second World War has ever been published. Somewhere between the military histories and the autobiographies and biographies of individuals lies an altogether different kind of history for which the Mass-Observation papers could provide a very useful corner-stone.

In September 1939 the National Service (Armed Forces) Act made all men between the ages of 18 and 42 liable for military conscription. Registration commenced the following month; men were expected to attend a Labour Exchange when instructed and, provided they did not hold a job which was listed on the schedule of reserved occupations and they were classed as grade 1 or 2 out of the four grades of medical fitness, they were directed into the Armed Forces. It was usually possible to specify a preference and it seemed generally accepted that the Royal Air Force was the best option. The number of men claiming conscientious objection on political grounds was quite high during the first months of the war. Many conscripts lacked motivation and resented their enforced position.

The writer of the following report was himself a reluctant recruit, as is evident from his earlier diary for Mass-Observation. Before being called up he had been a civil servant in Essex with moderately socialist views.

20. National Panel member: Conscripts' attitude to war politics, April 1940

GENERAL REPORT ON CONSCRIPTS' ATTITUDE TO WAR POLITICS

First of all I must say that I have to generalise a great deal in this report and that these generalisations should not be taken as applying to every conscript. They merely give the broad impression I have received from the contacts I have made in the few months I have been in the RAF. These impressions may not be typical. I imagine, for instance, that on the whole a more intelligent type gets into the RAF than in the Army or even the Navy. I have compared notes, however, with a friend in the Navy who is also a Mass-Observer and his impressions have been much the same as mine.

The first impression then is that, as shown by M-O's survey of those about to be called up, there is no enthusiasm for war as such and not a great deal of enthusiasm for this particular war. Also without exception, the conscripts, and also many volunteers, want the war to end so that they can get back to civilian life. They are not deeply in love with life in the RAF, tho' of course they like certain aspects of it but on the whole they bear it because they know that it is preferable to life in the Army, who are generally acknowledged to have the worst of everything. A number of conscripts have confessed to me that they would have been 'COs' if they had 'had the guts' but on closer questioning they nearly always revealed that they had no conscientious objection to war (tho' of course they thought it rather silly and pointless), but merely an objection to being in H.M. Forces at all.

There is not a great deal of hatred expressed against the Germans. Hitler of course is generally referred to as a bastard. In the last few days since the invasion of Scandinavia, I have heard more condemnation than in all the rest of the time. Neither is there in the RAF that tendency so common in civilians to underestimate the enemy. It is realised that we have a hard nut to crack. Indeed to listen to some RAF men talk you would imagine we had practically no chance of winning at all. I believe that a good deal of this pessimism is affected.

Conscripts I have met have not often been what the Communists call 'politically conscious' and they seldom talk politics. There are exceptions to this tho'. I have met Communists, Socialists, an ex-Fascist and so forth. But mostly conscripts do not talk incessantly politics. When they do, however, they seem to display a good deal of political intelligence and many can argue quite coherently.

The foremost characteristic of their outlook is a cynicism about everything. They like democracy but they know damn well that all we are fighting for is British capital. Patriotism, the Flag and the Empire are a lot of tripe – only they don't say tripe. Mr Chamberlain's ears must be red at some of the nouns and adjectives I have heard applied to him. Churchill is far and away the most liked member of this government. Indeed his was the only talk I have heard a barrack room listen to on the wireless.

Conscientious objectors cause a good deal of heartburning and I have heard many heated arguments about them. Many dismiss them all as unnatural and meet to be shot but the more thinking usually concede that it requires a good deal of guts to be a CO and that we have taken the easy way out by following the crowd. Complaints usually made over the fact that many COs are merely swinging the lead. There is probably some justification for this complaint but I have heard the more uncompromising assert that 95 per cent of COs were not genuine. Generally speaking, broad streak of tolerance runs thro' opinions of most of the conscripts I have met.

OPINION-FORMING MATERIAL IMPACTING UPON CONSCRIPTS

Opinions are formed entirely by the newspapers and by wireless. First the newspapers. Papers may be bought in the camp and there is a reading room containing all the leading dailies. The reading room is well patronised by the studious type of conscript. Papers are bought by perhaps 20 per cent of the conscripts but probably quite 90 per cent of the conscripts read a paper daily, for when a paper is bought by one member of a barrack room it is invariably read later by most of the occupants of that room. Far and away the most read newspaper is the 'Daily Mirror'. I should say that over 60 per cent of the newspapers sold are 'Mirror's. Surprisingly enough the 'Herald' seems to be next with perhaps 15 per cent of the total sold. Then the 'Express' with about 10 per cent, the 'Chronicle' about 7 per cent, the 'Telegraph' perhaps 3 per cent and the rest nowhere. I have not seen a 'Times' or a 'Daily Sketch' in the RAF since I was called up. It is probably true that the more serious papers are read here (i.e. by a greater number of people) than the less serious papers. I myself buy the 'Chronicle' daily and perhaps the three other occupants of our hut containing 20 buy the 'Mirror'. An 'Express' or 'Telegraph' also occasionally finds its way into the hut. My 'Chronicle' is usually read carefully by about eight members of the hut and perhaps scanned by five more. The 'Mirrors' are scanned by nearly everyone.

On Sunday, there is a great multiplicity of papers, the 'News of the World', the 'Sunday Pictorial' and the 'Sunday Express' predominating in that order.

As in civilian life there is far more concentrated reading of newspapers on Sundays than on weekdays but on the whole the almost solid phalanx of Conservative newspapers does not seem to unduly affect the conscripts. I confess that I quite shamelessly buy the 'Reynolds' in order that it may have at least a neutralising effect on opinion in my hut.

That cynicism I mentioned in politics also affects the views expressed about newspapers. There is that tendency, which M-O noted in their survey of News-Letters, to treat with considerable caution most newspaper reports about the war – particularly those about British victories. They believe the papers when they say we've lost five bombers (tho' they fancy it might be more than that) but they rather doubt reports that we have destroyed five enemy machines. Nevertheless there has been a very great demand for newspapers since the German invasion of Denmark and Norway.

Then there are the wireless news bulletins. Wireless sets are not supplied by the authorities at our camp so that each hut that wants a set has to club round and get one. About 25 per cent of the huts have wireless sets but when there is important news (and again this has been particularly noticeable since the German invasion of Scandinavia) people from other huts come in to listen to the news bulletins. There are also radio sets in the NAAFIs at this camp so that a fairly large percentage of personnel hear an English news bulletin from London once a day at least. But again there is that cynicism and disbelief of our news bulletins. Of course, this cynicism (perhaps that's rather an unkind word) is a necessary prerequisite of a healthy public opinion and I welcome it.

The sometimes nauseatingly complacent air of the BBC news bulletins does not go down well. 'All our aircraft returned safely', 'No damage was sustained in a raid in which 20 German aircraft took part' are usually greeted with 'Oh Yeah' and the like.

In our hut at least we also have the German news bulletins in English almost every night. A typical remark at 9.15 after we have heard the news from London is 'Let's tune in to Lord Haw Haw [a German propagandist] and hear the truth'. The remark of course is made semi-humorously at least. His version is compared with our version of events and except in his more extravagant claims, the tendency is, or seems to be, to believe Lord Haw Haw. But his version of the invasion of Scandinavia was not swallowed. The fact that he was listened to at a time when there was more dislike of Germany expressed than at any previous time, does show that there is a definite desire to get at the truth and not an unquestioning swallowing of the British version. And that much at least seems to bode good for the future of democracy in this country.

The only Observer to send in continuous reports from the Royal Navy was Able Seaman George Hutchinson, who became well known in the years after the war both as a journalist (he worked for the *Evening Standard*, and *Spectator* and *The Times*) and for his connections with the Conservative Party. Hutchinson came from Bradford where he had already embarked on his career in journalism with the *Yorkshire Post* before being conscripted at the age of 20.

He was posted first of all to Skegness in June 1941. He altered his original plan of becoming a signaller and decided to train in seamanship in the hope of gaining a commission. He was sent to the Royal Naval Establishment, HMS *Raleigh*, at Torpoint in Cornwall and from there to HMS *Valkyrie* at Douglas on the Isle of Man to undergo a three-week training course in RDF (Radio and Direction Finding, later in the war to become known as radar). Hutchinson had previously worked for Mass-Observation both as a volunteer and, during 1940, as a paid investigator. His reports to Mass-Observation from the Navy took the form of letters usually addressed to Mr Harrisson but some of them begin 'Dear Mother'. Since there is little difference between the two sorts of letters and nothing to indicate that some letters had been donated to Mass-Observation at some later date by his mother, it is difficult not to suspect that 'Dear Mother' was a subterfuge. In the HMS *Raleigh* handbook for ratings, rule 30 states 'Keeping diaries is not allowed'. There are references in other parts of the correspondence to suggest that Hutchinson had to go to some lengths to ensure that Mass-Observation received his contributions.

At the time of Hutchinson's training, the Admiralty was just beginning to install the newly developed radar equipment into its ships. The earlier form of anti-submarine detection, 'Asdic', was capable of giving only distant warning of approaching U-boats and could not detect surface vessels. The new short-wave radio sets were capable of detecting U-boats at several miles' range and since U-boats could move faster on the surface than under water, this was a strategic technical advance for the British Navy.

George Hutchinson's reports begin in June 1941 and stop when he is posted to Gibraltar in 1942. He spent the rest of the war serving mainly in the Arctic and North Atlantic. The extracts below were written during his three weeks' training on the Isle of Man, where many so-called 'enemy aliens' were still interned. 6928 were held in October 1941, of whom 3091 were in Category 'C'. That is, they were refugees from Nazism, and others judged by tribunals to be harmless, but nevertheless rounded up in 1940.

21. George Hutchinson: Naval manoeuvres on dry land, 1941

NOTE ON RDF (RANGE AND DIRECTION FINDING) TRAINING

RDF personnel are trained at the RN Signal School, Portsmouth or at the school's Isle of Man establishment, the *Valkyrie*.

There are several types of RDF set and the details are secret, but it can be stated that by means of this device (which includes a transmitting and a receiving aerial) surface craft (and with some sets aircraft also) can be detected.

The course normally lasts for three weeks. The first week is devoted to the theory of electricity, magnetism and wireless, and at the end of the week there is a written examination. The second week is devoted to the practical part of the work – how the set works, how to adjust or tune it, how to operate it generally. All this is shown with an actual set (not aboard a ship though), and at the end of the week there is a practical examination. During the third week trainees go to sea, and with the aid of a target ship, learn to operate the set in more or less normal active-service conditions. Those who fail in the theory or practical examinations aren't allowed to continue with the course; they are invariably made members of the ship's company (i.e. the people who 'work' the establishment, as distinct from those training there, though the latter have certain work-ship duties when they are [on] watch aboard) and after a month or two are sent back to Portsmouth, where, they say, they have to take another course in seamanship. Those who pass out in RDF are generally rewarded with a week's leave. Incidentally, an RDF operator is classed as a wireless operator.

Monday, Nov. 24

'Lash up and stow' is piped here at 6.30. Most people stay in bed til about 6.45, however, then slipping on trousers, boots and jerseys, dash downstairs to have a cup of cocoa before falling in at seven o'clock. At seven the captain of the top (i.e. the P.O. in charge of the division) details hands off for sundry jobs about the house before breakfast at 7.45. My job, to which I'm permanently appointed this morning, is to sweep out my bedroom – a five minute duty. Other jobs include sweeping landings, cleaning out w.c.s, washing up cocoa cups.

After breakfast we're free till 8.45 when we fall in for ten minutes P.T. in the roadway (fenced off) in front of the houses [. . .] Immediately after P.T., divisions; as soon as divisions are over, we fall in in classes to march to Douglas Head Hotel, which has been taken over by the Admiralty and is the place where we actually receive our training – we only live in the *Valkyrie* proper. I notice that a bus takes P.O.s and officers and any ratings on light duty to Douglas Head. Douglas Head is about a mile from the *Valkyrie* and it's an uphill walk. We stop halfway there outside a little shop which must be coining money since the Navy came to Douglas, for about 50 people buy a bag of sweets each (2d a bag), and I'm told it's open when we return to Douglas Head from dinner at the *Valkyrie*. Apparently the woman who keeps it only opens up nowadays when the Navy's due to pass. She hasn't got much in the way of cigarettes or tobacco, but there are always plenty of sweets they say, though little variety (I believe there's no shortage of sweets in the Isle of Man generally). A good number of people also buy bottles of pop (4d a bottle). On this little-frequented road this shop would normally be closed down at this time of year I should think.

Arriving at the hotel, my class is alloted a classroom to itself. Our warrant-school master is Welsh, about 30. A pleasant chap and highly articulate. First of all, we have a ten-minute written intelligence test (simple – questions like is a point East or West of another point when you have some more information about both points). This is followed by a 30-minute general knowledge test (also simple – meaning of letters C.I.D., P.M.G., R.S.V.P., etc.; why do you poke a fire when you want it to burn more brightly; what are the colours of the Royal and Merchant Navy ensigns; what is the mile limit – I answered this, like the rest, correctly, but can't now remember whether it's a three- or four-mile limit). These two tests over, the school master lectures us on the theory of electricity till 12.30 (stand-easy of 15 minutes from eleven).

Leave Douglas Head for *Valkyrie* at 12.30. Dinner at one o'clock. After dinner we're free till 2.20 when we fall in and march back to Douglas Head again. After dinner I go into the NAAFI canteen for a cup of tea (1*d*) and a couple of excellent cakes (1½*d* each). Quite unimpressive canteen this – formerly the public bar of a hotel.

Arrive back at Douglas Head about 2.45 (again stop for five minutes outside little sweet shop). Remain there til 4.30, and march back to *Valkyrie* for five o'clock tea (two slices of bread and butter, bun, cup of tea).

We're allowed ashore alternate nights here, from 5.30 till midnight (natives 7.30 next morning). There are liberty boats at 5.30, 6.30 and 7.30 (they talk about liberty boats here too but of course there aren't even buses here for we're right in the centre of town to start off with).

I go ashore with P at 5.30. We have a look round the town, then go to the Salvation Army Forces Canteen for something to eat. They offer us egg and chips or meat pie and chips, and there are, of course, buns and cakes and biscuits and tea as well. We choose egg and chips, and are, to put it mildly, rather surprised when the woman helper asks if we want two eggs each or one. There's no shortage of eggs here apparently and naturally we have two each. So for 1*s* 2*d* we each have two fried eggs and a large plate of chips, a cup of tea and a slice of bread and butter (not so sure that it is actually butter, but it tastes alright).

After that we go to see an appalling film called 'The Common Touch', the only good thing in which is Mark Hambourg's playing. In all Douglas cinemas troops are allowed in at children's prices – shilling seats for ninepence, ninepenny seats for sixpence. After the pictures, a drink then back to the *Valkyrie*.

Tuesday, Nov. 25

Same daytime routine as yesterday. At dinnertime hear classic example of shore establishment make-believe. A bicycle is parked alongside the kerb outside the houses. Along comes Sub.-Lieut. Pertwee. He looks at the bike, turns to a few people standing around and asks 'Who tied this dinghy to the ship's side?' He asks in all seriousness and I have to turn away to hide my laughter.

Watch aboard tonight. Fall in at 5.30 and with five others am detailed to sweep main deck, i.e. the roadway. Go to P.O.s' [Petty Officers'] mess to get brushes. Closet they're kept in is locked up. Key turns out to be lost. So we're told we can carry on [...]

Sunday, Nov. 30

Captain's inspection this morning [...] After inspection C of E people told to prove (i.e. put hands up), but guessing they're forming a church party, I don't. Those who put their hands up go to church about half an hour later [...]

Watch ashore today. Can go ashore soon after dinner but P and I don't go till 4.30 (have a sleep in the afternoon). We have a walk along the front past the internment camp (boarding houses). The camp is fenced off with several rows of barbed wire and a sentry guards each entrance while another marches up and down along the front. Through the uncurtained windows we can see the internees – mostly working-class, small café-proprietor type, I imagine.

Sunday, Dec. 7

Reaction to Japanese declaration of war on US: considerable satisfaction that America is at last in the war together with some dismay on account of Japanese Navy's strength. On the whole regarded as a good thing for Britain [...]

Some of the most detailed reports on morale in the Forces were written for Mass-Observation by Henry Novy while he was a private in the Royal Army Medical Corps. Henry Novy had begun his assessments of war-time morale from a Mass-Observation outpost in Worcestershire where he had lived with at least two other paid Observers during the early part of the war. His almost daily bulletins had formed the basis of some of Mass-Observation's reports to Home Intelligence at the Ministry of Information. In December 1940 he joined the RAMC and was posted north.

The report below was written in September 1941 as part of a diary for Mass-Observation and it describes the first attempt on his station at Shotley Bridge, County Durham, to institute informal discussions on current affairs. The recent creation of ABCA (Army Bureau of Current Affairs) had prompted the organisation of similar classes and talks throughout the Army. Adult education facilities had been available in the Army prior to the setting up of ABCA under the direction of the Central Advisory Council for Adult Education in HM Forces but the quality and the accessibility had varied from unit to unit. A growing recognition in Army circles that the modern soldier should understand why he is fighting, coupled with the desire to assuage the boredom among men based on home soil, convinced the new Adjutant General, General Sir Ronald Adam, that initiatives were essential. ABCA recommended that there should be at least one hour's compulsory education per week and that platoon commanders should lead the sessions using ABCA publications, *War* and *Current Affairs*, as background material.

At first the discussions tended to be rudimentary (as the following account illustrates) but ABCA courses soon proliferated and by the end of 1941, six out of every ten units ran discussions both at home and abroad. So popular and stimulating did they become that official eyebrows were raised. The lively debating groups were considered hotbeds of subversion and on at least one occasion, Churchill tried to curb ABCA.

22. Henry Novy: Army education, September 1941

Also we had a 'talk' given by a Major, the boss of Medical Division and quite an eminent specialist. He has been made the unit's education officer, and now he will give weekly talks to the men, on topics chosen and outlined by the Army Bureau of Current Affairs. As the men cannot all be spared at the same time there is a plan to have the same lecture given two or three times, so that all, or most of the men can be detailed to attend. This has been well-arranged and on the whole the organisation is satisfactory. About 40 of us attended, and we heard all the Major had to say. He is a tall serious-looking man, very straight, and a bald patch on his head, though young. He speaks with a definite varsity accent, and most definitely stands out as very different from the men. He has the reputation of being a good MO and also a good officer, strict, but with a keen sense of duty, and responsibilities towards his men. He is in no sense a Coy. Officer or a disciplinary man like an adjutant. His first words were revealing: 'It is the wish of the Colonel that these talks should be as informal as possible. He wants you to enjoy them and it is his wish that you may smoke.'

Old Harry beside me whispered 'Yes, but not mine' and I felt it was somewhat resented by the men. Actually I read since that these were instructions of the ABCA to the officers giving the talks, '"ammunition" for short, interesting talks to your men at suitable times in their training' . . . 'we shall make these texts as interesting and "human" as possible. The rest is up to you.' Allowing the men to smoke, to lounge back with their feet up had no doubt the desired effect to make the talks seem informal.

The text of the first number of *War* – the production of ABCA – was about the *War in the Desert*. It gave a few broad outlines of Wavell's tactics, his difficulties, his splendid achievements. Before any comment can be made on the talk itself, one must mention that the ammunition was pretty poor. The great question of the moment is Russia, the fight for Leningrad. The ABCA gives material for related comments on the first British success [in North Africa] (followed by reverses never mentioned, but only too well remembered), and absolutely non topical. The officers have instructions to keep to these texts.

The Major lectured as well as he could, a little in the way he might have lectured a medical students' class about the new ways discovered by Pasteur to fight disease, and how important they were. Only he talked about what Wavell did, not about the possible results of his strategy on warfare, or lessons to be drawn from it.

It was just a poor rehash of a poor text. Knowing nothing about tactics he could not illustrate. He had a keen sense that the illustrations given in the text were worn and would only seem stupid to the men. Therefore he talked about the little incidents he remembered in the last war. The only vital and interesting question asked was about 'the purpose of a medical unit in a fast moving tank force' asked by Harry out of his slumber, and that he could answer, saying something about armoured cars and ambulances, but that after all nobody knew very much about it. There was a complete absence of questions and an embarrassing pause each time he tried to get them going.

The reaction of the men was what one could reasonably expect. They rested as comfortably as they could in their chairs, some of them dozed off, others looked at the ceiling, and few smoked and listened. When at the end the Major delivered an impromptu tirade on the efficiency of the German soldier telling us that what won wars was efficiency and discipline and that unless we were prepared to be efficient and disciplined there could be no victory for us, the men looked up, half amused. Getting up they passed a few comments, where I heard 'like a lot of school children', 'Sunday School boys', 'Christ you must be good', 'Bloody Hell . . .' and other remarks no more favourable. When the Major felt he had nothing more to say, and that he couldn't get the men to ask questions, then he began to round off his lecture with a talk about the Germans, following hard and without link up on the Wavell tactics and the Italians. The Germans were efficient, they were disciplined and they'd kill refugees if they were told to. That was the difference between them and us, we wouldn't kill innocent people. But we couldn't win the war unless we were prepared to be disciplined. He repeated himself a few more times than I have here.

I asked as many as I could 'What did you think of it?' Here are some of the answers: 'Oh it was comfortable, I had a nice sleep.' 'Not bad, it's a change from work. I didn't mind.' 'All right but who wants to know about the bleeding Italians, they're done and finished with now.' 'Oh hell, we're not bloody kids to be told how good we're got to be.' 'No bloody good.' 'I said it'd be like that, pre-war 1914 stuff.' The good comments were extremely few. I have a very long one which I did my best to remember:

> 'What did you think of the lecture this afternoon?
>
> Not bad, was it? I reckon it was interesting really. Good stuff you know. It tells you about Wavell and what they did in Egypt. It was a Major, he was good I think. What are they for? I suppose it's for propaganda like, to make us understand the war. It was good about getting in between those two forts. I never thought it. He was a clever man, Wavell, wasn't he? Yes, I thought it was a very good talk, very interesting like'.

This was spoken to me at supper, quite spontaneously, by a man who is a complete ignoramus, very backward indeed. It points out that the talk was more fit for a School talk than talk to soldiers. It savours too much of 'what's best to tell them' spirit. Someone remarked: 'I suppose they can't touch politics. But then the war's all about politics. So what can they do?' One of the clerks who went to the lecture today said that it was 'quite good in parts. Major . . . was very good. He told us about Egypt and Libya. It was good in parts but in other parts it was bloody piffling . . . there were VADs [volunteer nurses] there, about 10 of them, and two sisters, Major . . . of the lab. and the RSM [Regimental Sergeant Major].'

In conclusion, one can say that the talk had an encouraging beginning. I think it has tremendous scope and future, if it is organised as well as it was, during working hours and yet not vitally interfering with work. A man with interest and liked in the unit is giving them, and the only thing needed is a different policy, one of truth, current affairs instead of buried phases of the war. If the ABCA wakes up and is placed in the right hands, then the 'Educational Talks' have almost as much future as films. I certainly don't hope to see such facility for reaching the men in a unit. The detailing was excellent, the atmosphere good, the lecturer did his best (though he wasn't really suitable), the only real thing that was wrong, hopelessly wrong, was the text, that is, if the purpose is to 'stimulate soldiers' interest in the war in general' [. . .] I spent quite a time talking about the lecture but it is important, can be the real foundation for a vital answer to a vital need, the war consciousness of the troops. I hear there is another bulletin issued by ABCA called *Current Affairs* and dealing with American help to Britain, also quite as hopeless and conservative as the *War* issue. Still it is a beginning.

The value of the Anti-Aircraft defences lay not so much in shooting down enemy aircraft as in the prevention of accurate bombing of British targets. The AA gunfire compelled German planes to fly at a higher altitude, effectively interfering with their ability to keep a straight and even course necessary for reaching their objectives. The AA guns and searchlights also indicated positions of enemy aircraft to British fighters. Two types of gun were employed, the 4.5 inch, which hurls high explosive shell to a height of eight miles, and the 3.7 inch gun, which has a faster rate of fire and uses a smaller shell. Location of aircraft and charting future courses was assisted by the Vickers Predictor (a calculating machine) and the height-finder.

AA batteries were often situated in lonely and isolated spots; the men and women who worked on the sites had to be prepared to move frequently, hence the use of tents for accommodation. The following diary extracts were written by a young architectural student posted to the Bristol area in March

1941, just as a period of very severe bombing was coming to an end. He had worked for a time under a Camouflage Officer, and resented being moved to routine duties. His resentment flavours his account. After much frustration and poor health he eventually got the commission as Camouflage Officer which he craved. He was one of Mass-Observation's long-serving Panel members, and his rather morose diaries and Directive Replies are full of interesting detail. 'Having been brought up in Aberdeen,' he once wrote in a Directive Reply, 'my attitude to money has always been a careful one.' He went on to note that he had saved £126 from his pay during twenty-nine months in the ranks; one wonders if any other man in the army matched his frugality.

He refers here to the débâcle in April 1941 when the Germans tore through Yugoslavia into Greece, where a British contingent mounted an ill-advised and ineffectual attempt to resist them, falling back on Crete only to be expelled from there in turn. He also alludes to the fire which had destroyed London's famous Crystal Palace in 1936.

23. National Panel member: Bullshit in Bristol, March–April 1941

Saturday, March 22

Up at 09.00. Spent morning cleaning up my room and packing my haversacks. Took 13.15 train to Bristol, read *It's a Battlefield* on train, crowded but got a seat. Bought dates and nuts at Paddington for lunch. Others in train had meat sandwiches and chocolate which they said had been quite plentiful at Maidstone where they had come from. It was fortunate at Bristol that I asked the RTO [Railway Transport Officer] where 364 Bty [Battery] was because 1st Division told me an address from where they had moved. Took a bus through Bristol which had been badly bombed, there seemed to be no shops in the centre of the town. The battery was in two halves, we had 3″ guns (4) and tents to live in. The usual business of no place to sit and read or write in one's spare time. I packed my stuff in tent and went out to a canteen with two friends. It seemed that everyone was pretty fed up chiefly through the primitive living conditions and lack of useful occupation. I was fed up because I could think of no reason why I was sent back from doing really useful work to merely fatigue work with occasional spotting, etc.

Monday, March 24

[. . .] As I was in manning team we examined equipment in morning,

I had been put on a 3″ gun although I had never touched one before. In the morning I moved over to learn something about the Vickers Predictor. I was then asked to take some figures on the heightfinder and stand in for someone in the afternoon. A WVS [Women's Voluntary Service] tea van called – it was very popular. Cigarettes are difficult to get. Suggestions they are being held up till the budget comes out [. . .]

Went to Bristol, got a lift down, bought candles [and] battery; friend bought stripes and lanyard. Had tea in nice tea shop. Bussed back, collected towel and washing things and writing book, and went to WVS canteen, wrote two letters and had a bath. Had egg on fried bread and chips. It was the last egg and chips, the lady complained she couldn't get enough rations and many people had to be content with baked beans. It is a cheap place and baths are free as the lady who runs it pays for all the gas and electricity. In Bristol there were two or three scrawlings on wall 'We want bomb proof shelters'.

Tuesday, March 25

After breakfast went in lorry to Bristol public baths for hot shower (a weekly procedure). I didn't have shower cause had bath the previous night. People enjoy larking at girls as the lorry passes. Did sandbagging in morning. It is unfortunate that the officers do not attempt to make a plan of combat as this is what makes people so slovenly and so unenthusiastic for work. One is continually getting different instructions from different people, they seem unable to commit themselves precisely. I learnt that from my six weeks camouflaging 1st Division gunsites that the keen officer produces the best gunsite. I can't help feeling that they mostly have had such an artificial education and have such an artificial cultural background that they have more clerical ability than ability to plan work and see that it is made interesting and done well. Judging by the messes they seem more interested in the girls or getting the picture with the most sex appeal than running the war, in fact I think that goes for all.

After lunch I was told to camouflage a machine gun post, but when it came to it they had no materials for it. They had the paint for tents but it started to rain so I couldn't do that.

People's tempers were not improved by trying to accommodate themselves in tents in the pouring rain. No officer turned up for 'lining up' in the evening, so God knows where we'll shoot if there's a raid. I think there is spit and polish disease. They don't know what efficiency is, they are afraid of the site not looking pretty for the inspecting officer. We've been scraping camouflage paint off handles so that we can polish the brass underneath.

Wednesday, March 26

[The Captain] assembled battery and told us Major was not satisfied with kits and tents. We had to blanco and polish brass more thoroughly. He also said we must always have our steel helmets with us because the enemy could easily see our tents from a great distance, and we might get bombed. Here . . . expressed in a nutshell the two opposing policies and it is the spit and polish one that is always carried out.

After dinner it started to rain hard, so the site commander foregathered half battery in marquees to discuss the question of indiscriminate bombing. There was an air raid alarm before a show of hands could be made but there would have been a majority for indiscriminate bombing of civilians.

Thursday, April 3

[. . .] Yesterday we erected this marquee which had been used to cover straw and was soaking wet. Our new section sergeant helped and I felt the best of everyone came up in this job. A shipbuilder in Glasgow demonstrated his skill in tying knots which was grand to watch. Another, farmer, demonstrated with amazing skill how to form bunches of straw out of a rough heap for thatching. After a member of the party said he enjoyed a job like that with a definite object. It's better than blancoing.

[. . .] Air raid siren and firing about 9. Literally hundreds of explosive incendiaries were falling on camp as we returned. We immediately started running after them with sandbags. Had clean suit on. No. of bags was hopelessly inadequate to deal with no. of bombs.

Friday, April 4

[. . .] The raids started at night and I was in heightfinder so didn't have much to do, got heights and ranges on planes and on diving plane which crashed in flames about 7 miles away. Many incendiaries around but only a few at one end of the camp. A plane came over camp at a few hundred feet and machine-gunned a site just beyond us. We don't know whether it was making a forced landing or deliberately attacking low. We finished at two after an exhausting night [. . .] We are short of non-manners at camp as there was a dance at RHQ [Regimental Headquarters] where one of the officers injured his face putting out a bomb. Our site officer came round the guns and command post drunk, cursing everybody and making an awful nuisance and fool of himself [. . .] We all got to bed safely at 2.00 but I had to be up at 5.30 spotting for one hour. Reveille was put forward one hour from 6.30 to 7.30, I sat in partial command past five then washed for breakfast. We had fired 570 rounds.

Wednesday, April 9

[. . .] We had a troop parade after breakfast and many people were told off for having dirty respirator cases and boots. I was alright. A full kit inspection was announced for tomorrow morning causing much annoyance and remarks that would shock CO [Commanding Officer] if he heard. How will kit inspections help us to win the war?

The improvement to be made in AA must come from the top and not the gunners. There were despondent remarks about the war situation. People were saying we are losing and kit inspections won't help us to win.

Thursday, April 10

[. . .] The last few days the raids have not been on Bristol but they pass over on the way to the Midlands [. . .] We had a lecture on Greece in afternoon from a young man who gave a kind of travel talk on Greece. He avoided the usual thing by saying that the marvellous character of the Greek would prevent him from being beaten. He admitted there were no mechanised units there and left us to draw the obvious conclusions about the outcome of the war. While walking back from canteen my friend said 'I hope we do win the war, I just can't imagine what'll happen if we do lose.'

Friday, April 11

[. . .] Went to Bristol with Bdr [Bombadier] M to find a flick. Saw 3 cinemas only Mark of Zorro and such like films we couldn't bear to see so finished up by having a few teas in a cheap and grotesque café in Odeon cinema. Bristol seems more unreal and shambly than usual. Reminds me of going over the Crystal Palace after the fire [. . .] In bus people were lamenting the pathos of seeing wrecked houses and furniture left about in piles. There were ARP [Air Raid Precaution] squads busy clearing debris in Bristol on Good Friday afternoon. Asked a bus driver the way and air raid damage was soon the topic of conversation. It affects almost every movement in the city.

Most of the war-time recruits into the women's auxiliary branches of the Armed Forces were volunteers. By 1943, over 400,000 women belonged to the ATS (Auxiliary Territorial Service), the WAAF (Women's Auxiliary Air Force) and the WRNS (Women's Royal Naval Service). Mass-Observation was fortunate in having an enthusiastic contact in the WAAF. Her name was Nina Masel and she sent in reports on WAAF life from April 1941 until mid-1943.

Nina Masel was only sixteen when she began keeping a diary for Mass-Observation in September 1939. Within a year after that, she had left her family home in Romford and was working as a paid Investigator. Most of her reports during this period described the effects of the blitz on London's East End. She was a radical and independent-minded young girl with a talent for seeming able to get along anywhere – a skill which had particular advantages for a Mass-Observer.

The letter reproduced below was her first report for Mass-Observation from the WAAF. She worked as a 'plotter' in the Operations Room of the RAF camp where she was stationed in Lancashire. The Operations Room was the nerve centre of the camp for it maintained radio telephone contact with the fighting aircraft. The plotters' task was to chart the course of aircraft on a vast map spread out on a table in the centre of the room by moving counters with long poles. The work was, naturally, secret.

The second extract, dated 1943, is a reply to a question which Mass-Observation put to its National Panel three years running from 1941. The 'results' are summarised in *The Journey Home* (John Murray, 1944), a study of people's hopes and anxieties as peace approached. It was the fourth *Change Report*, in a series made on behalf of the Advertising Service Guild. This body consisted of seven, later of five, advertising agencies who aimed to keep in touch with war-time movements of feeling and opinion. *Clothes Rationing Survey* (1941) was followed by *Home Propaganda* (1941) and *People in Production*, on 'War Industry' (1942). The last named was a particularly ambitious study. The patronage of the Advertising Service Guild helped to keep Mass-Observation going in difficult times. In 1941 the Ministry of Information ceased to draw on Mass-Observation's services for reports on morale, and though it got work from other Government departments this was a sad blow.

24. Nina Masel: Confessions of a WAAF, 1941–3

(*a*) WOMEN AT WAR

442448 ACW2 Masel, N.G.
Broughton House
RAF
Preston Lancs.
25 April 1941

Dear Tom,
Although my departure from M-O was somewhat tempestuous, my six subsequent months of knocking around haven't yet knocked the observational habit out of me.

Now a member of the WAAF, I find myself with an extraordinary amount of free time on my hands. My job consists for the most part of sitting at a table with ear-phones on my head – WAITING. The majority of the girls are intensely bored by the job which is extremely interesting when work comes through, but in which there is very seldom any work to do. We work on shifts of 5–8 hours each and nearly all the men and women keep themselves awake by talking or reading [. . .]

One aspect of this life which interests me immensely is the division of the girls into rigid cliques. A month ago, 42 of us were called up and met together for the first time in a large room in Victory House, Kingsway. *Immediately*, cliques were formed. The moment you entered the room, you knew exactly which group to join, almost instinctively. The noisy group in the middle was the working-class one: barmaid, waitress, mill-girl, domestic servant and a few others. At the side, the Colonel's daughter was surrounded by an admiring semi-circle of actresses, a dress designer and 'ladies of leisure'. A hairdresser, accountant's clerk, school teacher and mannequin formed another group. Others paired off, skirting one or other of the main groups. As the week went on, three main circumstances modified the cliques:

1) trade and social class,
2) hut, squadron, flight,
3) physique.

We had no control over which hut we went to, which squad we joined, etc., and if a friendship was broken up by the partners moving into different huts, it usually meant the breaking up of the friendship altogether. You were apt to be most friendly to the girl in the next bed.

It was surprising to me to discover the great importance of physique in group and pair forming. Fat girl went with fat girl, pretty girl with pretty girl, small with small. Moreover, if two girls were of similar type, faces the same, hair the same colour – they often formed inseparable friendships and no division of huts or squads could alter this.

The reasons girls gave for joining up – between ourselves of course – not to the officers, – had very little to do with 'doing one's bit'. General boredom with life was the keynote [. . .] nearly everyone said that on the night before she left, she almost decided to back out and that all the way up on the train, she kept thinking 'What a mug I was. Why did I join?' Afterwards, opinion was divided according to how the girls took to the life. There were two deserters one week. But on the whole, those who hated it – small minority – wouldn't go home because of the 'I told you so's of their friends. They had all been discouraged from joining up by their friends.

My friends also discouraged me from joining. In the East End it was considered a fine thing to do, almost an honour, but my friends told me I'd be bored. In Romford, on the other hand, the information was received with raised eyebrows. 'The WAAF', I was told, 'is merely the groundsheet for the Army'. There is a WAAF camp near Romford and its reputation was terrible.

2.8.41

M and I got along famously. We discovered that we were born in the same street and had lots of mutual acquaintances. Next day, [after meeting] we went for a walk together and she told me her life story and showed me her snaps.

She married six years ago, regretted it the following year. Her husband was a school teacher and his mother bought her two beauty salons. But she became very bored with beauty salons and married life and her husband was a drudge. He became a head master and she found it necessary to make up to the Vicar and the local councillors. She talked over the position with her mother who advised her to join the WAAF.

'I'm glad I did,' she said, 'it's terribly interesting and it changes you. At home, if I wanted anything, I'd shout my head off until I got it. Here I know it's no use shouting at the other girls so I just don't. But it makes you – well – loose, in a way. I'm a married woman, though I admit I don't feel like it, but at home I shouldn't have dreamed of carrying on with Geoff like I do.' Geoff was her Canadian boy-friend and they'd been going round together for two months, 'a record', said M, 'on this camp'. Geoff is tall and broad and handsome. 'I like being loved by big men', she admitted, 'my husband is *so* small.' It was M who first advised me to keep in with the Canadians for cigarettes, to steer clear of the Welsh Guard, especially the officers; to watch my step with the Sergeant Pilots.

Afterwards she displayed another rather surprising side of her character. She confessed that she'd always wanted to be an MP and that she'd talked it over with her school-teaching father who had advised her to wait until she was 35. 'Meanwhile he told me to go out and get experience [...] Then, this joining up is also an experience. You see, my idea is that we women – we haven't fought hard enough for equality. And, of course, the men won't give it to us without a fight. Why should they? I mean – housing, that's the worst. I think if all women had had better houses and more say in the matter, we wouldn't be at war today.'

ON KEEPING SECRETS

26.9.41

Our work is confidential. We have to sign a pledge of secrecy before being initiated into its processes and we are impressed time and time again by posters, lectures and notices about the importance of holding our tongues [...]

Most female plotters I have met have been extremely conscientious about this matter. Often a girl will say 'I'd *love* to tell my mother about my work but of course I can't.' When, hitch-hiking, we have been asked by the [...] driver 'And what exactly is your work?' My companions have often replied 'Oh we're cooks' or 'clerking' or just 'Sorry but we mustn't say'. It's a great temptation to divulge the interesting occurrences in the control room and a real act of will-power to suppress the 'I know something you don't know urge'. The men on the other hand, are not nearly so discreet. I have heard men describe in detail all the workings of the control room. Occasionally, plotters from this station are sent to a neighbouring one for a special 'hush-hush' cause. It is always from the returning men and never from the returning women that I hear details of the cause.

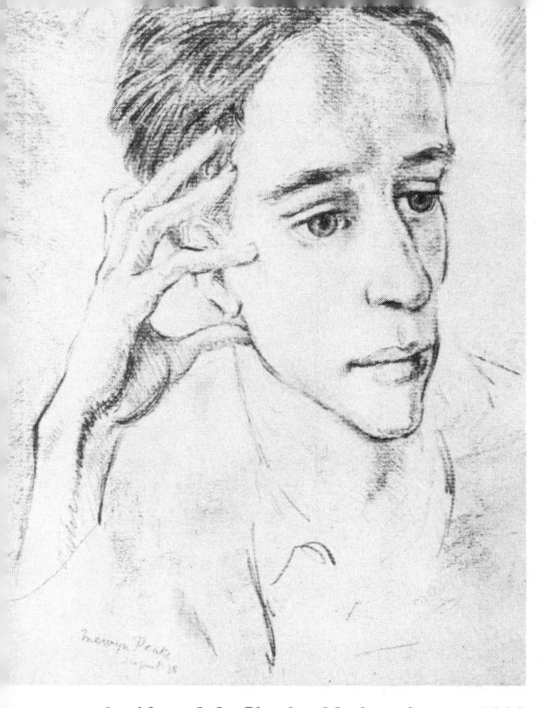

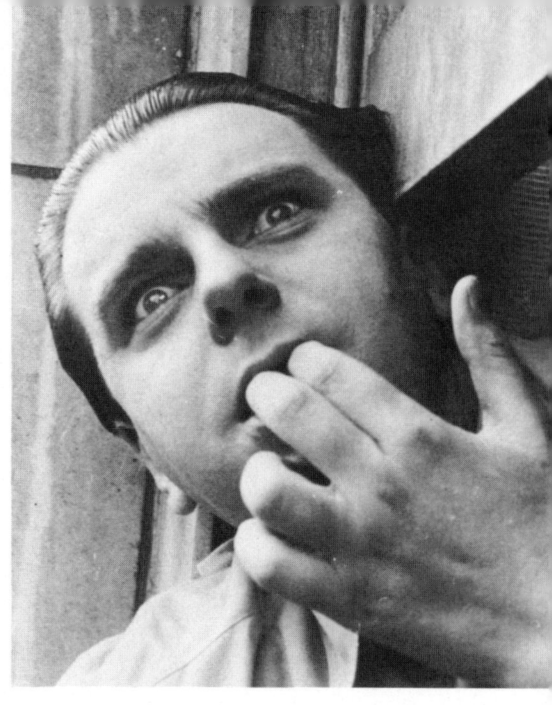

8 *Above left*, Charles Madge, August 1938: drawing by Mervyn Peake

9 *Above right*, Tom Harrisson feigning fear in an air raid, *c*. 1940

10 Humphrey Jennings filming *The Birth of the Robot* (from *Humphrey Jennings*, edited by Mary Lou Jennings, BFI, 1982, p. 12)

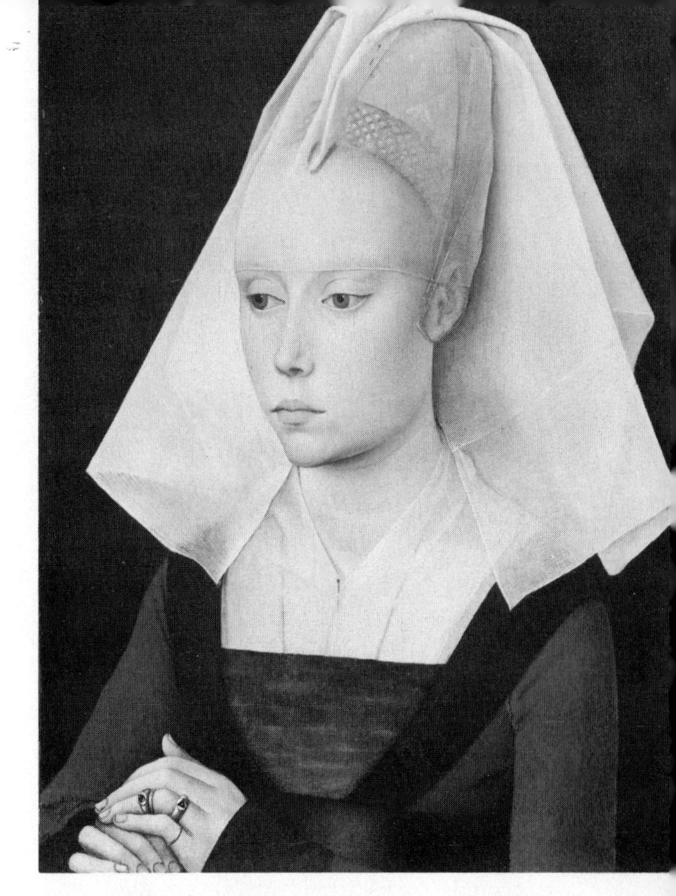

AN EXPERIMENT IN TASTE:

WHAT IS A

PIN-UP GIRL?

11 Twelve pictures were hung in a Services club and (*left*) members were asked which they would most like — and least like — to decorate their billets. *Above, left to right*, 'Jane', the *Daily Mirror* strip cartoon heroine, received 22 votes; Roger Van Der Weyden's fifteenth-century portrait scored minus 24; Roye's photograph came first with 46 votes; and Leighton's 'Bath of Psyche' received 13 points. *Picture Post* feature, 23 September 1944.

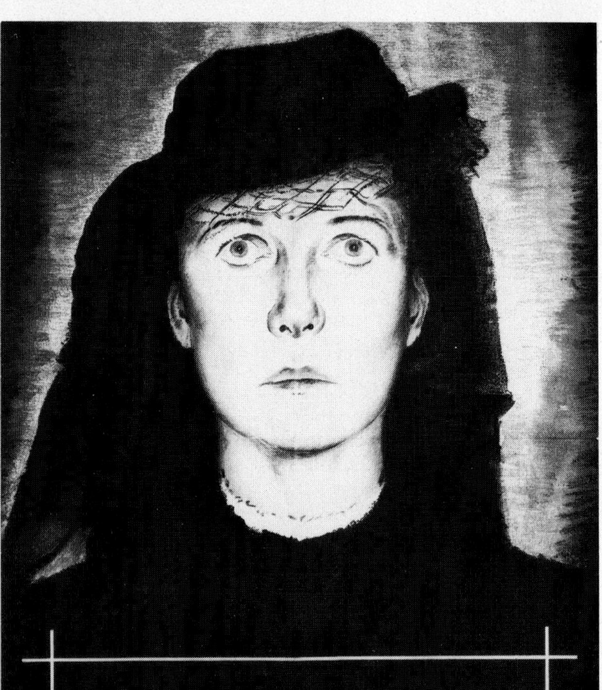

12 *Above*, studio portrait of Tom Harrisson (left) and Charles Madge, *c.* 1937, by Howard Coster

13 *Left*, Road Safety poster issued by the Department of Transport, 1946. See pages 240–5.

THE GREAT MAN-CHASE

28.12.41

The main consequence of a lot of women living together seems to be that since everyone realises that everyone else's emotions, aims and actions are similar to their own – conventional barriers and restraints are torn down and conversation gets down to bedrock.

The presence of both sexes always imposes restraint in conversation. The soldier's fumbling excuse for hard swearing is always 'Oh, well, when a lot of us lads get together [. . .]' Similarly when women are together in our circumstances, we use words we wouldn't think of bringing out in public.

Not only in choice of words, but also in choice of topic and depth of discussion is this new candour created. Even at women's tea parties [. . .] women are on their guard against each other and don't admit their basic feelings [. . .] But here we've got to know each other well: we're all in the same boat and we're all after the same thing. So why kid each other?

And what is this thing we're all after? Obviously, a man. Preferably an officer or a sergeant pilot. I should say that 85 per cent of our conversation is about men, dances (where we meet men), 15 per cent about domestic and shop matters and a negligible proportion on other matters.

But to get a man is not sufficient. It's easy to get a man. In fact it's difficult not to. Competitive factors in the Great Man-Chase are under the following headings:

1. Quality: The desirable qualities are rank, wings, looks, money, youth in that order. Rank is unbelievably important. There's a Wing-Commander here whose only redeeming feature is that he's young. He isn't good looking, he's owned to be a great bore and he's extremely 'fast' (which is *not* a recommendation) yet he could go out with any woman on the station he cared to ask. No one would refuse [. . .] The height of sex-rank is commission and wings. Higher commission, the better. Sergeant pilots and ground commissions tie for second place. This includes army officers. Ground stripes come a poor third. For the rest as far as most Ops girls are concerned, there is little hunting-value. In the term 'looks' I include charm, personality, etc. This counts only as a narrow comparison viz P/O [Pilot Officer] A is better than P/O B because he is more charming, but we'd rather go out with P/O B who is *not* charming, than with Sergeant C who *is*, (and he's good-looking too). Members of the Army without commissions don't get a look in at all [. . .]

2. Quantity: Naturally the more men one can fasten to one's train the more prestige one gains in the Chase.
3. Intensity – a deliberately vague term embodying length of affair, extent of ardour and its manifestations.

Of course the longer you can keep your man, the higher up you are in the competition. It's better if he's madly in love with you. He shouldn't be seen in public with other women. And telegrams, chocolates, cigarettes and really 'classy' evenings out all put you one step higher on the ladder. As far as physical manifestations are concerned, the average Ops girl admittedly likes a man who can kiss well, eyes 'wandering' with suspicion and definitely abstains from actual immorality. Technique in kissing is of first importance [. . .] Further than kissing is not eyed favourably. 'I *like* Bill and he *is* a Squadron Leader and all that but I simply can't face the coping I have to do every evening'. ('Coping' having become the accepted term for dealing with unwanted passion.) So the eligible men are those who kiss well but 'know when to stop' [. . .]

It seems to me that practically the entire object of the Chase is a matter of vanity and prestige [. . .]

Becoming of necessity subjective: I allowed myself to drift into this chase for the past few months and have discovered:

a. That I am happiest when I am conducting two or three successful affairs with eligibles as above.

b. That I am second happiest when I am *pretending to other girls* that they are successful affairs as above [. . .]

A girl in our Control had been trying very hard to get a date with a new officer. She was sitting next to him in the Ops room one day full of concentration in her conversation when suddenly she smiled, looked across at me, and mouthed the words 'Got him!'.

(*b*) SUBJECTIVE ANALYSIS OF POST-WAR DREAM

In my mind (March 1943), I have a hazy sort of plan about what I would like to do after the war. When people ask this of me I always say 'I'd like to have a beer-garden in Prague, where left-minded intellectuals could come and hatch revolutionary plots over their glasses'.

Analysis reveals the following:

1. *Why Prague?*

My interest in Prague is stimulated at the moment by the fact that my grand passion is a Czech. Unless I think carefully, I imagine I always wanted to go to Czechoslovakia. But this isn't true, because had I been asked last year, I should have said I wanted to hitch-hike to Russia.

2. *Why beer?*

Since I've been in the WAAF I've explored the field of alcohol and found it highly desirable. Nice to be on the premises!

3. *Why beer-garden?*

Like the rest of the WAAF, I'm inclined to build my plans on romance – coloured shirts, Czech violins, love and stuff.

4. *Where do the left-minded people come in?*

They were there before the war – this is the only part of the plan which has a foundation in Civvy Street.

5. *What about a job in England?*

Not much chance. I would rather have a good job in England than a bad one abroad, but if it's going to be bad anyway, it might as well be where I want it.

6. *Are you really going to do this?*

Of course not. I don't deeply believe that I'll do anything extraordinary, probably an office job in the end, but it's nice to write about.

7. *Marriage?*

As before the war – doesn't enter my plan.

8. *More lofty ambitions?*

I had them before the war – but the WAAF has shaken all personal ambition out of me.

The NAAFI (Navy, Army and Air Force Institutes) was responsible for providing the material comforts for the Armed Services. The work fell into two categories: the Home Canteen Service and the RASC Expeditionary Force Institutes which followed the troops abroad. The Home Canteen Service, unlike the Expeditionary Force Institutes which were staffed entirely by men, was composed mainly of women, who wore a distinctive butcher-blue uniform. NAAFI workers were all civilians but many of them, including the Observer whose diary is reproduced below, lived on the camp which their NAAFI served and were seen to be an integral part of military life. The NAAFI not only ran canteens and clubs but also provided entertainment facilities through its subsidiary organisation ENSA (Entertainments National Service Association). ENSA put on plays, concerts, films, cabarets, music recitals and so forth for both the troops and the factory workers throughout the war. NAAFI defrayed the extensive costs and its canteens were run on a non-profit-making basis (despite contemporary rumours to the contrary).

The extracts below are taken from the diary of an Observer in her late thirties who decided to train as a canteen manageress at the Army camp nearest her home in North Yorkshire. The diary begins with her first week at the canteen in November 1941 and ends with her leaving just after Christmas, disillusioned and exhausted by the long unsocial hours of work and the petty rules and restrictions which affected her and the young women she supervised. Her husband, to whom she refers as 'M', was a teacher living not far away. He also kept a diary for Mass-Observation.

25. National Panel member: Rats in the NAAFI, 1941

Nov. 2

Sunday seems to be the hardest day for NAAFI Girls. Extra scrubbing of stands and trays and since tomorrow is stock-taking the work has gone on until midnight. This happens every five weeks – complete check up on the smallest details. One of many snags of being manageress.

Spent the afternoon by myself in comparative quiet and got down to study of book keeping demanded in NAAFI. Got a few things cleared up. Wrote letters and then went alone to play 'Rope' where friend was performing. My word how the 'pips and the crowns' did shine on the uniforms. Poor batmen! One specially 'blimp' had a row of pips dancing attendance while he puffed an unbelievably 'blimp-ish' cigar stuck in a Xmas pudding face. How I loathed all the lick and spittle and thought of the canny little girls here working so late to get the stock checked. I had been asked to stay behind to be introduced to Major H and family – friends of my friend but I just couldn't, so sent apologies saying I must catch my bus. [. . .]

Nov. 3

Have begun to collect superstitions among the girls. The chief source, however, has given in her notice today. Sure to be friction among people living and working together in such small space, little privacy and exhausting hours. Stock-taking so I found myself pushed on the counter. Alarming but satisfying work and the soldiers were most helpful when I didn't know the prices. After NAAFI I'll be able to run a grocer shop, tobacconist shop, chip shop, café, hotel. Secretly I'm longing to serve in the bar. The huge barrel awes me but I'm longing to get at it. Doubtless that will come later. [. . .]

Nov. 6
No singing, the canteen staff quarters quieter than since I came. The weather is depressing and most of the girls and men have colds or spots. Spots worry the girls very much. They spend a great deal of time on their make-up. Venereal disease seems to be the bogey – it is never mentioned by name but often darkly referred to. One girl told me she had shingles a while ago and was afraid this rash was 'something else' and had got into a very nervous condition before she told anyone. Fear that VD is carried by money common. Another girl who is riddled with superstition (as most are) told me that one of the men she served had his nose tied up. She had told the others he must have been in 'trouble', but her punishment came next day when she was peeling potatoes and the knife slipped and cut her nose. She had to be bandaged by the Medical Officer and had suffered agonies when she had to serve, like that, in the canteen. Find a great deal of 'nerves' among the girls and manageresses and sick leave is common. Notices are often handed in at all canteens, but most often withdrawn when the supervisor offers a long weekend's leave or rise in pay. This happened here yesterday.

Nov. 10
No difficulty in waking! Rats in the skirting boards of my bedroom kept me awake most of the night. As soon as I arrived I saw the woodwork of kitchen and scullery was moving with beetles and the girls hinted at use of many cats but it was nice of them to let me down gently and so I slept in peace and ignorance while the rats were away. Now that I mentioned my adventures of last night the girls told me stories of sleeping with the light on, throwing shoes at directions the sounds come from and of cat catching and eating rats in the bedroom. My goodness, it's a rough life. I find the rat bit of it revolting. The cook feeling depressed with her cold and the unbearable heat of the kitchen so we visited the bar and enjoyed a large shandy. More books – 'indents' and 'goods received' solved today. Would like canteen of my own so that I could unravel the problems on my own.

Nov. 11
Forgot it was Armistice day until two ATS came selling poppies at 11.10 a.m. Girls all bought one, but showed little interest and no conversation followed. Soldiers wearing poppies in their caps and union jack flying. Heard of no one observing the 11 o'clock period: – or was it not recognised this year? I don't know.

Attended demonstration by area super on NAAFI cooking. Correct cooking urged in order to raise the profits – the 'People' newspaper articles, which criticised NAAFI, referred to – we must be able to say that NAAFI needs profits and more profits to make up for 'evacuation' losses in France, Crete, etc. I feel dead tired having worked continuously from 8 a.m. till 11 p.m. – with good deal of walking to and from demonstration and this is to be repeated other two days.

Nov. 13

Visiting manageress and the resident one exchanged horror stories at breakfast table on NAAFI women and soldiers who lose their reason – it's not to be wondered at and at supper tonight Miss S related scandal of the anonymous letter variety here. I prefer the girls' wit when they sing to the old hymn tune!

> We are but little children weak
> We work for NAAFI seven days a week
> The more we work, the more we may
> We never get any overtime pay.
> Yes Miss Todd loves me (Area Super)
> Yes Miss Todd loves me
> Yes Miss Todd loves me
> The D.M. told me (District Manager)
> Swing it sister.

Worked from 8 a.m. till 11 p.m. with time off for meals and a visit to the bank to deposit NAAFI money. It poured all day and when some of the men came into the canteen wearing topees the cook remarked 'The monsoons must be on!' Surely the topees must have been a joke by the men – the army officers cannot be so crazy as to make that an order. Nobody is encouraged to order Horlicks because it has to be made individually and the girls have little enough time, so should any poor man be rash enough to insist, when the order is shouted into the kitchen the girls begin to sing 'What! night starvation! Oh how he misses his missus', etc. (A popular song) The girls often hold conversations by using lines of songs and it reminds me of the cotton-pickers singing.

Nov. 17

Saw 'Night Train to Munich' at canteen film show – enjoyed it very much, but felt it all belonged to a former life. Here although living in a military camp I feel remote from war and politics. Others have remarked on this. Tonight, while unpacking supplies found two letters from girls in the warehouse [in] Darlington giving their names and addresses and asking two men of fixed age and complexion to write to them (they evidently thought this canteen was run by men). The cook and manageress intend answering in male names.

Thursday, Nov. 20

Reached height of ambition – drew my first pint of beer and what a froth! Very sympathetic soldier congratulated me on the 'finish'. An ATS's 21st birthday party at the canteen brought out the bad feeling between NAAFI and ATS – the latter look down upon our girls, who felt self-righteous as the ATS began to pass out (certainly not a beautiful sight).

Nov. 24

11.30 p.m. Have just finished work – began at 8 a.m. with 3 hours off in the afternoon which I spent in bed. All work was kept late due to a visit from supervisor who raised hell over nothing. I was not blamed since I had only done as I was told by manageress – but I was addressed in the most insolent manner I've experienced. When I smiled at something she said I was told it was no laughing matter. When asked if I was ready for a canteen of my own I said 'yes'. When asked if I could do the books I said 'yes I think so' I was told I should not *think*, but *know*. My God and from a supposedly educated woman of over 60 years of age! Asked if I would go to Doncaster. I refused saying I had pointed out when I joined that while I still had my husband and a home I wished to be within reasonable distance of them. Told that when I'm a manageress I must say 'Sir' to all army officers and see that my staff do likewise. With difficulty I refrained from smiling!

Dec. 1

A strange day. Set out before daylight to my new canteen where I'm to manage for one who is ill – the usual nervous breakdown.

Dec. 2

A most happy day. The staff are efficient, pleasant and helpful. I find I can leave them while I devote the whole day to mastering book-keeping, indenting and issuing goods. Life is much quieter here. Probably because they are older. The place is cleaner and of course I enjoy my own room with a fire and meals when I can read. Went back to my old canteen for the rest of my belongings and realised how very different a canteen can be even with the same building to start on.

Dec. 3
[. . .] Slept badly last night – rats here as well. Quite the noisiest gnawing on record. Spoke about it this morning but there girls are evidently not encouraged to air this grievance and merely said there were lots and they were afraid. I prefer the hearty cursing at the other canteen. But in neither place does anyone seem to do anything about it.

I'm afraid I got black looks (from the chargehand) when I asked the corporal (who is not popular I don't know why) to do something about it. He was only too willing, got a cage trap and it's duly set. However since they seemed to be in the roof, a trap in the larder seems of little use. Still at least a beginning is made.

Dec. 8
Was in my room when 8 o'clock news was broadcast. One of the girls dashed in to tell me that war had begun between USA and Japan. About half the girls mentioned it during the morning, 'now we might get something done' attitude.
6 p.m. BBC news. Canteen had just opened and more men than usual at that hour. All listened intently. No remarks.
6.30. Only a dozen men in canteen. Girls all stopped to listen to R[oosevelt]'s speech. One man began to demand his pie and chips but the girls just ignored him, and the men looked coldly at him and so he gave in. I was thrilled to hear Robeson sing 'Ballad for America'. Felt a little homesick when I remembered our record of it and then downright miserable when I realised not one person in the canteen even listened.
9 o'clock news. Full canteen. Talking carried on a while after C[hurchill] began and then men called for silence. A few still whispered orders to girls who at first ignored them then turning weary of the broadcast began to serve the men on tiptoe. Then one girl boisterously began to rattle the beer bottles, she was 'shushed' by the men but they were not annoyed with her. Towards the end few were listening and business was in full swing. Heard no comments afterwards [. . .]

Visit of the District Manager. I had phoned for him last Friday – because our cigarette allocation had not arrived and still has not. I asked plenty of questions answered amiably enough since he has volunteered for overseas. I asked if there was any hope of the staff getting an increase of wages. They are shocking. There seems to be no fixed rising scale. In fact I don't know how wages are increased apart from manageresses asking D.M. He promised to put forward the matter. An officer called to see if everything was alright so I reported no heat in the central heating of the staff quarters. Saw the corporal again about rats – we don't seem to be getting anywhere. [. . .]

Dec. 9

Good deal of talk about compulsory service for women. On the whole the girls here think it a good thing and they all prefer to stay here (although they grumble about the conditions) rather than join ATS, etc. I find this general on NAAFI – despise ATS.

Dec. 17

[. . .] Told that wages will go up if work goes up, that NAAFI profits must go up to cover losses at Norway, Dunkirk etc., – a history of British failures. Thank God Russia can stand alone. At night group of little boys carol singing at men's bar, brought in and fed on cakes and tea by the men. Cook's remarks – they'll not be so thrilled in a few years time when they're in the army. Her remarks on Russian news tonight 'Aren't they wonderful? I'll never forget Russia'.

Frequent talk among the girls who question why NAAFI is not in a union. They 'itch' a great deal and like all others have no pride in NAAFI. None of them wear their uniforms except on work days. The cooks hate their white caps and are always being told to wear them by the supers. I don't know why they stay on as they do. Perhaps I see it at its worst with the girls who join to escape the services.

[. . .] Notice from headquarters telling of death of one of the girls and warning the rest against taking risks with colds. Refusal from the P.R.I. to grant our girls permission to use the canteen on Xmas night after we close in order to have a little party. Girls furious and then so dispirited that when an offer came for a free dance tonight in nearby hall and I gave permission they said they were too tired to go. They compared this life to reformatory conditions and I agree. Then telegram from cook to say she's not returning just capped the night. It may mean that she is not returning tonight or that she has just walked out. When we closed, everybody just melted away. No gossiping and I was left to battle with all accounts and money. However they balanced and I feel good. This upset seems the general thing in NAAFI. All work and no play can produce nothing else.

Dec. 21
[. . .] Sometimes I think I can't stand this endless strain of work and worry much longer. If it wasn't for the affection of the girls I would have to leave. We met most of them while we were walking and they think M is wonderful – he talked to them as equals – and all day they have fussed over me because I looked so miserable. Could eat no meals – feel wretched. So had hot bath and a big sleep in the afternoon and feel more normal tonight. Wish Xmas was over.

Dec. 23
A huge mail from friends who write only at Xmas and birthdays. Tales of those who've gone into the Forces, of deaths, etc. I'm so detached here that they have little meaning. Have not seen a paper for days and rarely the wireless – have had to shut myself in the office to add up my figures lately. Did I hear aright that Churchill and Roosevelt met in the White House? Scrap from wireless gave me that impression.

Girls in the depths, not only have they to work on Xmas night but the unit orders which we saw tonight says there are two houses of pictures here that night which may mean that we have to keep open even longer than usual! If so, will ring up District Manager to see what he can do. [. . .]

Dec. 26
Twelfth anniversary of our wedding! Most wretched morning. All staff in bad temper and chargehand unbearable. Decided to tell M. that I must go home when I see him tomorrow [. . .] However, the fresh air and the sight of our unit on the square taking the salute revived me immensely. I poured all the hatred I have for this war and the brass hats which add to the misery of our girls into that pair of plum trousers that marched past. It was he who personified 'authority' which refused our girls their party and made them work yesterday, I feel I am fighting feathers – no visible damage is being done to me but I feel suffocated in this job. It's easier to fight for than against. Letter tonight from that pair of plum trousers to say the girls close work at 8.30 tomorrow so that they can go to the carnival. When I told them they whoopeed and danced about til one cynic said 'You'd think you'd got the day off instead of a bloody hour'. Any concession would please them and so little makes them happy.

Dec. 30
After a most unhappy, emotional Xmas I went to my parents' home

with M. for the weekend. There I got my balance again and decided that I have been exploited enough in NAAFI. Called at our house for the last night (strange being a visitor in your own home – where two rooms remain as we had them and the rest I do not recognise as ours) and called at the Labour Exchange to see what job I could do and live at home until M. has to join up. (Seems to be likely that it will not be soon.) Miss K. — a complete stranger to me, heard my story was full of admiration of my leaving my home for NAAFI and suggested nursery school work as being most suitable. I still hankered after catering and she said she could give me school meals but did not recommend the job or works canteens where she thought I was wasted. Took leaflet on nursery schools work and am thinking it over.

Just over a year after Mass-Observation had announced its birth in the letter pages of the *New Statesman and Nation*, a new picture magazine was launched under the editorship of the Hungarian journalist, Stephan Lorant, and published by the Hulton Press. The first issue of *Picture Post* appeared on 1 October 1938 with the now famous cover picture of two girls in brief versions of cowboy suits photographed leaping in mid air.

The publication of a feature on pin-up girls (23 Sept. 1944) was a natural choice for *Picture Post* which was by this time being edited by Tom Hopkinson. The strengths of the magazine lay in the balance between excellent photographs and texts which were occasionally humorous, often entertaining and consciously provocative and controversial. The parallels with Mass-Observation were obvious and Tom Harrisson was a regular contributor to its columns. This article, however, is not by him.

'What is a Pin-Up Girl?' is a neat piece of unconscious propaganda. It doesn't tell you anything about what members of HM Forces *actually* put up on their barrack room walls nor does it shed much light on the men's relationships with real women. Any suggestion that pin-ups might provide sexual titillation for heterosexual men deprived of women's company is discreetly sidestepped (unless you count the corporal's delicate reference to 'mental' excitement). In fact poor Betty Grable comes off badly, one suspects, precisely because of her sexually explicit costume and pose. Like the usually very popular cartoon character, Jane, Betty Grable has the somewhat tarnished air of a woman shared around and is no rival to the remote inaccessibility of Roye's nude. Mass-Observation, unwittingly, set up its survey so that it was bound to get the 'results' it did. Years of communal life could not rob the British soldier of his desire to find a woman for his *private* possession – 'home girl, sister, sweetheart', 'the idealised wife-to-be'. Mass-Observation claimed as one of its conclusions that to the soldier, 'the Pin-up girl is a person' but there are no Land Army girls here, no munitions workers or housewives, no ATS or WAAFs or WRNs in uniform . . .

26. Mass-Observation: What is a pin-up girl? (Picture Post, *23 September 1944*)

The twelve pictures above were hung in an all-Services club, whose members were asked which they would most like to decorate their billets. Mass-Observation's report of their findings provides some shocks and many surprises.

In a recent article in Picture Post discussing the work done by the Council for the Encouragement of Music and the Arts (CEMA) in supplying pictures to the Forces, Osbert Lancaster suggested that the Council should provide pin-up girls painted by first-rate artists to compete with those culled from cinema magazines. What would be the reaction of the troops to such pictures, we asked, and in order to find the answer we commissioned Mass-Observation to conduct an inquiry into the opinions of men and women at a Service Club.

The pictures from which a choice was made included old masters, screen favourites, and pin-up girls popular in this war and the last. All printed up the same size and all reproduced in black and white, they were hung, in no special order, in the lounge of the Nuffield Centre, Soho, where members of all the Forces are catered for. No clue to the identity of subject or artist, nor any indication of period, was given. Sailors, soldiers and airmen were asked to mark A, B and C against their first, second and third choice, also to indicate by a cross the picture they would *least* like to have around. Three marks were given for first choice, two for second, and one for third. Three marks were deducted for each cross. About one-fifth of the voters were NCOs, the rest 'other ranks'. Rather over half the votes were from the Army, over a third from the RAF, and the rest from the Navy. No officers were present, and women's votes were excluded from the total.

The vote totals were reduced to percentages of a possible hundred marks, which would have been obtained if everyone present had voted A for the same picture. On this basis the voting was as follows: – The picture numbered (1) secured 6 votes: (2), 22; (3), 13; (4), 5; (5), minus 24; (6), 0; (7), minus 12; (8), 7; (9), 10; (10), minus 12; (11), 46; (12), 39.

Apart from Psyche, Roye's photograph was the only picture which no one disliked, says Mass-Observation, in its report. It did not get as many first votes as Dorothy Maguire, but it was well ahead on seconds and thirds. Nearly seven out of ten men put it among the first three choices. People liked this photo because it was: Full of Life, Natural, Refreshing, Good Photography, 'Some figure,' 'The girl I'd like to be stranded on a desert island with.'

A 22-year-old army private commented on his voting form: 'I choose Roye's photo, because in my opinion it portrays womanhood in its real beauty, and I think a very good title would be 'Worth Fighting For'. I don't think anyone would ever tire of looking at this picture, and, unlike the Kirchner girl, it is something clean and decent.'

A young corporal in the RAF: 'A modern girl, fresh, full of the joy of life. Exciting, and reminding one of the fun derived from open-air life and the joy of female companionship.'

Dorothy Maguire scored a straight hit as a reminder of home, an idealised wife-to-be. These were typical comments: a REME private: 'No. 12 reminds me of home, of somebody beautiful, but not anybody like Jane. Perhaps just all the good and beautiful things and people I expect to find in my life.' An Ordinary Seaman: 'Although she tends to be serious, it gives me a feeling of home.' An NCO: 'Very pleasant to look at. Typifies for me the person I hope one day to meet and wed.'

Part of her success was due to the fact that the Janes, the Royes and the Betty Grables are to be seen so frequently in barrack-rooms and papers, that people are getting bored with them. As one soldier said: 'Those other girls are ordinary, I like a nice open face myself.'

A young sailor commented: 'She's different from the rest. The others – you can see them anywhere. But her – there's too much glamour these days; it's nice to see a girl without too much glamour.'

Jane did well on second and third choices, but didn't get many firsts. Nearly everyone recognised Jane and Betty Grable. The only other picture which was at all widely recognised was the last-war pin-up-girl by Kirchner. These three formed an interesting contrast. Jane got most of her votes on her familiar and friendly figure. A soldier said: 'Oh, she's the girl. I'll tell you why. All the lads in the barracks go for her – every time. It's the "Daily Mirror" you see. When I was in Civvy Street I had a full book on Jane.' Another private said: 'Jane has become an institution, and many of us follow her adventures with more interest than, for instance, the war against Japan. She would do well in our canteen.'

The Kirchner girl, favourite of the last war, scored more votes as *worst* of the lot than any other picture except No. 5. A few gave her as first choice, practically no one as second or third. She was considered 'indecent', giving a wrong conception of womanhood. In contrast with the unembarrassed undress of 1944 Jane, her coy semi-nudity struck many people as repulsive. The same private who voted for the Roye photograph as portraying 'womanhood in its real beauty', said of the Kirchner girl: '. . . a French pin-up girl of the last war, and the best place for this type of picture is in the dustbin.'

A 40-year-old soldier, who voted for the Roye as expressing 'gaiety and life in its full and exuberant aspect,' said of the Kirchner: 'would cause one to have a false idea of the opposite sex and her ways.' Betty Grable and Jane created the most discussion of all the pictures, but Betty Grable scored a high proportion of anti-votes as well, which pulled her down the list. She might provoke a fight in the barrack-room.

If Betty Grable is the most explosive material for exposure in a billet, No. 3 is the safest. No one voted against number 3, and very few voted for her. She reached high position entirely owing to the fact that she provoked no violent dislikes. She was least commented on of all the pictures. Perhaps she owes her unchallenged position on the walls of boarding houses to this inoffensive quality. Votes for Psyche seem to have been more of a gesture towards Art than anything else.

It must be remembered that the men were not asked which they thought the *best* picture. They were asked which they would like to have around them back at their units. Clearly the vote goes to the modern, the real, the idealisable and the identifiable. One soldier put his views like this: 'Heaven preserve us from re-issuing ancient pictures. The main objection is the hair style. It looks dated. Unless the picture is modern it won't hold much interest for those who are not interested in art; which I am not. I think that the fact that a picture is old will put the un-artistic off altogether.'

A Leading Aircraftman said: 'Ancient art annoys me. I can't understand how artists ever painted people like No. 5 – doleful features, the face is too pointed, the lips pursed – it stinks . . . I like Roye's nude, because it looks clean, the model has a really good figure, which interests me (being a man), and the background is good. Betty Grable is – just Betty Grable; lighting bad, harsh, which makes Miss Grable's brassière even more pronounced . . . I like Jane, not because she's Jane, but because she typifies modern art – of a kind. Dorothy Maguire is natural. No. 10 – more art from the Ark.'

But perhaps an NCO in the RAF puts the whole case of the barrack-room wall in a nutshell when he says: 'I prefer a flippant surround in a serious life.' 'Man in close contact all day with other males,' says another Corporal, 'wishes to be reminded of the females that he wants to be with. He wants to be excited mentally. But at the same time the picture must have its artistic values, or it becomes crude and thereby does not refresh.' His ideal barrack-room picture would have the layout and figure of Psyche, the face of Dorothy Maguire, the freshness and boldness of the Roye photograph, a little of the coyness of the features of the Kirchner girl.

It is the Venus of Mile End, not the Venus of Milo, which men like to have around in the barrack-room, gazing at them when they sink on their beds after an exhausting day, looking at them as they open their eyes to another round of masculine routine. Someone they can think of as perhaps meeting sometime. Of course she won't look as good as that, but she may have something of the Roye figure and vitality, of the Maguire homeliness and unelaborate beauty, mixed with a little of Jane's boldness and adventurousness.

These choices sum up the evolved yearnings of soldiers after five years of war – a war which, for home troops, has often been bizarre and muddled, encouraging homesickness, a bit hot-and-sticky and quite un-Hollywood. Restfulness, naturalness, the open smile and the open sky – their first choice. Civvy Street, home-girl, sister, sweetheart – their second. Adventure and relaxation from the too real adventure of war, unelaborate sex, vicarious impossible girl-friend – their third.

The Pin-up Girl is a person to the soldier; she represents all absent, longed-for femininity. We didn't use the phrase 'pin-up girl' in this investigation, but willy-nilly that was what we were investigating.

The Masters get nowhere, because their subjects are not people. They're Art, and their hairstyle's out-of-date. The pin-up girl is the dream-come-true in two dimensions. Maybe, tomorrow, when the war's over, and the real three-dimensional dream-girl's no longer far away, at the end of a hundred-mile train journey on a 48-hour pass, the Masters will adorn the home-walls of the same men who today blow them a barrack-room raspberry.

Demobilisation was a key political issue during the second half of the war. The disaster of the First World War, when men had returned from the Front only to face possibly years of unemployment, was still a bitter and recent memory. It was quickly recognised by Mass-Observation that a well-organised demobilisation scheme was a 'bridge into the future' (*The Journey Home*, p. 7) and that the morale of men and women on active service depended largely on an optimistic view of the post-war world.

The first demobilisation plans were announced in 1944; releases began on 18 June 1945 according to a carefully conceived system of priorities. Builders and other skilled workers required for reconstruction work were designated Class B and were released first. For men in Class A, release depended on age and length of service. Hence it was known as the 'A and S' scheme. On the whole, it operated successfully although there were 'demob strikes' in the RAF in the East.

The following report describes some of the reactions to the demobilisation procedures in SEAC (South-East Asian Command). It was written by a 28-year-old Observer who had been conscripted into the Royal Signals in 1940 and had been stationed in Rangoon for a year at the time of writing his report. He had originally joined Mass-Observation's volunteer Panel in 1938 while he was a reporter on a provincial newspaper. When war was declared, he responded to Directives from Tom Harrisson and commenced a prodigious war diary which unfortunately lapsed not long after he was posted abroad. His contributions to Mass-Observation in later years took he form of occasional spontaneous reports and replies, like this one, to Mass-Observation's special Forces Directives.

27. National Panel member: Demob in the Far East, 1945

[. . .] When I came out to SEAC in Nov. 44 I was expecting to have to do two more years and it is merely stating the obvious to say that the Jap war ended unexpectedly soon. I'm enough of a realist/pessimist to see that the mere end of the fighting doesn't mean we can all go home; but the fact remains that in SEAC (as in other theatres) the men who have had the worst hardships – the actual fighting men – are those who do find themselves now definitely unemployed, and therefore have a double cause for resentment. It's clear, for example, to us as Signals, that we still have a job to do here; and to some extent being busy on a job prevents us from brooding on our fate resentfully.

BUT the fact remains that demob is the daily moan of 99 per cent of all British Forces out here (the 1 per cent of course are the Regulars who are quite happy in Army life). There is a lot of wild theorising, and a lot of the mainly emotional 'thought' (if one can call it that) which finds expression in all-round resentment, expressed either in sentences which start 'Why should we . . .?' or in violent anger against a scapegoat (e.g. the 'bastard Yanks').

Being, I hope, a bit more objective in my mental processes, I find myself always getting involved in arguments with these dissatisfied blokes. In argument one is always liable to say $2x$ when one really believes x and I'm often shocked to find myself saying things which would lead any listener to assume that I like the Army and want to stay in it.

In point of fact – as page after page of M-O diary earlier in the war would show – I have always managed to keep a civilian mentality intact in the Army, and I want to go out into the kind of job which will involve the use of one's intelligence in the ways for which the Army has little scope (or at least such branches of it as have been within my reach). And I want to get out of the Army to get married to a girl who is herself still in the grip of the uniformed machine. In short, I have just as much reason as anybody to want to get out of the Army. But I do realise that being out of the Army will be a bitter freedom if I go out to an England that'll be in the depths of industrial crisis owing to the too-sudden demobbing of the Forces. I'm group 27 and at the moment hope to be out about Feb. (earlier if there's a fresh speed-up, of course); so I ought to be fairly well in the running for the great Job Race (I need a better paid job than the one I left if I'm to support a wife). But I think I can take an unselfish enough view to say that there *will* be dislocation throughout the UK industrial/occupational framework if mass-demob is forced on the Govt by any powerful interests who have the power to do it. One of the most dangerously fallacious moans that the soldier is heard to utter is 'They got me into the Army quick enough, why the —— can't they get me out just as quick'.

We in SEAC have a special grievance which had assumed dangerous proportions until satisfaction was to some extent given by Jack Lawson [Minister at the War Office] when he came out here – the TUC resolution calling for the scrapping ('modification') of the A & S scheme and the 'compensation' of men in SEAC for being let out only when all the troops in and near the UK had been demobbed irrespective of group. It was specially disheartening to notice even so objective and intelligent a newspaper as the 'Observer' adding its editorial weight to the proposal. As I say, Jack Lawson has promised 'over my dead body' . . . and I think he's made a very good impression out here and the boys believe him.

I don't know much about Charles Dukes [secretary of the National

Union of General Municipal Workers], the bogeyman of the whole episode; but it's clear that he – and presumably the delegates of all the unions which supported his resolution – is grossly lacking in imagination. He sees demob *only* in terms of figures – work available for *x* million men *x* thousand men in group *y*, men in SEAC to be compensated £*z* for their extra £*n* months out here. I haven't had any of the hardships of SEAC except the universal ones of climate and ever-present risk of disease. But a man who can seriously suggest that a soldier of 14 Army who's fought through all the Burma Campaign can be compensated in cash for (*a*) what he's been through, (*b*) 3½ years separation from home, (*c*) getting home when all the best jobs have been snapped up by UK and BAOR soldiers – that man is completely lacking in any knowledge of human factors.

As Tom Driberg [Labour MP] pointed out at a meeting here (Rangoon) last night, the Govt isn't bound by any TUC decision and there is no longer a majority of union-sponsored MPs in the Parl. Lab. Party but the fact remains that the TUC resolution was a slap in the face to thousands out here who had voted Labour in the hope that Labour would speak for us. There is also a grave danger that because 'the Govt' is always thought to be to blame for everything, the great stock of goodwill with which (in Forces' eyes) it came to power will automatically dwindle if this vital demob question is handled at all badly. It is, of course, in the interests of Tory papers to encourage this suspicion . . . but not many of the boys out here read Tory papers except (notably) the 'News of the World'. 'SEAC' our daily newspaper run by Frank Owen is magnificent and admirable. Its sane impartiality at election time made the English papers when they reached us stink of the gutter; and now as always its attitude towards demob is firm, objective, free from cheap emotional appeals and in every way a worthy voice of the boys out here.

V

Women, 1937–1945

Charles Madge, who was chiefly responsible for setting up the voluntary side of Mass-Observation, claimed in an article he wrote in 1937 ('They speak for themselves', *Life and Letters Today*, 9, 1937) that one of Mass-Observation's aims was to give a voice to those people in the Britain of the 1930s who had been deprived of effective forms of expression and communication. He was thinking primarily in class terms when he wrote and there is no evidence to suppose that any special effort (at least at the outset) was made to attract other 'silent' categories of the population. Oddly enough, and not at all anticipated by the early Mass-Observers, the group who seemed to get the most out of Mass-Observation as an outlet were women.

By the latter half of the war, women outnumbered their male counterparts in the composition of the national panel of Observers. The contributions they were sending in were longer, more regular and more detailed than those from men. Despite changes brought about by war, life for the majority of women was dominated by the private sphere: the home and the family. Here was a means of self-expression – writing diaries, letters and personal reports – in keeping with women's traditional skills and inclinations, which at the same time enabled them to transcend their domestic insularity and speak out through the collective voice of Mass-Observation. There was another special appeal which Mass-Observation had for women. Its insistence on the importance of the details of everyday life and the value of recording even the mundane and routine activities gave a new status to the daily preoccupations of most women engaged in housework and childcare.

The central core of Mass-Observation's full-time staff was also preponderantly female in the 1940s. Originally the team had been composed mostly of men but conscription and other demands had gradually whittled down their numbers. Bob Willcock still directed the research but the

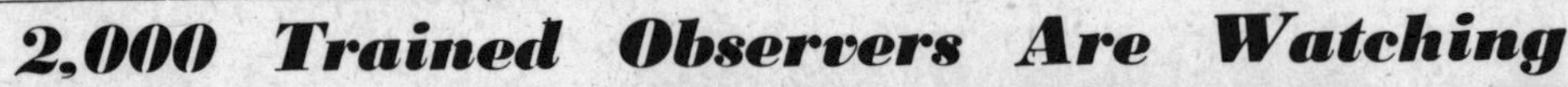

Page 12.—SUNDAY GRAPHIC and SUNDAY NEWS, October 30, 1938.

2,000 Trained Observers Are Watching

– By –

T. HARRISSON

CAN science answer the riddle of a woman's charm?

It is doubtful. But the researches of Mass Observation, the science of everyday life, have disclosed many startling new

fashion-shop, movie-show and multiple store, hairdresser and home . . . the unnoticed shadow is with you all day long.

Madam, we've made a graph of you. It may be ungallant, but it's Mass Observation!

You are not good at telephoning:

A G.P.O. executive told me: "Three times more women than men give wrong numbers, five times more women than men make complaints."

You are not good at driving:

Ministry of Transport told me: "Last week, out of 7,000 men taking their driving test, 4,400 passed; but ou; of 2,200 women, only 1,300 passed."

losing them but giving up the wrong 'alf or the whole of the return ticket."

But those are small things.

Marriage matters most.

More than eight out of ten of you are married, and the average age you marry is 25.

. . . And the happiest women are married.

One in five couples don't have children; and the average number of children per family has fallen from 4.8 to 2.7 in the past 70 years.

But one in ten of married women earn an income outside their homes.

Six million women do this in Britain:

30 per cent in domestic service;
30 per cent. in factories;
16 per cent. in commerce;
5 per cent. in local government.

Since 1911 a million more women have become wage-earners!

And the average wage of the British working woman is 27s.

Though there are very, very few of you who don't regard marriage as your real career.

(And just to show how much I know about you and your sister, it's 15 to 1 you did not marry the first man who kissed you. As a Peckham girl said to one of our observers, delicately investigating this difficult problem: "I didn't marry the first one I kissed by a long chalk, and they never did, and they certainly don't now."

How You Spend

And when you have a home, what then?

Mass Observation asked hundreds of housewives what was the biggest difficulty in running your home.

First of all came "lack of adequate space," second came "lack of efficient electrical appliances," next came "complaints about the furniture," and next "trouble with clothing and cleaning."

5 *Sunday Graphic* feature, 30 October 1938

reports and observations conducted at the time are marked with the initials of mostly female investigators: Mollie Tarrant, Celia Fremlin, Priscilla Novy, Gay Taylor, Stella Schofield, Nina Masel, Marion Sullivan, Doris Hoy, Diana Brinton Lee, Veronica Tester, and many others.

Feminist readers may find themselves disconcerted by the sometimes patronising tone which Mass-Observation writers adopted in their treatment of women. It is partly for this reason that a distinction should be drawn between the two different forms which the papers take. On the one hand there are writings about women: the publications (*War Factory* and *Britain and her Birthrate*, for example, deal predominantly with women's lives) and the many unpublished reports which summarise studies on women or women-related issues. On the other hand, there is an abundance of first-hand material such as the diaries which were sent to Mass-Observation by the panel of volunteer Observers.

The two forms of documentation cannot be entirely separated of course. Many of the articles and research reports are written by female members of the full-time staff and therefore might be expected to contain some element of personal identification. And the Panel material was frequently drawn upon to complement the results of more formal research. It is tempting (and we haven't resisted this temptation altogether in the choice of items for this section) to concentrate on the first-hand material. These diaries and questionnaire replies have an irresistible attraction which increases with years. They also have the advantage of being available for re-interpretation and re-integration with other sources of data. But it would be a pity to be completely dazzled by what might be regarded as the more 'authentic voices' of our mothers and grandmothers and to ignore the considerable and original work carried out by the professional Mass-Observers. The accounts of their research on women's issues (evacuation, rationing, the conscription of women, family planning, women in industry, etc.) are a testimony of the times in themselves. Mass-Observation continually emphasised the importance of addressing women's needs. In an early critique of government war-time policy, Tom Harrisson wrote, 'I believe that women are bearing the brunt in this home-fronted war. I believe that the way they react to the strain may largely determine the outcome. And I see everywhere . . . very little sign that the woman's point of view matters nearly as much as the man's. This war is being led by men and run by men, mostly old men. They are appallingly ignoring women's problems' (*Industrial and Personnel Management*, vol. XXI, 1939). Mass-Observation may have been bound by contemporary prejudices about what it meant to be a woman but it has nevertheless left behind a valuable insight into how women themselves experienced a period of significant social change when the demands made upon them were severe and sometimes conflicting.

When Mass-Observation arrived in Bolton, the Lancashire cotton industry had suffered for some years from the effects of the economic recession and in particular the decline in world cotton markets. But in 1937 the mills still dominated the town and continued to provide employment for over half its population. The workforce had traditionally included a large proportion of women and although the supervisory and highly skilled jobs were jealously guarded by the men, women and girls performed a range of tasks in the spinning and weaving processes. It was quite usual too for women to continue work after marriage wherever they were able to make provision for their children.

Girls usually started at the mill at the age of fourteen. The hours were long (7.45 a.m. until 5.30 p.m.) and included Saturday mornings. In the carding rooms, where the highest proportion of women worked, the health risks were high. Pieces of cotton fluff produced during the combing and cleaning of the raw cotton filled the atmosphere. Work in the winding room (described below), where the cotton was wound from cop to cone ready for the weaving process, was considered much more desirable. Each winder kept a record of her work in a notebook which was examined weekly together with examples of her work. Pay-day was on Friday and the amount paid depended upon the skill and speed of the individual woman. Not long before the following account was written, Mass-Observation reported that women recently promoted from the card room into the winding room had worked so fast that the management had reduced the piecework rate, preventing even the fastest winder from earning more than 38/- per week; the average wage was 35/-. Relatively fewer women than men were trade union members.

Penelope Barlow, the Observer who wrote the following account, spent several weeks at one of the mills owned by the Musgrave Spinning Company, learning the different processes and writing up her experiences for Mass-Observation. She was the daughter of Sir Thomas Barlow, a Lancashire mill owner, and had received her education at Cheltenham Ladies' College and Newnham College, Cambridge. Like her father, whose philanthropy had led him to give financial help to Mass-Observation, Penelope Barlow was genuinely interested in the day-to-day life in the mill and her explanation to 'Eileen' quoted below rings true – 'I only came . . . to get a practical background to a theoretical education and to see how another class of people lived, worked and thought.'

It is unusual for the full-time Observers to reveal very much about themselves in their observations. It is even rarer for there to be much evidence about the way Bolton people responded to being 'observed', but in this case we can discern in 'Eileen's' polite reserve and quiet competence a friendly acceptance of Penelope Barlow. Perhaps the strongest impression to be gained from this account is the lack of opportunity which faced a young woman as lively and talented as 'Eileen Braithwaite', particularly in contrast to Penelope Barlow, who was doing mill work temporarily in the course of moving on to better things. Hemmed in by the restrictions on her class and gender, 'Eileen' says with resignation, 'I started to wonder what was the point of ambition and getting on. So followed the family into the mill.'

28. Penelope Barlow: Introduction to winding, c. 1937

I asked in the watch-house for C. as instructed. He led me into the adjoining mill and up to the top floor. As we went up he said, 'I hear you've never done any winding before. I've decided you shall learn with Eileen Braithwaite and her sister.'

Then he handed me over to them. Eileen took from me my dinner, mug, towel, etc. and then showed me a peg for my coat. Then we started. The ends are pieced by means of a knotter fastened by a strap to the left hand. There is quite an art in getting the thing to make knots at all. Also it seems to be something you learn yourself – you are simply shown how it is done and it is hopeless, when you imitate unsuccessfully, to try to point out where your mistake lies. I started to learn the art on one of Eileen's winders and occasionally, more by good luck than good management, succeeded, but generally failed. Most of the time she left me alone. Sometimes she came and made encouraging noises. Once she said, 'Your name's Phyllis, isn't it?' and after that she used it. Then I moved on to try her sister's machine. They work on two adjacent winders, so that in effect they are working back-to-back in the same alley-way. The sister called me 'Love' throughout the day, and seeing me in difficulty tried my knotter, which was new, and very stiff. I got on better with hers, and after a time changed back. Eileen tried the new knotter, and decided it was no good, so took it off to C. (overlooker), who gave me one of another pattern which was easier to use.

I spent all the morning mastering the art of knotting, with gaps of clearing cones off old labels. About 9.30 Eileen said 'Do you like tea?' I said 'Very much – I've brought some'. So we put tea in our pots, which were fetched and filled for us by a girl from downstairs. Eileen had a bottle of condensed milk, which she offered to me but I declined it. She gave me some wedding cake which she said was from Emily farther up the room.

At dinner-time, our tea was again made. The majority of people dashed off at 12.15. The Braithwaite sisters sat on boxes for used labels and insides of cops. Eileen said 'Would you like to sit with us?' I said 'Very much' so we turned a skip upside down. Eileen produced a spare copy of *Woman and Beauty* and we settled down to eat and read in silence. Another girl (Minnie?) joined us sitting with me on the skip. She talked about the potatoe pie she had just bought and what local shops were good for what. Then she talked about films – *The Prince and The Pauper* particularly – and criticised it intelligently on historical grounds – that Edward VI was too weak to have been the tough lad he was made out to be in the film. Then Eileen decided that the new girl was too disturbing so found her another magazine, and again silence.

I went across to see Mabel at the card room. They said 'Have you worked in the card room?' in tones of surprise. 'How long?' 'Is it very dirty?' None of them had worked there; only one of the three of them had ever set foot inside it.

When I got back they were talking about keep-fit classes on Monday evenings and were joined by several other people. One from an adjacent winder called Margaret smiled at me several times but no one spoke to me. Eileen was knitting. They talked jumper patterns. Minnie (?) said that she heard of a school where all the boys are taught knitting and had seen a photograph of them. This so amused Eileen that she exploded into her tea, upsetting it.

After dinner, I pieced up for the sister (name unknown) as she had a coarser thread and therefore more frequent changes of cops. I gradually got better and by the end of the afternoon could do it without a hitch, though not at standard speed. The sister said at intervals 'That's champion' 'You're getting on fine' and as she sat on a skip for a few minutes, 'I've got a labourer this afternoon'. Towards the end she went to look at the time and came skipping back saying that it was a quarter past five. So we changed our shoes and combed our hair in front of a mirror hung on a pillar. At 5.25 we put on our coats but continued working right up to the last minute though everyone stopped punctually with the engine. I had got so used to the feel of the knotter that I forgot to take it off, and had to creep back to the dark and deserted room to return it. Just as we were ready to go Eileen said 'How have you enjoyed it?' I said 'Very much so far'. How did she enjoy it? She said 'Not at all'; she used to like it, but she was bored with it now. She'd been at it 8 years. She was now 24. How old was I?

I told Eileen that I was going on Saturday; that I only came for a month to get a practical background to a theoretical education and to see how another class of people lived and worked and thought. I might one day do the sort of work Miss W is doing. She said that of course she knew from the first moment that I was not an ordinary new winder and wondered how long I would be staying. She thought perhaps I had been training to take Miss W's place or become her assistant. Everyone had been wondering about me and some had pestered her, but of course she knew nothing and had said so. And they, being an exceedingly decent lot of girls, hadn't bothered me. (It's quite true, no one has asked me any whys or wherefores since I entered the winding room) . . . She said, 'I didn't think you'd stay very long; you're too intelligent.' I said, 'I'm not half as intelligent as you.' She said, 'I've no ambition. I used to care a lot about elocution and did a lot of it, but suddenly I started to wonder what was the point of ambition and getting on. So followed the family into the mill.'

EILEEN

Youngest of 7 children, only one now at home. Has been a winder for 10 yrs, but has not worked all that time at Musgrave's (7 years I think). Sister, aged 32, married 8 months, also working at M's, on adjacent winder. Brother in Air Force. He started in mill but was on short time and so enlisted and went to Cranwell. Is now in Ireland and has been in Air Force 2 years. Is training to be a wireless-operator.

[Eileen is] Bolton's Personality Girl No. 1. Also England's according to Miss W. Engaged to an engineer who went out to Australia for good at Easter. She was supposed to follow in 6 months, but doesn't expect to go until sometime next year. Is not in any hurry as she doesn't want to leave her family. Said 'I shall be married a long time'. Wears no engagement ring. Meanwhile she leads a gay life in Bolton and in particular with a boy called Frank. She says that he is a 'nice' boy but too attractive and too good-looking and conceited as all the girls run after him. So she has adopted him and is trying to get him to think and to read a bit. They often dance, sometimes at the Palais; the other night at the Co-op.

She dislikes discussion of 'Personality Girl' business. When young she had elocution lessons and was very ambitious. She won a Shakespeare competition out of about 90 people once. The Personality Girl competition was at the Palais de Danse. There were several girls and one was particularly attractive but she was showing off to some people and afterwards discovered that one of the judges was among them. Anyhow, Eileen was chosen and was fêted all round, but hated it and disliked the people she met. 'Your class', she called them to me. The result was that she lost all ambition and was pleased to live peacefully at home again.

The Mass-Observation directive for the month of June 1939 was concerned with people's attitudes to class and to race. No further work appears to have been done – at that time – on these subjects and it is likely that plans to extend the study were overtaken by the advent of war. The results of the Class and Race Directives, about 400 detailed reports each time from the members of Mass-Observation's volunteer Panel, remained largely unused and unpublished although there is no doubt that the class replies in particular are an exceptional source of insight.

The replies sent in by female Observers have a peculiar distinction. It had been standard practice to locate a woman's class position according to that of her husband – or father, if she is unmarried – rather than according to her own employment or wage-earning capacity. It is instructive to see how women themselves related conceptions of a class structure in which they were regarded as adjuncts to men to their own experience of life.

The example reproduced below is one of the most elaborate of the Directive replies on class. The first part, the carefully constructed list of no fewer than twenty-eight 'grades', has been included because it underlines the writer's own climb from grade 28 – 'crude, dirty and irresponsible' – to grade 19 by marriage to someone in Grade 10 – 'the nicest people of all grades'. The writer was a married woman with one daughter living in Marlow, Buckinghamshire.

29. National Panel member: Escape from Social Class 28, 1939

'CLASS'

I can only see civilised society as a culture scale, which is divided into grades but with no clear dividing lines. Generally income and early training are the principal factors in determining the culture grade. There is more culture among the masses now than there was in the past, due to increased opportunity, and this adds to the difficulty of defining the gradations. A natural inclination for higher culture in some people creates grades that are not much influenced by income and low-class ancestry. The accompanying scale is a crude one when one considers the complexity of the subject, but it is better than defining society as lower, middle and upper 'classes'.

THE SOCIAL SCALE

1. Royalty.
2. Nobility.
3. The outer edge of the inner circle.

4.–9. I know nothing about these except from books (6 grades for convenience).

10. Income £8–£12 per week. These are the nicest people of all grades. Cultured, but not being too well educated they can also be intelligent. In the higher grades persons must be of a very high mental order to surmount their education.
11. Income £8–£12 per week. Same amount of money as 10 but by birth belong to a higher grade.
12. Same amount of income but by birth belong to a lower grade.
13. £5–£8. They will have a car or bust. Life would be easier without the car but this symbol of superiority is more important than comfort.
14. £5–£8 income but by birth belong to a higher grade.
15. £5–£8 income but by birth belong to a lower grade.
16. Income £4–£5. They are not very much different to grade 19 except that life is considerably easier for them and they are better dressed, well fed and can have holidays.
17. £4–£5 income but by birth belong to a higher grade.
18. £4–£5 income but by birth belong to a lower grade.
19. Income £3–£4. These have some idea of higher culture and a few interests. Probably the lowest stratum of the reading public.
20. Income £3–£4 but by birth belong to a higher grade.
21. Income £3–£4 but by birth belong to a lower grade.
22. Income £2–£3. Children better fed and look more intelligent than those of lower grades.
23. Income £2–£3 but by birth belong to a higher grade.
24. Income £2–£3 but by birth belong to a lower grade.
25. About 35/-–£2 per week. Too poor to be 'respectable' and wisely perhaps, most of them don't try to be.
26. Income 35/-–£2 but belong by birth to a higher grade.
27. Income 35/-–£2 but belong by birth to a lower grade.
28. People who are crude, dirty and irresponsible. Have no community feeling outside their own grade and 27. Quite content to live and produce children on the dole. Of their circumstances they would say 'It's good enough for the likes of us'. It seems they know their own value.

'CLASS', PART ONE

(1) *Try to define exactly the 'class' to which you feel you belong, and give your reasons in detail. How far is it a question of income?*
Accompanying this report is the social scale as I understand it. I really don't know to which 'class' I belong. I was born in grade 28 with relatives in grade 27. My husband was born in grade 10 with relatives and ancestry in a higher stratum. We both live in grade 19. This is the grade to which we belong if it is income that counts.

(2) *Do you tend to move in a different 'class' from that of your* (*a*) *parents,* (*b*) *grandparents? Describe the steps that have led to such a change.*
Parents and GrandParents in grade 28. This 'class' revolted me and I determined to get out of it. When I was 17 I decided the best way would be to work in an office. (I started work at 14.) But I found this very difficult because when I went for interviews and was asked 'What is your father' the answer 'A bricklayer' condemned me immediately. I was usually shown the door at once. I thought about it quite a lot and then hit on the idea of saying my father was a builder (a bricklayer is a builder). This did the trick and I got an office job.

(3) *With what 'classes' do you feel most at your ease? With what sort of people are you liable to feel embarrassed for 'class' reasons? Try not to answer this question theoretically but to give actual examples.*
Although I am a little shy at first I feel at my ease anywhere, being a classless person naturally (having no sense of class distinction). It is the individual that counts with me every time. The only thing that does embarrass me is the extreme 'Haw Haw' voice.

(4) *Do most of your close friends belong to your own 'class'? Describe any exceptions.*
Most of my friends belong to the same income 'class' as myself.

(5) *If you are married, engaged or in love, state the part played in this situation by consideration of 'class'.*
This is a continuation of Question 2 as far as I am concerned. I decided not to marry unless I found a decent man. I couldn't bear the idea of a gross man like my own menfolk. Luckily I found my dear hubby [. . .] Just before we were married I determined to tell him the truth about my people (he had never been to my home). I asked him to guess what my father was. He made some guesses (all wrong) and then asked me to tell him. I was terribly embarrassed and when I told him 'a bricklayer' he said Oh! He took a minute or two to think it over and then said 'that makes no difference'. So I

married a member of an old family. The coat of arms of the [Blanks] is hanging a few feet away as I write this.

(6) *If money were no object, would you rather give your children a public school or secondary education and why? (Answer this question whether or not you actually have children but mention if you have them, and in that case what are your actual plans for them?)*
If I had a son I would not want him to go to a Public school unless he was super intelligent. I would send him to a good secondary school and then to a training college to develop any special talent he possessed. Also if I had the courage to be cruel enough I would say to him (about the age of 20) 'Here is a £1 note come back home in six months time'. I think he would learn more of life and people in that six months than any school or college could teach him.

If we can possibly manage it we hope to send Eileen to a business training college for about 1 year when she is 15.

(7) *What do you think of the working-class attitude to money? Illustrate from your own experience.*
Their attitude to money is conditioned by circumstances. They live from hand to mouth because they can't do anything else. Besides why should they try to save? If they do and fall out of work, under the means test they must spend it to live, while the man next door who perhaps has been earning more but hasn't a penny, gets Public Assistance.

(8) *Which 'classes' do you think are (a) meanest about money, (b) most generous, (c) most thrifty* (d) *think most about money? Give your reasons and give examples of the sort of thing you mean.*
I don't know.

'CLASS', PART TWO

(1) *Give your reasons and analyse your motives for living in the district where you do live.*
We came here because about eleven years ago Hubby was out of work and was offered a job here. We don't like Marlow there is too much snobbery. Everyone is categorised according to income. But we have a comfortable little house and big garden in lovely surroundings and that is the chief thing that keeps us here.

(2) *In what ways do you consider yourself different from your neighbours?*
I don't know much about my neighbours. Outwardly there is not much difference.

(3) *When you go into pubs, which bar do you use and why?*
I don't go into pubs.

(4) *What priced seats do you use at the cinema and why?*
On the rare occasion that I go with Hubby (he doesn't like Pictures) he pays 1/6 each. He doesn't know I pay 9d when I go alone – I do this because I feel I must economise.

(5) *What forms of food, drink or amusement are thought 'infra dig' or not quite the thing in your circle?*
Fried fish and chips (from fish shop) tinned food (a small amount is permissible) and margarine.

(6) *Are you sensitive on the subject of accent and have you made any attempt to change your own?*
I am a bilinguist (English and cockney). I use English as a rule but find myself speaking cockney on the rare occasions that I am really angry. This usually has the effect of pulling me up as I abhor an accent. I even swear sometimes on such occasions although I am quite ashamed when I do so and I think I shock my husband terribly. (His womenfolk are Ladies.)

(7) *Do you make a habit of using the following words and phrases? If not, what is your reaction when they are used by others? Cheerioh, Bye-bye, Toodleoo, Okay, Okidoke, Not half, Ta (for thank you), Old Boy, chum, pal, mate.*
I use Cheerioh but not the others and sometimes wish that people who do use them would find some alternative expressions.

The extract below is composed of short and often unrelated sentences which sometimes seem more like notes jotted down at odd moments during the day – which perhaps they were, for a housewife's life during the war was usually busy and demanding. The writer lived in Tyseley, a poor working-class district of Birmingham, in a road not far from the engineering works, British Small Arms, which was heavily bombed in the blitz.

The diary starts on 3 September 1939, the day war was declared. It was continued, with some breaks, throughout the war. The entries were always hand-written and the first one was sent to Mass-Observation in a small red-covered notebook. The punctuation and spelling have not been changed.

30. National Panel diarist: War begins at home, 1939

3 SEPTEMBER 1939

A momentus day.
11oc–11.15 a.m.
The Prime Minister is about to break the news of the war. It is inevitable, I have been convinced of it since last September. Hope against hope for peace, impossible with the greed and evilness of humanity spreading.

War, – how ghastly, we must live a day at a time and never think of all the plans for the coming months.

I am glad I have nearly finished bagging the front of our shelter, it will be as near gas and splinter proof as it is possible to make it. I have a great admiration for Poland, during this conflict I hope England regains the prestige it has lost.

The evacuation has gone off smoothly, this part, although fairly dangerous, has not gone.

Have decided to keep Jacqueline with me, no one else would bother with her special diet.

Sept. 4
News of the *Athenia* [torpedoed by a German submarine] has just come through, I hope to God the world leaves Britain and France and Poland to wipe Germany from the face of the earth, until we do we shall never have any peace.

Fancy Jacqueline deciding to run a temperature, can I take her down in the shelter should an air raid come? or do I have to stay in the house?

I have done one bag too many for the shelter I have strained my side a bit, it never rains but what it pours, the tank has decided to leak and father says (worried like) 'if you have been working too hard it is a sign of hysteria', my retort was 'I didn't know one had to have hysteria in one's foot to cause it to slip on slippery clay.'
10.30 p.m. Have gone to bed hoping there will not be an air raid tonight, I'm too tired to care anyway.

Sept. 5
The world around me has settled down, the women don't stand around quite so long gossiping. I see the same faces going to work

every morning at exactly the same time, the only difference is, now they all carry gas masks.

The windows every night become a little darker. The children play in the streets exactly the same. They still pop to the Hucksters for '½ of flour and 2d of corned beef'!

The shopkeeper told me that that class of people do not shop a day at a time but a meal at a time, they had no stock in [. . .] That class of people will muddle through the war the same as they muddle through in peace time, the one shining light will be that the sons that go to war will find themselves in time and so save themselves their parents' existence. I heard that at the Co-op shop they had sold three weeks' sugar supply on the Thursday and Friday before war was declared.

Sept. 6

I am running a temperature now, I have been working too hard and caught a chill, the only interest I show in the war tonight is to hope to goodness there isn't a raid because I couldn't go down to the shelter if there was. My husband, generally most reserved has done more talking this past fortnight than I've ever known him do in his life.

I am very conscientious it annoys me when I talk to people asking them if they fill the bath every night, have they a case ready with every thing in ready to dash to safety, the different answers, 'I trust in the Lord', I said, 'If you haven't prepared the Lord can't save you from gas nor any thing else.' Another says, 'I don't really think anything will happen do you, its a long way from Germany.' Next door is a young baby 4 mths, they haven't had a shelter it would mean spoiling the garden, 'the Lord will look after the baby.' Next door the other side they haven't one, too much trouble, what do I do, that's my problem? offer mine.

Sept. 7

I feel too ill today to take an interest in anything.

The French and British have started, although their seems to me something, I can't say what it is – seems to be playing for time. A Proffessor of Psychology said this was being looked at and treated from a Psychological angle, well up to now it evidently hasn't worked but it seems to me they are still hoping. The British when put to the test are the finest in the world and to me the French have acquired poise and character.

Sept. 8

Things are still carrying on, I notice the people who come home at night later than 11 o.c. do not have to whistle and sing to keep their spirits up in the blackness, they did the first few nights. How quickly we adjust ourselves. The ARP [Air Raid Precautions] have my greatest admiration, they give one – the civilian population, I mean, a feeling of strength. When I have returned to normal health I for one shall not be afraid to venture abroad occasionally.

Sept. 11
I think I have got the turn thank heaven, shall be glad when I can mix again with people. Mrs B. next door came in for 5 mins to say that in Wales from where she had just come life went on just the same, no talk of war. She thinks she will go back when the fireworks start. Have just listened to Antony Eden, I'm glad he's back, he's more vital.

He spoke very well, what will the Germans' reactions be when at last our motives and plans leak through to them.

Fancy failing to tell them that war had started on the Western Front. A few more shocks and dissillusionment and a much tighter belt will wake them up with a jerk.

Sept. 12
Sat sewing my net curtains, everything quiet, as Jacqueline says, 'There might be a war on but I'm glad it isn't here.'

Hardly imaginable there can be a war on, such lovely weather and peace around us. The Poles, how ghastly, I'm convinced when at last it sinks into Hitler's numbskull that we are a force to be reckoned with, he'll have one great burst and send all he's got over, it will do a deal of damage but it will be the reaction of what he is, 'Thwarted Man'.

Sept. 13
I have just looked from my sewing out of the window.

The beauty of the sunset – whatever comes one cannot be robbed of that, except by death.

It changes rapidly the golden living vanishing and the great floating clouds, always my 'Castles in Spain' since childhood billowing up and merging into just a great sky.

I have just listened to Lord Eton, he has and he is only about my age attained a great philosophy on life.

Sept. 16, Saturday
Not being well enough yet to go out I spent a quiet evening.

Mother came this morning, I was surprised to see her, I feel she won't weather – War as it will come, her health is so poor and she will fret about all of us. She bravely says I'm not worrying, we must take things as they come, yes but whatever will be the effect on her nerves and they are in such a bad condition.

Sept. 17

Sunday – its just 12 oc noon and the news has come through that the Russians have walked into Poland my heart turned sick.

Whatever will be the outcome – the Armagedon decended on us I think. Poland just now, wiped from the earth, Russia rushes in to get her share, England and France pressing Germany back and further back into Poland, Germany takes Polands place, the sandwich between Russia and us.

What will it mean Democrosies versus Reds.

Who will win, or shall we nearly all be in Kingdom come and not care anyway. Another beautiful sunset tonight.

If I feel strong enough tomorrow I shall make an effort to go out, fancy I have not been outside the door since the declaration of war. Some hopes of my doing a job of work when just helping to finish own Shelter has strained my heart and my side and sent me nearly deaf.

I wish to heaven I was strong. Never mind I must write for M-Obs —

Compulsory service for women was not formally introduced until December 1941 when increasing labour shortages, especially in munitions work and in the auxiliary branches of the Armed Forces, made conscription necessary. Prior to this, a number of campaigns had been launched to recruit women voluntarily into essential war work and in March 1941 the Regulation of Employment Order invited all women over school age to register at an employment exchange. Any woman between 20 and 45 was under a legal obligation to register when called upon.

The writer of the diary below was one of those women who decided to avoid compulsory conscription (which might have resulted in her being directed into uncongenial war work) by arranging her own form of contribution to the war effort. Both she and her older sister had been petrol pump attendants in the family business in Norfolk but the introduction of fuel rationing together with the increasing pressure on women to do something 'useful' prompted her decision to train as a gardener. This extract from her diary is a record of her first month's work on a manorial estate in Dorset. It illustrates well how war-time conditions might provide both an escape from the confines of the family and an opportunity to develop an independent life. (But this diarist was lucky – contrast the experience of the woman who wrote item 28.)

31. National Panel diarist: Digging for victory, 1941

Easter Monday April 14
Great preparations for latest adventure tomorrow. I shall be glad to get away from our business as it is so depressing seeing it so unlike our beloved business of the piping days of peace. Feel full of excitement and anticipation of going and wonder what my fate will bring. I have never been so far from Norfolk before. Everyone here keeps saying they will miss me. This depresses me more than leaving as they all seem so sad about it. I tell them I shall probably be back in a month sick of the soil and gardening. I am looking forward to getting there and finding out what it is like. I have not seen London in war-time and hardly know what changes to expect. Lots of bombs dropped near here this morning. We heard them shake the house [. . .]

April 15
Rose at 6 a.m. and caught 7 a.m. train to set out on great adventure to Dorset as a garden apprentice. B [her sister] upset me crying a little when she saw me off but I soon got over it. Crowded train and elderly female relation as travelling companion. Arrived in London 10.30 a.m. Dissappointed in balloon barrage. I was expecting to see something much bigger. Saw lots of bomb damage, but on the whole London looks much the same as before the war. The people do anyway. Taxied to Waterloo with luggage and then walked around ending up at Lyons in Regent St for some lunch before catching 12.50 train which I nearly missed. Arrived Salisbury 2.30 and found a bus directed to after some difficulty and parked luggage. Spent 1½ hrs until bus, went looking for food office for emergency ration book (which was wrong district) and labour exchange for insurance card. Very rural bus and market day crowd. Arrived 5 p.m. and found another young lady was going as well from Devonshire. Met off bus with car by Lady L, owner of manor house where I am to work and Hon Anne (daughter – ATS Officer on leave) and cart to bring luggage. Delightful to us and charming old house and garden.

There are five girls here and head lady gardener, quite young and very nice. All girls are very nice, one from Kent, Yorkshire, Letchworth – and all over between us. We live in a charming 'ideal home' old cottage and have sweet bedroom each and bathroom (h & c), kitchen where we share washing-up and lounge common room. All delightful. I can see I shall be quite happy for a month here. Food is sent in ready cooked from Manor House and is plentiful. We had high tea when we arrived. 6.30–7.30, the lady gardener who lives with us gave a lecture on pests and spraying. After that, light supper and I had a bath and bed at 10 p.m. I am quite satisfied so far with my 'war work'. Wish I was here for longer than a month. I haven't done any gardening yet though! Tomorrow I start.

Wednesday, April 16
Have had my first day as a gardening apprentice. Got up as instructed at 6.45 and found nobody else got up until 7.15 a.m. Went with the other new student and Head gardener into garden and had some elementary digging instructions. 8 we came in for breakfast. 9.15 we went out again after having instructions on the boiler store which I have to make up with another girl this week. N, the other new girl, and I learned the correct way to dig and manure trenches. About 10.30 we helped water greenhouses and then potted tomatoes till 12. All very interesting. Lunch 12.30 and wash-up after. New students rest until 2.30 for the first [week]. Then we dug all afternoon until 4.45 p.m. Every time we felt tired, we leaned on the yew hedge for support. Digging quite tiring but we laughed and talked so much we quite enjoyed it. Then tea after which N and I went for a walk until 7. Then we had supper and talked till 9.30 p.m. and so to bed very tired but happy after the first day's work in the gardening profession. I can see I shall enjoy this work. We have excellent food and plenty of it.

Saturday, April 19
Spent morning sweeping paths for weekend visitors and return of the Colonel, the master of the Manor. Then we pollinated the peach trees by tickling them with rabbits' tails on canes. We finish at 12 on Saturdays. I caught the 1.10 bus to Salisbury to shop. After shopping and trying about 3 shops for nearly everything, I inspected the cathedral and close and several of the ancient streets. I thought the close lovely and the cathedral. A very quaint old town and quite decent shops. I went to the labour exchange to find out if I had to register. I did not think I had to, but did not want to be fined £50. An elderly gentleman met me at the door and said 'Have you come to register, Miss?' I said I did not know and said why — about being 20

and born in '21. He patted me fatherlylike and said 'If you go upstairs, my dear, the young lady will tell you'. I did and met another girl coming down. She smirked at me and giggled as though it was terribly funny and she was nervous as though she had signed her death warrant. The girl at the desk said 'Not this week' and I retreated hurriedly in case she changed her mind. I met several more girls on the way out who all smiled nervously. The elderly man was fatherly ushering them all in and he asked the verdict and was very sweet about it. I always thought one was bullied at labour exchanges but today and last week I was treated with absolute kindness and almost love! I had never been inside one before.

I returned from Salisbury by 5.30 p.m. Everyone was sitting by the fire, talking and reading. Miss C, the organiser returned today and brought her radio, so I heard the news tonight for the first time since I left home. We have the 'Times' every day brought for us but no one but me seems to read it. Miss C does but the others don't seem interested in the international situation and are very vague about the war. Here we should certainly not know there was a war on if it was not for the fact that we have our butter on separate dishes with our names stuck on with stamp paper and our jam in jars likewise.

Monday, April 21

Gardening all day. I love it. I would not have believed it. At home it was just not any fun and so dull and it seemed dirtier. Here it is interesting, very interesting. Of course this is perfect weather for gardening but I don't fancy it will be too bad in mid-winter. I think I shall keep it up but it depends on the next place I am at. I shall probably be only a month here and then 5 months somewhere else. After the 6 months I shall be trained and be an under-gardener if I still like it and will probably then have a new post. It rests a great deal on where I am landed then and in what company I am. I am glad I did not go teaching. This is much nicer, so far. I have been here a week. The war has brought me here. Some good things come out of the evilest.

Tuesday

[In the] evening, myself and 3 other girls here, the Land army girl off the farm and the engineer's daughter went to the village 2 miles away to the dance. Great fun and quite a change as I had not been to one for so long. Held in a wooden hut and dancing to the Radiogramme in aid of Salisbury infirmary. All sorts of dances including old-fashioned ones and the Air Raid Warden's something or other which was new to me. Partners consisted of sons of the Dorset soil and a bus load of soldiers. I danced mostly with soldiers, practically every dance. Did not get out once and great competition from 2 soldiers to ask me first every time, [in] the excuse me I was changed backwards and forwards. One soldier had to be in by 12 and so after then was left to the other who offered to bring all 6 of us home in his army van. We began to walk (we had gone in a car from the manor) as it was out of his way, but he had left the soldiers he was supposed to take home and brought us. It was much better than walking and we got in at 1 a.m.

Friday, April 25

Gardening and very cold indeed. N and I all morning raking stones out of a newly dug bed which was a rose garden and this year is to be an onion bed. On Monday we are to be photographed for the press and they want us to be setting out onion plants for the new bed. We call it 'the onion bed' but Lady L. says it is to be known as 'the old rose garden' to show what she has sacrificed I suppose. Great amusement today as the butler turned out in a brand new boiler suit and cap and is to learn to work the water pump from the engineer. He is usually dressed à la butler and very pompous. We understand it is to avoid military service and be called an engineer and essential to the water plant.

Monday, April 28

[. . .] We were preparing the garden with some trenching for the press photographer's promised visit for the afternoon. We hurried lunch and then were told to do our hair, etc. and pose ourselves artistically in the sitting room ready for being taken 'at leisure'. All the afternoon we were photographed and photographed. It was more fun than gardening although some frightful ordeals of being taken separately and posed about in unnatural gardening poses with tools and wheelbarrows and then doing things we never do or are ever likely to do and we had a lot of laughing. To our horror the photographer said they would probably be in Picture Post or some other illustrated. I shall never lift my head again in my home village if I am in Picture Post looking a sight and I know I shall look a sight in my dungarees. Everyone in Snettisham takes Picture Post and I know all my friends will laugh.

Tuesday, May 6

Sweeping up and doing the drive ready for the return of the Col. Aft. everyone but me went to Salisbury. I stayed in to do some washing, to keep the fires going, save my money, write some letters and get the tea and welcome a new student who was coming. She missed the bus she should have come on so no one could meet her by car. I walked to meet her and the district nurse gave us a lift back. She is only 16 and been in London since war. She is very pale and nervous and looks as if a month here would do her no end of good. She had not had an egg for 6 months and was delighted because we had 2 each for tea. We nearly live on eggs here. At least one meal a day is eggs, often two . . . Milk is fairly plentiful. We have been slightly short one or two nights and had to make the cocoa with ½ water. Otherwise milk and eggs flow like water.

Thursday, May 8

Working in garden all day. The days fly. Evening washing hair for great departure. Brought out case and did some washing. Cannot think how I shall pack things in. They seem to have increased and multiplied since I came. Then the 3 of us went for a walk in the bluebell wood . . . We are planting onions frantically these days. Thousands of onions we are growing. Beds and beds of them. I had a ducky letter from my Lt. Col. whose garden at Empingham I am going to. He is meeting me off the train Sat evening. I keep wondering what it will be like as the girl that went on Mon. wrote and her lodgings lack only the asperidisdra and the canary we imagined for her. The hip bath sits outside her door and there are texts and 'vorzes' all over her bedroom. I hope mine is not like that. I could not bear it after my nice room here with oak beams and modern 'antique' furniture.

Friday, May 9

Last day in the Manor garden . . . I have to make up the greenhouse stove no more. It was the only thing at W Manor I shall not be sorry to leave. Even that this weekend has behaved first class [. . .] In the evening I had an exam before leaving. 10 questions on gardening. I answered them all and did quite well I understand. I passed anyway and qualified in the 1st round as a gardener. Tomorrow I bid farewell to the girls and Miss D and C. I am sorry. I hate saying goodbye to people you know you will only by chance see again. I feel it is the end of another chapter. Tomorrow I begin a new one. I have been very happy here. The month has flown. I am now used to working in the garden all day and I must say I love it. I adore the sun and the fresh air. It has been a rest cure. That is a rest from the war. I have worked harder than ever before in a month. If I had been at home, the days would have dragged especially as the war news has been so depressing.

The decline in Britain's birth rate between the wars had excited much anxiety and speculation. Mass-Observation, never an organisation to stand on the sidelines of such a worthy public debate, weighed in with *Britain and her Birthrate* (1945), a book which had been more interestingly entitled, before publication, 'The Reluctant Stork'.

Mass-Observation had conducted a survey of women's attitudes to family life, to having children and to the use of birth control, and in March 1944 had asked its Panel of volunteers to write at length on the subject. It was in such areas of private opinion and experience that Mass-Observation's Panel revealed its strengths. By 1944, many of the Panel members had been corresponding with Mass-Observation personnel in London for some years and there is reason to believe that Mass-Observation had become an old and trusted friend to whom confidences could be told. Whatever the truth of this matter, it is certainly clear that this Directive elicited some of the fullest and most detailed material of the whole investigation. The autobiographical account below was by no means unusual in its candour, and although there is not a great deal of information on the writer's own opinions on the pros and cons of having children, there is instead the much more valuable context in which such choices had to be made.

The writer was a woman in her mid-fifties who had worked as an elementary school teacher. At the time of writing, she was employed in London in the preparation of educational film strips.

32. National Panel member: My marriage, 1944

I married at the age of 22 and that marriage lasted for fifteen years. There were no children. Now incapable of having any, as uterus was removed on account of fibroid tumour. In any case age would have prevented by this time.

Why did we not have children? Temperament, I should say, two people rather under than over-sexed, and to the child by his first marriage. For he had been married before, very happily by his own account, and there was the one little boy. She was an artist, doing pretty well, illustrations for press and miniature painting for a living, and more ambitious efforts in wall painting after that. A pleasant home a little way out in Kent, a fine garden, pets, etc. All prospects pleasing. Then, without any warning she died from a brain clot, one night when the child was fifteen months old.

It was three years later that we met. There was a good deal of mutual interest, he was interested in politics from the socialist standpoint, and so was I. He, at that time was running an antiquarian bookshop, which fascinated me. We both loved the country, especially bird-watching. He knew lots of people that I was thrilled to meet, Edward Thomas, W. H. Davies and others. He was, I think, attracted by some versatility of mind, and by the simple fact of youth, a time which gives the plainest of us a sort of bloom. And, perhaps above all he wanted a mother for little H. His thought was more or less consciously like this: 'She is young, reasonably intelligent, and with congenial interests, ignorant of many things, of course, but that is all to the good, as I shall be able to shape her as I want her. And of course, there will be no conflict in dealing with H. as, naturally all decisions will be mine. Indeed, I might do worse.' A little unjust, perhaps, but about the shaping to his own will, certainly not so. It was declared many times, manner half playful but none the less real for that. So his decision was made, and I soon knew of it, and saw what was coming. And a kind of fatality possesses me. I knew that I should have to go through with it. Not altogether unwillingly but certainly with no passion of enthusiasm. His loneliness was dwelt upon, the task that would be mine in building up what had been broken down, the interests in common and so forth. I was too young and inexperienced to stand against it. Less worthily, somewhat flattered too, maybe, as his strange personality made a great appeal to many women. My parents pleaded with me. They could not think his 'intentions were honourable', his dark saturnine personality seemed so alien to them, that they thought he must be a designing villain. Nothing could have been farther from the truth. Not morals but a sense of fastidiousness kept him absolutely clean, and my mother's obvious doubts were resented and led me to an estrangement which lasted for years. So that when we were married we were a good deal alone, as he had cast off most of his own family, too, save one brother.

H. was brought away from his maternal grandmother, whose influence was said to have been unfortunate. But I am sure that nothing she had done would have been approved of, as they never cared for one another. So plans for home making, the boy's education and the rest went forward. He desired no other child. Partly the coming of one would have interfered with his plans for H., and might, I think he believed, have taken some of the affection he wished me to have for the boy. And, rather more intangibly, the sense of insecurity, the former home, the coming of the child, and, in little more than a year, the end of it all.

Was I consulted? It is hard to say. It was so much taken for granted that I should acquiesce in such matters that decisions were announced as if we had both made them. But actually I had no wish for a child. Three reasons, I think. In the first place I had much to do, young, and with fairly heavy responsibilities, for he was away from home a good deal, sometimes weeks at a stretch, and I was keeping on with teaching at that time, as well as looking after the child. Then, lack of sexual urge. Had I been passionately in love with my husband doubtless all fears and shrinkings would have weighed little, but I argued to myself that my lack of desire was an indication that I was not well adapted to bearing children, that I should have a very bad time if I did so (tales of my mother's were remembered here), and that if my husband wouldn't welcome it, its prospects would be pretty poor, anyhow. Thirdly, I was beginning to sense an abnormality in H. himself. His father's people were, for the most part, eccentric, but some of his traits seemed to me worse than that. And I felt in my bones that it was a stock which was on the down grade, on the whole better not perpetuated. This last was quite real, but probably less a deciding factor than the second. There was no question of birth control, fastidiousness again. He knew a good deal of physiology and imagined I think, that he could manage as he wished. But on one occasion, after a bout of influenza, when less observant than usual maybe, there was a slip-up, and I learned two or three months later that the unwished for had come to pass. He was very upset, for reasons given above, and suggested ways by which the 'mischief might be undone'. Not surgical or really harmful ways – old wives' tales rather, very hot baths and so on. Whether such had any effect, or whether a long walk was responsible I don't know, but, while we were on holiday over in the West of Ireland I had a miscarriage after some three–four months. I shall never forget the primitive village and the pious woman called in to attend to me throwing drops of holy water over the bed 'in case there may be life in the poor, wee, thing'.

So that was that, and it never happened again. I had been told before our marriage that it would probably last for about seven years. He had an idea, partly in joke, but with about as much seriousness that the individual was remade about every seven years or so, and that different tastes and habits inevitably developed. Be that as it may, in earlier days when having chosen me, he really wished to make a success of the business, things were possible, and happy enough. While I was really wanted, not so much physically but in so many other ways, I was content, but when that need relaxed I knew that, on my side, I could not supply the necessary urge.

We never had word at issue about money, or such like matters, and never disagreed openly about the boy. But in my heart I *did* disagree about many things concerning him. Yet not on this or that, tangible things, but a whole attitude of mind. The standard set or expected was too high for poor H. to live up to. He had quite a good deal of ability, but was expected to be outstanding. When he showed a good ear and some appreciation of music, he was at once destined to be a musical genius. Must hear nothing but the best – so with books with furnishings and the rest. Much of it was so right – and yet. There was nothing homely about it. I got the clue when I saw how he used to love to go in next door, where they had wallpaper on the walls, and calendars hung up, and it didn't matter much if you broke a cup because it wasn't Rockingham, and so on. Whether this was a contributory cause, and to what extent, I can't say for certain, but I think so. Any how H.'s 'conflicts' took the form of stealing, the oddest, most wholesale and embarrassing incidents succeeded one another. One got to know it so well, new contacts, initial enthusiasm, puzzlement, cooling off, and silence, or worse. Calls for little friend on way to school, clears breakfast table while C. puts on his coat, spends tail end of long holidays at school camp in country, stamp albums borrowed and best stamps missing. Every hobby, ordinarily beneficent had its dangers. Did I give him a garden plot for his own. The neighbours gardens were ransacked for plants. I knew that an aunt had been expelled from school for same thing. Was it hereditary? I consulted a psychologist, for opinion, not treatment, as this wasn't available then. But no help. Possibly due to having no mother of his own. Maybe, but that couldn't be put right, so what? The real underlying conflict between father and boy was so difficult to explain. With me he was as well as with anyone, indeed in his way he was fond of me, and would rather come out cycling with me, for instance, than with other boys. His father a 'turned Catholic' thought formal religion might help him, and he was given instruction, seemed to take to it, and a little later entered the Choir School at Westminster Cathedral under Sir Richard Terry. Did pretty well as far as music was concerned, but distinguished himself by taking one of the priest's watches and some notes. So that influence was no more successful than the rest. Later when seventeen, and trying to make up his mind whether to do this or that, he more or less settled the matter by taking a neighbour's bicycle and selling it. We managed to avoid proceedings, but his father all the bitterer by having such high hopes, declared that he would and could do no more. As a result of many counsels it was decided that emigration under one of the approved schemes might offer the best chance, an entirely new environment, and chance of really beginning a new reputation.

So he went, and for two years we heard pretty regularly. He liked it, his rather wide, but not deep ability came in useful there, he could drive a car, but didn't want to be an engineer, could play and sing well, but didn't want to be a professional musician, liked horses and cattle, but didn't like the idea of arable farming, so his job on a cattle station was pretty much to his taste.

With the need for looking after him and the predicted changing of interests, I felt that we were neither of us doing the other any good. 'If it becomes a sham, we will end it' had been said at the beginning. And now it was so. A trip to the South of France in search of health, an acquaintance struck up with a nurse there, and that was that.

I have never had any regrets, it was a job I took on, and tried very hard to do. Perhaps if I had felt more and tried less it would have been better. Who can say. This seems to have been a long story, and not altogether relevant maybe. Yet I could explain in no shorter way why there were no children. If I could live the same life again I should feel the same. If everything had been different, if I had married someone else, I could not, of course, say how I should have felt. But I think that on my side, I should have wished for three children, 'Two to fight and one to part them' as the old country saying goes. But it would rather be from sense of duty and the wish to go through all normal human experiences than a physical urge. Never an only child. That may have been some of poor H.'s trouble – too much attention focused upon him. I was one of three children myself, and know how much that helped in our growing up.

'Will the factory girls want to stay put or go home?' was written in 1944 by Diana Brinton Lee, a member of Mass-Observation staff who was for a while employed as Tom Harrisson's secretary.

For anyone who is still puzzled by the apparently willing retreat of women into domesticity after the war, the article provides important clues. The war may have offered adventure, travel and professional training to certain women, mainly to those in the higher ranks of the Forces, but for many others, particularly women with family responsibilities, it imposed a double burden – that of combining an often strenuous job outside the home with the task of rearing children and managing the housework.

Attempts to enable women to cope effectively with the two roles (such as the provision of nurseries, communal eating facilities, flexible shopping hours, part-time work, and so forth) were uneven and sometimes half-hearted. It was always assumed too that men could not or should not share in the domestic burden. The women interviewed by Mass-Observation did not seem to be opposed to the idea of employment itself but rather to the long hours and boring routines required of them. As Diana Brinton Lee pointed out, the women who had been working part-time were much more favourable to the idea of working after the war.

33. Diana Brinton Lee: File Report No. 2059, Will the factory girls want to stay put or go home? 1944

The demobilisation of the special industrial effort after the war will have to be of a positive as well as a negative nature, maintaining a balance in favour of what we want over what we no longer need. The shifting of women out of war industries as these become no longer necessary, and the drafting of both men and women into the industries of peace, will require nice judgment as well as immense organisation.

Mass-Observation, in a recent survey, has tried to examine the wants and expectations of the women themselves. Do they wish to stay in industry, to what extent, and why?

That women's place is the home, is a slogan that has been used dishonestly in many contexts and circumstances. It is true, nevertheless, that the average human being's idea of a life centres round having a home and children. It is more or less true also that the average human considers the bearing and rearing of a family, combined with looking after a house and husband, a full-time job for a woman, leaving her little time to go out to earn an independent living. In general, therefore, the ranks of female labour have always been recruited on a short-term basis from young unmarried women who wished to keep themselves for a few years with marriage in view, and from a minority of women who for one reason or another had been left without a provider.

The war has changed all this, and has forced women of all classes, and all ages from 18 to 50, to break or neglect home ties, and embark on an independent wage-earning existence. What are these women's own feelings about their job after the war?

Among those interviewed in the course of this survey were those who had worked in the same factory before the war; those who had come to war industry from luxury trades; young girls who had left school during the war, and would have wanted a job anyway; those who were directed or conscripted into industry, and those who went in from feelings of conscience, or because their husbands were on active service and they were lonely, or couldn't manage on the army allowance.

All this adds to the complexity of opinion, which is further confused by doubts as to what conditions after the war will be like. Of the people questioned about their post-war plans, few gave any unqualified answer.

> It all depends . . . It's very hard to say. I was here before the war, and you don't know how things will turn out at all. My husband's not in the Forces, he's at home. Perhaps I might have a baby, after the war . . . and we might be selling matches in the streets, – you never know. I only know I'm lucky to have my husband with me.

There is no doubt, however, that a large majority of the women factory workers look forward to settling down and making a home after the war. A minority of less than a quarter were ready to continue in their present work. Most of these were women of 35 to 50, unmarried or widows, who had either been in factory work before the war, or found that they preferred it to their previous job. Very few of those who want to stay on at work mention the possibility of marriage; most of them seem resigned to a single existence, and to have arranged their lives accordingly. In spite of this, there is no career-urge towards factory work; one gets the impression that those who choose it have given up ambition, and want a quiet life. An ex-waitress who had risen to be under-manageress says:

> This job is a sort of relief, really, a nice change after that other. I don't mind factory work at all. I share a flat with a girlfriend; we've lived together for twelve years now, and we suit each other, neither of us wants to marry.

These women have been driven into industry, and conditioned to it, by economic pressure, and as one of them puts it:

> I was here a long time before the war, and I'll go on when it's over, so it really makes no difference to me. I was always in industry. I've got used to it, and I don't mind it. It's quite different with some of these young married ones that have been made to come in. They're not used to it, they've been put under orders, and they don't like it.

For such workers the only peace-time problem is whether, having found a job under decent conditions, they will be able to keep it when the war is over. A single woman of 50 says:

> I've been here 25 years this very month. I hope I'll stay on after the war. You get used to your one job, and I don't think I'd like to do any other. I'm still on the shelf, – most likely I'll be coming here with me cloak and bonnet on.

These people represent a permanent nucleus of factory labour. An entirely different attitude is taken by another group who want to stay in the job – the war-experiment part-timers. Many of these are middle-aged women who have not worked before, and part-time work has given them a new interest in life, a social activity, and a little money of their own.

> When you get up in the morning you feel you go out with something in your bag, and something coming in at the end of the week, and it's nice. It's a taste of independence, and you feel a lot happier for it.

The division of their time between the house and the factory bench makes each part of the day's work seem a rest from the other, so that they can undertake both without undue fatigue.

> I have everything to do at home, and so all I want is to get on to part-time. It's just what you can manage nicely when you get to middle-age.

Nearly all of them express the hope that part-time will continue after the war, and it seems a pity that their enthusiasm is likely to be wasted. The different attitude towards the job expressed by those who work four or five hours as against ten to twelve reminds one of the Utopia foreshadowed by pre-war economists, in which the needs of mankind would be met by everyone working five hours a day.

Among those who wish to stay in industry we must include those who want to get back to their own jobs after the war. These, and not the factory workers, are the careerists – people who have learnt a trade which interests them, and in which they hope to improve. They are surprisingly few, and the majority who mention their old job in office or store do so without much enthusiasm, except to say that it was less monotonous. Many of these have no very definite intentions about the kind of work they want to do, except to say they want a change, but the nature of the change is only vaguely expressed, and they are not very optimistic about their chances of getting it.

> I'd like a real change after the war, but I'll have to see what jobs are going. I think a lot will leave this country after the war – those that have married Americans and Canadians, and those that have heard about what it's like over there – I know a lot would like to get right out of this country, they think there'll be more freedom over in America or Canada. I should think a lot more will want to go than can get. I'd like to myself.

This restlessness and dissatisfaction comes mostly from the younger girls; those over 25 are much more sober and realistic in their outlook. These are the vague aspirations of a girl of twenty, unmarried, a piece-worker on the day shift:

> I don't want to stay on here myself, I wouldn't like to stay at home either – I'd get too bored. I'd really like a job that took you out of doors. I don't quite know what. I used to work in a leather factory, making handbags, so I was used to factory work before I came here. But it's very monotonous sitting all day at a bench; I'd like something with more variety.

The desire for change and travel is much less pronounced in the factory than it is in the forces. This is partly due, no doubt, to the fact that the average age in the services is lower than in industry, and also that the services, from the beginning, have attracted the more adventurous type of girl. But the putting of young women into uniform certainly seems to have had the same effect upon them as it does with men. Just as soldiers often dislike the idea of settling down to a routine civilian job, so service girls express revulsion at the thought of a return to their pre-war life. In the case of men, however, the feeling is often sublimated in a determination to occupy a position in 'civvy life' higher both in the social and financial scale than before. In the case of women it appears to be more a desire for escape pure and simple.

Even in the services, however, and overwhelmingly so in the factories, marriage and domestic life remains the almost universal post-war hope. Those who have struggled to keep their homes going and do a war job are beginning to feel the strain. A woman of 43, who expects to be obliged to go on with her work, says:

> The two jobs of home and work are getting me down. *I'm tired*. I used to work here for several years before the war, and I expect I'll

Mass-Observer, Sept.1939
Housewife
Age 37
London SE3

(1289)

Three days after two landmines - small debris not yet cleared from lawn
Oct. 1940

Digging Trench Shelter
1938

Pond Shelter Jan.1941
Self in raid kit

Trench Shelter abandonned and this one built in 1939

14 Snapshots of herself sent in to Mass-Observation by a volunteer diarist

15 *Above*, Mass-Observers interviewing people in the queue for the Britain Can Make It Exhibition, Victoria and Albert Museum, 1946: photo by Michael Wickham

16 *Left*, Marion Sullivan (later Rickards), former full-time Observer, with her daughter Barbara, *c.* 1945

stay on . . . But the longer hours here, and the long time it takes to do the shopping, and rushing home to get your hubby a good meal, and I do all my own washing and I don't have a bit of help – well, what I feel is that when the war is over I'll want a good long rest. A real holiday.

Even those who like the work and enjoy factory life only look upon it as a war-time interlude. As one girl puts it:

Of course when we get married I shan't want to work; I shall want to stay at home and have some children. You can't look on anything you do during the war as what you really mean to do; it's just filling in time till you can live your own life again.

And this married part-time piece-worker:

I've got a home and a husband and a child of 14 still at school. I only came as a war-time thing – I wouldn't say I disliked it; it's a change from housework – but I hope I'll go back and lead a peaceful life when the war's over.

Though women do not seem as a whole so apprehensive of the condition of things after the war as do men, a good deal of doubt appears. The fear that there is going to be an 'awful muddle' and a 'terrible struggle' is often expressed, though some think that 'all the planning ought to help', and 'anyway, it's better to be hopeful'. Many women say that they would like to stay at home after the war, if only they could be sure that their husbands would be in work, or will come back to them safely.

My husband hasn't got a job to come back to, but if he can get a regular job, then I shan't go to work. I'll stay at home and have children. I may go on working for a bit, so as to save towards the children's education. It all comes down to money. If I had money I wouldn't want to work at all.

You can't afford to keep a child on the army money, so I've got to work. There's only me and the girl, now my husband's in the army. His job'll be there if he comes back. Providing he was all right I'd want to go back home, where I ought to be now.

Many of those without husbands express anxiety about their own future when the men come back; but do not seem prepared to insist upon their right to work:

I don't think things look too good for after the war. A lot of the girls would like to stay on, and the boys will come back and want the jobs. I think it's going to be just as bad as the last time, or even worse.

Another girl of 21, discharged from the WAAF and now a factory-worker, expresses the fears of both groups when she says:

> I think really there'll be a lot of unemployment – look at all the girls in the services coming back and wanting jobs, to say nothing of the men. *They* can stay in the army for a time, but the girls can't. I think we're in for a very difficult time.

Quite a number of women, however, go out of their way to emphasise their willingness to stand aside. Even girls who have no definite prospect of marriage feel that their future is best assured by having the men in full employment, like this one of 25, who is single, and who has always been in factory work:

> It's not so much what's going to happen to us, as what's going to happen to the men who come home. Will there be jobs for them?

Married women are even more definite on the subject. They know that their homes depend on the welfare of their men, and that having a job does them no good if their husbands are out of work. As one puts it:

> I'll go right home after the war unless they make us stay on . . . I suppose most of the married women will go back home. But it depends which of you is unemployed – the woman's got to work if the husband is unemployed.

And another adds:

> I just want to go on till my husband comes home, and then I'll be a housewife and glad to . . . I think there ought to be plenty of work for everybody after the war, if they manage it properly.

Both men and women agree, therefore, that men should be the breadwinners, and there is little sign of sex antagonism. It is on this foundation of goodwill that the future must be built.

By June 1943, not only did women make up a third of the workforce (compared with a quarter in 1939) but women were also taking jobs which had previously only been done by men. As in the First World War, labour requirements, particularly in the engineering industry, compelled the Government to consider the question of equal pay for women. In 1943, a Royal Commission was set up under the chairmanship of Sir Cyril Asquith.

In the same year, a dispute broke out involving men and women workers at the Rolls Royce works at Hillington in Glasgow. The employers were reneging on a 1940 agreement to pay women the same rate as men after they had been employed for thirty-two weeks. The workers won their case at Hillington. Elsewhere the situation was less straightforward, partly because increasing automation meant that women were often employed on unskilled tasks which men no longer performed and easy comparisons could not always be made.

The Royal Commission deliberated for three years without reaching any clear conclusions. Little pressure had been exerted by the trade unions and despite public praise for the contribution made by women to the war effort, no real progress was made towards equality. Winston Churchill himself was responsible for quashing a House of Commons amendment to the 1944 Education Act, proposing equal pay for women teachers.

Mass-Observation asked its Panel what they thought on the question in 1944. Not surprisingly – since the Panel composition was predominantly middle-class and tending towards the left – 95 per cent of the women believed in the principle of equal pay for equal work. The article below is taken from a Mass-Observation Bulletin for February–March 1945. Mass-Observation sent out regular monthly Bulletins to members of the Panel, usually summarising the result of an earlier Directive or providing information on Mass-Observation current research and publications.

34. Mass-Observation Bulletin: Equal pay for equal work, February–March 1945

Early in 1944, when the appointment of a Royal Commission to consider the question of equal pay for women was first announced, members of the National Panel were asked what they would say, supposed they were asked to give evidence before it. Nearly everyone had an opinion, but as one careful statistician said: 'I could give no *evidence*. I have very strong views and prejudices . . . But none of this is *evidence*.' As far as opinion goes, however, there is remarkable unanimity, at any rate among the women answering this question. Ninety-five per cent of them are in favour, and most of them think of it as a matter of simple justice, and are surprised that it should be thought necessary to have a Royal Commission to discuss it.

> It seems to me a matter of simple justice, hardly worthy of extensive discussion and conclusively proved without further argument.

> For true equality between the sexes, and freedom and justice, equal pay MUST be insisted upon. (Student)

> Equal pay has been the declared principle of the House of Commons. Govt. refused. 1944. The same again. The RC is in fact a disgraceful subterfuge ... This whole business makes one's blood boil. (Teacher)

Men, on the whole, are far less positive in their ideas than women; fewer are in favour, though the large majority are; many, however, with sweeping qualifications:

> Strongly in favour of equal pay for work on piece-rate lines, but not for time-rates, tho' in some cases women work faster than men.

> Providing that the legal code was adjusted so that there would be absolute equality of status and responsibilities ... also that the existing shibboleth of 'chivalry' towards women was abandoned. (Engineer)

> YES, provided govt. will accept whole responsibility for men's dependants.

Men are conscious in this matter of a conflict of interests, instincts and ideals, leading to muddled thinking:

> I am strongly against equal pay for women, not because I feel that women are inferior, on the contrary. The man is usually the wage earner, and as such should not be in competition with women for his job. There is also a certain type of woman who sponsors such an innovation, mostly old maids and others of a domineering nature. The main thing is to see that a man has ample to keep his family and should also have first claim on all jobs before a woman, then let women have an equally advantageous system of wages and conditions and all other amenities.

This conflict is more clearly expressed by another who has thought it out:

> I have worked for many years in an office where the pay has been equal for men and women, boys and girls. In recent years a scale of salaries has been introduced giving males a slight advantage over females, and I felt my self-respect soaring. I always felt a certain amount of resentment because the girls were getting the same as myself, particularly as they expected men to have money to spend

> on women. I think it is instinctive in human nature for men to lavish on women and the women like and expect it. This is apart from the fact that man is still in most homes the breadwinner. Nevertheless, I am prepared to tolerate equal pay for men and women so long as the responsibilities and burdens are equal. Pay being equal, employers would want men for men's jobs, and women for the jobs at which they are more efficient than men. (Clerk)

One girl frankly agrees with him:

> But I do feel that equal pay will upset the relations between the sexes. Personally I like a man to have much more money than me. It gives me twice as much pleasure to have a book or dress bought for me by a kindly male than to buy it for myself . . . and this is not because I am a gold-digger, but because I am feminine. I realise that it is hard luck on plain women.

Among those in favour of equal pay, the majority of both sexes agree that it will entail some form of increased family allowances, payable in respect of all dependants, either in income-tax relief or cash. Women are quick to point out how hardly the present system bears upon them, and here many members of the Panel are in a position to provide first-hand evidence, much of it very illuminating:

> Women have far more dependants than is supposed. I have one, and for several years had two, and that is typical of the older woman teacher. On the staff of a school where I was working just before the war, the nine men had three dependent children between them.

> We girls do exactly the same work, including a regular turn of night duty, and also perform regimental duties similar to that of the men; in addition we have 'barrack' nights . . . Thus, for exactly equal work, we receive precisely *two-thirds* the pittance granted to the British soldier. The wife and family of the married soldier receive an allowance. Surely it is logical that if his wife and children are allowed for, a soldier's expenses are no greater than those of the ATS girl? Do her cigarettes and snacks at the NAAFI cost only two-thirds of his?

> A temporary measure like the 'cost of living bonus' adopted by the firm I work for seems unfairly worked out when the male members of the staff get 23/6 per week, and women only 16/6, irrespective of their commitments as home-providers, payers of

rent and rates and school bills, etc. if they are widows. I confess this is a personal complaint.

If I had to give evidence before the Royal Commission I would cite my own case. When my husband died I returned to teaching, but of course at a lower salary than a man would get. Because of being absent I sent my son away to school, but because I was a woman getting less salary than a man I did not get reduced fees. A widow has to have a house to live in, but because she receives less wages than a man she does not get her rates reduced. Her expenses are the same.

My job is precisely the same for a woman as for men. I have always succeeded men and been succeeded by them in the various districts in which I have worked, and the amount and grade of the work has been identical. It is only fair in my view therefore that men and women should receive the same remuneration for the same job. But of course there is more to it. There is the argument that men have greater responsibilities. So they have on an average, but no one suggests paying bachelors on the same scale as women. The solution is equal basic pay and family allowance for men and women. It is hard on the women who have dependants to receive less for the same work than bachelors. Why should I with my mother and two children dependent on me be paid less for doing the same job than my predecessor, who is unmarried, and the only son of parents who are comfortably off?

After this it is a change to hear from a woman in a profession where the question does not exist.

It seems to me to be archaic and barbarous to refuse equal pay for equal work. I am a doctor, and I expect equal pay, and I get it.

VI

Aspects of Politics, 1940–1947

Though we include no material about politics in the 1930s, Mass-Observation was keenly interested in this subject from its earliest beginnings. Politics was a major area of study for the Worktown team, and Mass-Observation's account of public opinion in the Munich crisis gave *Britain* the same topical, urgent appeal as other Penguin Specials of its day.

Harrisson was, if anything, a Liberal; Madge first a quiescent, then a lapsed Communist. Other full-timers were generally left-wing in sympathy, and war-time books, notably *People in Production*, have a critical, anti-Establishment, 'populist' tone. The Panel were preponderantly left-leaning, though rather confused idealists were commoner than Labour or Communist activists, and there were Conservatives, even the odd Fascist, amongst those who wrote directive replies and diaries. Overall, it could be said that the fact that its organisers and volunteers were more 'politically-minded' than most Britons helped Mass-Observation judge remarkably well the trend of public – and private – opinion.

Our first choice in this section is a gem of 'participant observation'. Zita Crossman, last seen in this book being propositioned in Blackpool, had met Tom Harrisson when she went with her first husband, Professor John Baker, on the Oxford University expedition to the New Hebrides in 1933. She attended the momentous 1940 Labour Party Conference with her second husband, Richard Crossman, later Cabinet Minister (and diarist), and Alderman George Hodgkinson of Coventry. Comparison with the printed *Report* of the Conference reveals a few errors in her account – but no other record could give more of the 'feel' of this extraordinary occasion.

The context was one of extreme tension. On May 7, the House of Commons had assembled to debate the failure of Britain's campaign in Norway. The Labour Party, next day, had forced a division, in which forty-one Government MPs had voted with the opposition. The Tory rebels then insisted that there must be a coalition of all major parties. The Labour leaders, Attlee and Greenwood, went down to Bournemouth with Chamberlain's offer that they and others should join a new administration under him. At this very time, the German Army swept into Belgium and Holland. Labour's National Executive resolved unanimously that the party would serve under any leader except Chamberlain. As a result, Chamberlain had to resign, and Winston Churchill replaced him at 10 Downing Street.

We have not annotated all the names, some famous in their day, some little known even then, which appear in Zita Crossman's account. Regretfully, we have had to make cuts to reduce its length.

35. Zita Crossman: The 1940 Labour Party Conference

Saturday, May 11

Arrived at the Highcliffe Hotel, Bournemouth, just before 3 o'c. Many members of the L.P. Executive sitting out on the Terrace in front of the hotel in the sun. Philip Noel-Baker rushed up and gave us a great welcome. Ran into Laski in the lobby who seemed to have the whole conf. taped and said it would all be over by Monday evening. Dick (my husband, Candidate and Delegate from Coventry) and George (Labour Agent, Alderman and Head of Labour Group on Coventry Council) immediately dashed off to Delegates' private meeting where resolutions are pooled and sorted out.

Went for walk along Front and through the crowded Pavilion Gardens to City centre. Many holiday-makers walking about but I should guess very many fewer than in peace-time Bank Holiday week-end. Not many children about except at boating stream and very few men in uniform (all leave cancelled). During whole hour's walk heard no conversation at all about L.P. Conf. Surprising amount of German heard from prosperous-looking presumably refugee families. In the centre of the city large piles of evening papers had arrived which were being sold as fast as the two men could exchange pennies for papers. The placards were 'Allies bomb 50 enemy troop planes' and 'Rotterdam Aerodrome retaken'. The shops were all open but appeared quite deserted except for food shops.

Returned to very crowded hotel – seemed to be full of fat gents in black coats all talking very loud about 'Have you seen old George yet?' 'Do you know if Bill is turning up?' 'Don't miss the committee this evening.' In the lounges groups of from 3–6 were sitting round trays of tea, more men than women. The latter were mostly comfortable looking matrons of 50 or so. In one family there was a schoolboy of 16. Found Dick and George Hodgkinson, Noel Baker and Will Henderson having a great discussion about Enemy Propaganda. Wisecracks and serious suggestions mingled. George, who knows everything about running a city but not much about Propaganda was silent. There was a general feeling of Big Things are being decided as we saw members of the National Executive rushing to the telephones and having tremendous urgent confabs with each other. Hugh Dalton particularly looked strung up and just had time to shake hands and go on striding around and waiting for telephone calls [. . .]

Listening to the news is quite a ritual. At all the news times the wireless is turned on and the lounges crowd up. People sit on chairs or arms of chairs in very tense attitudes. It is a very loud wireless but even so some men crowd right round it and lean over it. People smoke a lot and the great thing seems to be to avoid anybody's eye. It was abruptly turned off as soon as the sport bulletin began. There was rather low subdued talk after, as if people weren't very happy. The word 'parachutist' was frequently heard. Forgot to mention – on our way out we looked through a basement window of the hotel and saw the Executive sitting – about 40 of them it seemed. All very solemn. Someone scowled at us for looking.

One odd thing is the number of chaps that seem to be called 'George'. George Ridley, Latham, Shepherd, Dallas, Catlin(!), Lansbury, Hodgkinson.

Dinner at 7.30. Most of the executive seem to sit at small tables for two either with their wives or someone who is not on the E.C. Barbara Ayrton-Gould dressed in evening dress is going from table to table speaking to different people about business of some sort. There is quite a cheerful air – people eating heartily and drinking beer. Herbert Morrison is in a far corner with his back to everyone – talking hard to Maurice Webb. Willie Gilkes comes up to us and Dick says 'So you chaps think you can send us home on Monday, do you. You won't find the Delegates as easy as all that. They've come for a holiday – it's their annual out and they're not going home until they've had their money's worth.' Willie Gilkes giggles a lot and says, 'We'll see, we'll see.' Rumours are going round that there will be a short debate on co-operation with the Gov. and then we will all be sent home. Delegates who have been mandated to speak for more free milk, Old Age Pensions, choice of Insurance Companies feel diddled. On the other hand there is a feeling that with the guns booming only a few miles away even the personnel of the inner Cabinet doesn't very much matter. It's the Belgian Front and the Dutch Front that matters [. . .]

A few comments after the news. 'Not too Good', 'These parachutists are hell', etc. Then Stephen Swingler and Dick started a violent argument on the effect on morale of civilian bombing. Stephen saying that the people would turn against their leaders and Dick that they would be fiercer against Germans; wanting to loot and smash all shops with foreign names. Wandered around and saw that every chair was occupied. Groups of people now fairly large. In most groups there were two talkers and the rest were listeners. A lot of beer was being drunk. At 12 another News Bulletin listened to intently and then most people wandered off with a few wisecracks about keeping Parachutists off during the night.

THE RALLY AT THE PAVILION, SUNDAY EVENING, 6.30, MAY 12

Arrived at 6.33 to find standing room only. Hundreds of people hanging about waiting for friends or still hoping. Went across to Regent which was already ¾ full and met Tom Baxter (former Agent in Kings Norton and now works for Transport House) who said he would get us a seat in the Pav. if we didn't mind the Platform. Back we went and we were all this time with George Hodgkinson and A. E. Thomas (the solicitor who works for Civil Liberties and T.U.s). He refused to come on the platform – he doesn't like being in any limelight. On the steps of the Pav. all sorts of literature being sold. Did not see anyone buy or reading any.

On platform, about 150 people, even men and women. Most women wearing hats and suits. 15 men standing in tight row singing. As soon as they stopped singing we took our seats. Orchestra next played Valse Triste [. . .]

George whispers to me 'Funny Bourgeois Bournemouth leading the way in socialised music – it's the only Municipal orchestra in the country'. Tremendous clapping at end. Orchestra stands up. Conductor goes and returns. People cheer. Orchestra retires.

Someone says, 'Now we can get down to business'. About 20 people leave but others crowd in. Someone says 'Did you hear 6 o'c news?' 'Just same as at one,' replies friend. Everywhere we go we see Vera Brittain and Geo. Catlin. Can't think why as a Pacifist she bothers to come. Girls appear in gangways selling chocolates and do brisk trade.

Table and 3 mikes set up; 5 gold armchairs placed in a row. Enter Geo. Latham, Hugh Dalton, Jimmy Walker, Ellen Wilkinson sit in chairs – someone missing. Audience claps.

Geo. Latham as Chairman gets up and says many great changes have happened since arrangements were made. He reads his speech [. . .] Gives excuses for absence of Leader and Deputy Leader. Some people say Oh – evidently disappointed. 'Tomorrow, however, they will be with us' (audience slight laughter of pleasure). Continues with speech – brave lads – titanic struggle all those who value freedom, etc., etc. A few interruptions from gallery which couldn't catch. Ends with some clapping.

Jimmie Walker speaking in Scottish voice without notes. Talks about the L.P. always standing for freedom – League of Nations – talks about its failure. It is a particularly socialist institution, each for all and all for each, etc. 'It's no good arguing with Hitler – he'd get the best of it.' Laughter. Some people think, give the lad another chance but he's broken every one of the ten commandments and there aren't any left (laughter).

The labour movement has made up its mind. Fascism has got to be destroyed (loud claps, interruption from gallery). Financing the war – I don't know if any of you have had the habit of dealing with banks (laughter). During last war when on Glasgow Council Banks asked Corporation to lend money to Gov. Glasgow Corp. had no money but the Banks said that's alright – we'll lend it to you and you lend it to the Gov. They made 1 per cent. More funny stories about banks – much laughter. Turned to flesh creeping – the vultures of the air may now be on their way, etc. We are not just fighting for our freedom – we are fighting for our very lives. Every single thing ought to be organised for defence. No time to argue when enemy is at the gate. Speaks about subversive movements which stop war efforts cannot be tolerated (loud claps). Talks about cabinet crises and Labour's opportunity (claps). End.

ELLEN WILKINSON

'Something very extraordinary happened in Parliament last week' history of crises – punctuated with claps and 'Hear hear'. 'No shots, nobody put in prison but revolution occurred.' Outside they were selling the *Daily Worker* and 2 bright lads sold *Action* [Fascist paper]. Deals with criticism of L.P. specially put forward by Member for Bournemouth namely Labour voting against re-armament until three years ago. Armaments must go with policy. Talks about the power of the ideology of Hitler. People listen very intently – she holds them [...]

HUGH DALTON

A few people return. He recalls being Chairman of Conf. in 1937 which ended cheerfully with heightened confidence in Labour. Now across the blue water an awful battle is being fought. Talks about unanimous vote of the executive to support a new national govt. (applause). Gives whole history of cabinet negotiations and Labour's part in it. Gradually gets worked up and starts shouting. Loud claps when mentions a million unemployed and shortage of aeroplanes. Medium claps when he finishes [...]

Arrived back at hotel to see Greenwood and Attlee standing in lobby looking rather tired and forlorn. Photographers from USA *Time* pounce on them and flashlights flicker as we go into lounge and hear of fierce fighting and continuous air raids on the wireless. Everyone is listening tensely as usual. Lounge fairly full.

Barbara Ayrton Gould starts looking after Greenwood and Attlee. She is dressed in black evening dress with striking gold leaves.

MONDAY, APRIL 13. IN THE PAVILION

Everyone in their seats by 9.30 [...]

Tremendous claps and cheers when E.C. walk on platform specially when Attlee and Greenwood are spotted.

On the platform about 150 people – many empty chairs – some appear to be candidates who aren't delegates. In the galleries 2/3 are women. Down on the floor among the delegates, about a tenth are women. Round the walls are posters advertising *Reynolds News*.

B. Ayrton Gould is Chairman. Next to her sits the Mayor of Bournemouth with gold chain then Attlee then Mayoress in gold chain. 25 members of the E.C. sit at platform table. It looks an awful squash. Chairwoman makes announcement of order of speeches saying that Attlee and Greenwood will speak before Mayor because they have to rush back to town [...]

MR ATTLEE (LONG CLAPS)

Reads resolution. 'Comrades it is a time of the greatest crisis for civilisation', etc. 'This is a tremendous moment. Every thing is at stake' (He has notes but rarely looks at them. His voice seems to have taken on a new power and authority lacking at former conferences.) Photographers flash lights keep on flashing. 'Hitler won't care whether this is an Imperialist war or not, he won't care if your wives and children are capitalists, socialists or pacifists' . . . 'Cabinet have given an account week after week and Labour has given constructive criticism. Our working people have supported the Gov with their unceasing work in factories and fields.' Talks about dramatic scene in Parl. Mentions young men who were about to die who voted against their party. 'It would have been much nicer for us to leave the decision of joining Gov until we could consult you at the Conf. but events marched too quickly. Holland and Belgium were invaded and we *had* to decide then and there' (loud claps). 'I said we come in only provided we have the support of our movement. We come in as partners not as hostages (claps). It is our people who are fighting and doing the work. We must get a mandate. That is what we are here for this morning.' 'You must keep some confidence in us. You won't get all you want. What T.U. has ever got all he wanted from a meeting. We've got some of them there we don't like but they've got some of us they hate very much (laughter) – I haven't the slightest doubt of our victory (cheers) but I haven't any doubt of the great price which will have to be paid' (Aye aye).

Talks about hopes of future. 'There can be no real equality of sacrifice in a war. Nothing can equal life but the other sacrifices can be equalised. We are standing today for Labour all over the world, in Czechoslovakia, in Germany'. Ends (several women in gallery are seen to be weeping).

Chairwoman suggests taking vote now. Terrible hubbub. Delegates shout. Shall the vote be taken. Tremendous shouting. Observer sees hundreds of hands holding cards but Chairwoman says 'The resolution is not carried so we will have a discussion'. More shouting.

We are asked to give Attlee a big send off. Conf. stands up and claps and cheers. Chairwoman suggests that we hear Haden Guest for 5 mins as he has just returned from the Front. Describes air raids and says how much the men at the Front will welcome Labour's decision. They all wanted a more vigorous Gov. Towards end shouts of 'Get on with discussion.' Rather abruptly ends (claps).

Standing Orders explains resolutions. Great rustling of Agendas. Chelsea's anti-war resolution must be taken as it is anti E.C. Resolution. Delegate complains. Laughter. Chelsea Labour Party to move. Chairwoman hurries him up (laughter). Time limit 10 mins. Name Schofield [Shufeldt], 50, plump, specs. Trouble with mike. People laugh. Is against entering Gov until Cabinet can be wholly socialist. Talks without notes. Is a gent. Few people clap, but fiercely.

Chislehurst, seconder: Aged 50, bearded, very dapper, slightly cockney voice. Speaks without notes. Seems to have learnt speech off by heart – never stops at end of sentences. Appears to be a pacifist.

Edinburgh D.L.P. MacDonald (mover of composite resolution): Conf. laughs when it hears very scotch voice. Says his blood will probably be spattered in fields of France within next few months. He is out and out against the war. Pacifists from gallery occasionally say 'hear, hear'. Few claps at end.

Norwood D.L.P. seconder: Aged about 28, short, specs, Anti imperialist war. It's the working class that suffers, etc. The fight against the ruling class of this country must be maintained. People get restless, a lot of talking. Few claps.

Miners Federation Will Lawther: 45 tall, dark, just going bald. No notes (many had tried to catch Ch's eye. She quickly picked him out). Speaks about miner victims of Nazi aggression in support of E.C. Resolution. Many hear hears from Delegates. Sneers at Chelsea who don't know what a struggle is. Has loud N. Country voice. Mentions miners having foregone their holiday to show that their support is not empty words. Loud claps. Few delegates want to speak. Ch. selects.

South Ayrshire: 45, thickset. Thanks E.C. for allowing minorities to voice their opinions. Says that resolution asks for a vote of confidence in Winston Churchill and that even too much in wartime (claps). First he heard of him was in 1910 when he was doing down miners (claps). Mentions his past history (small claps). Chairwoman says time being wasted in coming from seats. Would speakers queue up 12 men. Some backchat with Chairwoman, laughter.

Speaker (couldn't catch name): Speaks as representative of head of queue and against those who have spoken against the war.

A great defence of Churchill – loud laughter and shouts. Talks of little Belgium, Little Denmark, German swine (loud shouts of shame). Terrific shouter with bright red face. Claps and laughter.

Torquay Lathom [Blaylock]: 45, small, dark, thick moustache. Democracy in peril in our own country and France.

Half of the E.C. have left platform. Some delegates have gone out to have a chat or drink. Slight difficulty with Chairwoman who says only anti-resolution speaking.

New Forest Christchurch: Very tall, tweedy, 45, gent. Wants some assurances from Gov. about mandating colonies, freedom of India. If they give nothing then Labour will part. Speaks only 2 mins (claps).

Mitcham: 45, baldish, very loud cockneyish voice. Have been uneasy about utterances of leaders. Labour M.P.s have been saying that Gov. hopeless but have been supporting them. Points out that many of worst Tories still in Gov. War must be fought but who by? Wants to sound a cautious note. Claps. Bell had to ring twice.

Transport and General Workers Union: 30, young, sleek hair, tweed coat, flannel bags, cockney or midland voice. Supporting resolution. Talks of gravity of situation. First speaker to look at notes. Reads some of them (claps.)

[Sidney] *Silverman M.P.* (claps): 45 small, fat, fair. Supports resolution. 'Wars in a capitalist and imperialist world must be capitalist and imperialist. In a socialist world there would be no wars.' The importance of which side wins. Wants to know conditions of cooperation in Gov. Have been kept in the dark (claps). Specially we must know about peace terms (loud claps).

Society of Compositors of London: 35, dark specs, grey suit. We only deal in facts (laughter). The fact is that the house is on fire. Declaims against the people who said stand fast for Czecho[slovakia]. etc. and now throw up the sponge. Shouts of vote. Show of hands carried. Shouts of dissension from the floor. One delegate says his resolution has not been put. Calls on Arthur Greenwood, claps. Labour saw menace of war creeping up. (All delegates back in their places.) His speech is powerful, good-humoured. Some backchat with audience. A gibe at the Tory majorities of Chelsea, Chislehurst, etc. 'If they get us majorities there, then we can have the socialist Gov they want. We have the trust of the T.U.s They are not like twittering sparrows. Good Heavens if they all trust us, why can't Chislehurst? (loud laughter). Prolonged clapping at end of speech which ended on very serious note.

Chairwoman moves report page 8–10. Card vote in favour of Chelsea and Chislehurst. Gallery cranes forward to see voting. Motion lost by overwhelming majority. Gallery very angry with people who stand up and spoil view. Shouts of 'Sit down'. Everybody sits after some shouting. Loud hum of conversation. Oldish lady next to Observer says it's always the very Left that does the talking but they are nowhere when it comes to work on voting. She shows me list of Cabinet in the Times which she has added up. Talks to other neighbour about local Party. Few people from Gallery go away. Tellers are being selected.

After 3 mins, Delegates are asked to show cards. The Press are all leaning over rail and looking at delegates. People behind are discussing elections. They have Lancs. voices. Keep on hearing 'daft' and 'I sez'. Chairwoman announces:

For [Coalition] 2,413,000. Ag. 170,000. Says A. Greenwood going back carrying with him splendid figures. Gets big clap.

Told to return at 2 o'c. Everyone streams out. Hear remarks that Greenwood and Attlee were fine. 'Never heard him speak so well.' Also Silverman complimented. Outside enormous throngs trying to locate each other. 2 men and a girl selling *Daily Worker*. See no one buy it. People buying other daily papers. Brilliant sun. Everyone very cheerful.

Tuesday, May 14

Fred Thomson and his wife (he is a delegate for Oxford – Chairman of the Party and Chairman of the Trades Council and Co-op milk roundsman) came to lunch. I noticed them looking hard at all the celebrities staying in the hotel and getting a great thrill out of it. On the way to the hotel Fred said to me, 'This conference has taught me an awful lot. It makes me realise how ignorant the ordinary party member is. Those debates have made me see that it's no good talking if you have no knowledge of the stuff you're supposed to be talking about. And it makes all the difference seeing our leaders in the flesh. They're not just names to me any more.' We had a very cheerful lunch party and they weren't the least bit put out by the comparative grandeur of the Highcliffe. They are taking their week's holiday now and are in digs 3 miles away – the other side of Boscombe [...]

Hundreds of Delegates swarming outside. Everyone seemed very cheerful – lots of laughter and smiles. The *Daily Worker* sellers very much in evidence. A young girl was particularly energetic and a fat pleasant looking woman went up to her and said 'Now don't be a silly girl. You don't know what you're selling. Go and get a bucket and spade and play on the sands and don't be so silly.' The girl blushed scarlet and disappeared into the crowd with her *Daily Workers* [. . .]

Dick and George came away from afternoon's meeting very disgruntled as the motion on the control of the *Daily Herald* which Dick was supposed to move didn't come off. They said that the Chairwoman had been impossible. She had been curt and snappy and had created a bad-tempered atmosphere so that people had bickered and valuable time had been wasted. Before dinner Dick went up to Barbara A-G and asked her if she would make time for the D.H. to be discussed tomorrow and she said 'Oh no, that opportunity has gone and anyway what was wrong with the D.H.' She thought it was perfectly alright. Dick said that the Delegates wanted to know and discuss the real control of the *Daily Herald* as they had been disturbed when a socialist editor had suddenly been sacked. She said 'Well, it's over now.' Dick said, 'It's the principle we want to discuss.' She said, 'Well I'm afraid you can't and that's that' [. . .]

At dinner Dick tells us that Dalton is Minister of Economic Warfare. George Ridley told Dick before dinner that Dalton told him that at 6 o'c a call came through from London for him. He said 'Hello' and a voice said 'The Prime Minister speaking. Will you do a job for me Dalton?' Dalton said 'Certainly Prime Minister'. 'I want you to start on the job early tomorrow morning as Minister of Economic Warfare.' Dalton said, 'I will be there' and was rung off. He went to George and said, 'That's not much of a job they've given me' and grumbled a lot about it. In the end George said, 'Well you know some of us think we're quite good chaps too and have got nothing at all.'

After dinner and the news, walked down to the Pavilion for dance and cabaret. Noel Baker walked down with us. I said to him, 'I do hope there's a chance that you'll find yourself in the Foreign Office'. He said, 'I'd like to be there. I feel peace might be coming quickly and we want some socialists there to make the treaty – preferably people with experience of treaty making. But I don't think I'll have a chance.' Blum's speech tomorrow is discussed and hopes are expressed that Anglo-French relations discussion will get through without a shindy. Dick makes suggestions for the line that should be taken and N-B says he will see to it.

The dance was in full swing – little tables all round large dance floor. At middle table B. Ayrton Gould, John Wilmot and others. Not very many Conf people recognised. Dick and I dance. Joined at table by Wise (candidate for E. Norfolk, a farmer) then Dr and Mrs Stross who have difficulty in getting in as no one allowed in after 10 (police rule). (Tickets cost 2/6). Order ices, etc. Mrs Stross will only drink alcohol so won't have anything. She thinks soft drinks are funny. In Paul Jones I dance with some very good dancers and Jenner, candidate for E. Leicester – a big heavy Jew. Harold Nicolson holds his seat with a majority of 87. We express satisfaction that National Labour are now right out of the picture.

The cabaret consists of 20 small girls hideously dressed who do a Tap dance very badly. Then a large Jew in morning suit and Top Hat who makes verses when given a word – words given are Banana, Hitler, moon, democracy (which gets a big laugh and clap), etc. Then there is a young girl being clever on a bicycle and then 2 acrobats and then Stainless Stephen who comes on and makes a lot of wisecracks first of all about Dick Crossman of the *New Statesman* and Mrs Crossman (he appears to be a reader). Then Harold Laski, and quotes some of his sayings, Barbara Ayrton Gould, John Wilmot, Mr Middleton, his secretary, etc. He seems to know the party intimately and must have been at some of the debates. We talk to him after and he shows us his specs which busted when he turned a somersault. He is very polite and friendly at the same time.

As Zita Crossman's account shows, anti-war feeling remained quite strong in the Labour Movement. It was encouraged by the Communist Party which, until Hitler's invasion of Russia in 1941, denounced the conflict as an 'imperialist war' like that of 1914–18, and by the pacifist Independent Labour Party.

Labour's entry into Coalition meant that these small parties had a chance to capture support from those who, for whatever reason (inadequate shelters, shortages, profiteering), were at least temporarily dissatisfied with Churchill's Government. The ILP fought by-elections in Conservative-held constituencies and regularly secured around a quarter of the votes. The CP organised a 'front', the People's Convention, which called for a 'People's Government' and a 'People's Peace'. A large conference held in London during the winter of the blitz showed that these vague slogans had wide appeal.

Celia Fremlin was left-wing in her sympathies. The daughter of a medical scientist, she had read 'Greats' at Oxford, and had joined the Communist Party there but she resigned over the Nazi-Soviet pact of 1939. On leaving university, she had decided to find out what working-class life was really like and had worked for a couple of years in a series of jobs as a domestic servant. She wrote a book about this experience, which drew her to Harrisson's attention.

After some time as a waitress in Lyon's, during which she kept a diary for

Mass-Observation, she became a full-time paid Observer not long before she wrote the report printed here. Her role was important. She was one of a 'team' of four women full-timers (the others were Doris Hoy, Veronica Tester and Marion Sullivan) who worked together most days, questioning people in the streets. Eventually, they were all 'called up' for war service. Celia Fremlin went to work in a factory in Malmesbury making electronic parts. She turned her experience on the shop floor into one of Mass-Observation's most interesting books, *War Factory* (1943) – written by her, though her name did not appear on the title page and Harrisson's, as 'editor', did. Soon after finishing the book she married, had a baby, and dropped out of Mass-Observation activity. She became well known after the war as a writer of detective stories.

36. Celia Fremlin: The People's Convention, 1941

GENERAL REPORT

TYPE OF PEOPLE PRESENT

Very predominantly Cl[ass] C. About 25 per cent D, a small number B (many of these student and intellectual type). No A's observed. The age-group was, roughly, 20–45, the great majority being between 25–35. There was about a 3–1 majority of men.

There was, of course, a liberal sprinkling of C.P. and extreme left-wingers – particularly among helpers, bookstall assistants, etc. The vast majority of the rank and file were, however, ordinary trade-unionists, etc., of varying shades of left-ish opinion.

There were perhaps about 20 soldiers and airmen in uniform present – Inv. actually saw 11 in the course of the day. Most of these were in battle dress – Inv. only saw 3 in ordinary uniform. There were a certain number of other service men in mufti, but it was of course impossible to count these.

MASS ATTITUDE AND AUDIENCE RESPONSE

Inv. was struck from the outset by the high level of group-feeling attained – evidenced by *simultaneity* of response (as distinguished from intensity); general readiness of response – quick fluctuations of mood following the tone of the speaker; the general feeling of informal friendliness between platform and audience.* Inv. talked to a few of the speakers afterwards, and they were unanimous in describing the audience as an 'easy' one – quick to 'get across' its own emotions to the speaker, and quick to respond to his.

Inv. would attribute this state of affairs partly to the aims and nature of the Convention itself, but partly also to the fact that the majority of the audience must, in the nature of the case, have been well-accustomed to group activities and to find them congenial. A non-social individual would be very unlikely to have attained such a position in his organisation that he would be appointed delegate to the convention.

PARTICULAR ATTITUDES

Internationalism

Inv. was impressed, as she has not been before at left-wing meetings, by a genuine enthusiasm for internationalism. This was evidenced by loud applause for Indian speakers; at references to 'our comrades in Germany', 'the workers of the Soviet Union', etc. Also significant was the fact that during announcements of donations, the announcement of 3/- from 'a group of anti-Fascist internees' received one of the biggest ovations.

Enthusiasm for 'outside' representation

A curious mixture, soldiers and clergymen, received big applause simply on appearance. There seemed to be a similar feeling about both – that they represented deeply-rooted traditions in our society, whose support is of intrinsic value.

Anti-materialistic feeling

A marked feature of the proceedings was the fact that applause always followed remarks of ideological or sentimental appeal rather than materialistic. Talk about wages, food, ARP, etc. were listened to with general intellectual approval, but no emotional response. On the other hand, talk about new opportunities, the possibility of putting the whole of the present mess behind us and starting fresh, co-operation with people of other countries, etc., were received with strong emotional enthusiasm.

Further evidence of this feeling was obtained from interviews

* N.B. also high per cent actually singing 'International' at end.

after the meeting. A tailor from Leeds said to Inv.: 'It's fine eh, but I don't agree with all they say . . . Too materialistic. It's always the way with them, too materialistic. We want something to look up to, not look down at our food and clothing, eh?' And another man, from South London: 'Sometimes I feel depressed when they talk so much about Dependants' Allowances and ARP. What I want to see is a world where we don't need ARP and don't have to think about our allowances.'

POLITICAL FEELING

As has been said, the extreme left was not predominant. There was, in fact, a fair amount of feeling of regret that the Convention should be so much in the hands of the extreme left. That it is so seemed to be universally believed. There was a large section with the feeling that it is tiresome that whenever any really vital and vigorous political activity arises, the Communist Party always seems to be in the middle of it.

WHAT PEOPLE HOPE FOR FROM THE CONVENTION

The overwhelming feeling that had brought people to the Convention in such numbers was one of hope – a hope that somehow a way would be found out of the present mess – *into* exactly what was left very vague in most minds. They were people who find the orthodox prospects of war and plans for peace emotionally barren; people groping to find something worth either fighting for or making peace for. The force that brought them was not so much an intellectual appreciation of the merits of the programme, but a blind quest for something on which to fasten the social emotions which this war has roused but has not (like most previous wars) satisfied.

A feeling of hope was the thread running through it all – a feeling that struck one rather curiously with the realisation that for months past this feeling has been almost totally absent from public gatherings. It was expressed forcibly by a young clerical worker from the Home Counties with whom Inv. was talking:

'It's funny, it sounds queer, but do you know, it has occurred to me today for the first time that perhaps the war really *will* finish some time. I know people talk about "after the war" – I do myself, but I have always felt somehow that we were pretending – that we all knew in our hearts that it would go on for the rest of our lives, and only talked about "after the war" out of politeness – the way you talk about Heaven. But today I feel as if the end is in sight. It is extraordinary.' (M30C)

BEFORE THE CONVENTION, WOBURN PLACE

By 9.30 a.m. there was a queue stretching in both directions from the hotel entrance in Woburn Place. In one direction it reached to Russell Square, and in the other it went along Woburn Place towards Tavistock Square, round the corner into Byng Place, and round the corner again into Upper Bedford Place.

The queue was quiet and orderly. Only two policemen were in sight, and they were strolling about without finding anything to do. The people in the queue consisted very predominantly of men – mostly Cl[ass] C and some D, between the ages of 25 and 35. The atmosphere was cheerful and lively; a lot of people seemed to be feeling cold, but this was expressed more by stamping and talking about it rather than by looking miserable.

By about 9.45 there began to collect quite a number of miscellaneous sellers of literature and distributors of leaflets. The main literature Inv. saw consisted of the *Daily Worker*, *Labour Monthly*, and suchlike Communist and near-Communist papers; there were also a considerable number of 'anti-convention' organisations selling their literature 'debunking' the convention; the I.L.P.; *Tribune*; Social Credit; and so on. Samples of this literature is appended. Sales of most things seemed fairly good, and on the whole most people accepted the leaflets thrust upon them and at least glanced through them.

Conversation was varied in subject. Much of it was about details of getting here; some about last night's raid; a good deal of surprised greetings of the 'Fancy seeing *you* here!' type. There were also pleased comments on the number of people present. (N.B. Inv. may have noticed these unduly owing to personal prejudice). A good deal of technical T.U. talk about local shops, etc. Samples of talk follow.

The report which follows is the work of P. Ormsby-Lennon, an Observer, paid, we believe, for his work, whose style is distinctive and very lively. His own political position seems to have been fairly middle of the road.

37. P. Ormsby-Lennon: The King of Poland speaks, 1942

Surrey, Indirect, 8.11.42
MA(?)39–38.
Can't be disguised. Red robes and long hair. Polish Count, poet, been in gaol twice, Pretender to the Crown of Poland, lordship of Bialystok, Grand Duke of Lithuania, Bohemia and a few other odd spots. Suffers from Jewish paranoia, megalomania, satyriasis and a few other complexes. Known to Inv. very well indeed for quite 10 years. Until outbreak of war, one of the most picturesque characters in Bloomsbury. Now rusticating in Surrey.

Inv. and wife call on King and Queen of Poland when bound for a Sunday walk. King dressed in regal dressing gown about to change into a tweedy sort of suit. Going to town to see a Fascist Group for which he is printing on a private press at his cottage an attack on 18 b. Inv. gloats goodhumouredly and says that despite King's astrological predictions and Royal fulminations against the serfs who cast him in gaol, it appears that after all England looks like winning the war. King not so sure as he was. Thinks Hitler and himself great men. Says Hitler was once spurned like himself and look at him now, one of the really great men of history. Thinks Germany not defeated in Africa yct (but see above date). Says he would possibly have sided with the Democrats here only they wouldn't have anything to do with him, except in the way of persecuting him, and that now, in view of this, he has become a Fascist. Regrets he has to go to town, but that it is a question of LSD (apparently he has to try and collect a cheque).

Comes back dressed, with his long tresses tucked in behind his ears and under his coat collar. Dons a beret. Plays a bit on piano. After a while goes with many regrets. Says to be sure to wait till he returns about 7.

King returns very moody and depressed. Apparently his meeting has not been a success.

Before he went he takes Inv. to see his printing press in next room. He is printing advertising matter as well as a sort of love poem by Marie Stopes who lives nearby and for whom his wife is acting as a sort of Assistant Secretary at 50/- a week. Inv. asks him if he is going to revive his paper 'The Right Review'. He says he is. Plays the piano, talks a lot of royalist boloney and remains moody and depressed.

Swears revenge on the people who put him in gaol last. He was living at Pimlico and was showing lights in the blackout. Police asked him to put them out. Said he wouldn't as he enjoyed diplomatic privileges, being a King. Police break in, but he hits copper over head with a tomahawk and gets three months, wife a month for obstruction.

Man who has lent him cottage has just finished 6 months for being a conshie and refusing medical examination. Lost his good job in Civil Service for his ideals.

Accompanies Inv. and wife back to station.

Surrey, Indirect, 8.11.42
FB25, (Queen of Poland)
French, ex-schoolteacher, married for about 2 years.

Fears that she and King are not hitting it. Says he expected great things of his poetry, but as he did not make a success of it, he took the Kingly path. Feels they may soon be reaching the parting of the ways. Somebody else has come into her life. Doesn't know how it all will end. 'Somebody' had been a lodger with them.

Tells Inv. and wife all about Marie Stopes for whom she works. Rides a bike there and back every day. (Marie Stopes has a place down in Surrey.) Has to deal with letters writing in for advice re birth control, etc. Thinks Marie Stopes is getting 'dated'. Says M.S. doesn't realise that knowledge of birth control methods is fairly common property nowadays.

Goes a long walk with Inv. and wife.

Doesn't know how the Count will end. He must follow his stars! But she is finding his ways are not her ways. They have not lived as man and wife since September.

Thinks M.S. had a crush on other men. Written a long poem to a young naval man who lost his life in a famous naval engagement recently. Says her husband lives elsewhere. M.S.'s son studying science at S. Kensington. Thinks M.S.'s poetry pretty putrid.

Says she can't get the other man out of her system. Husband was not jealous at first. Now he is. (The King)

Thinks she is coming back to monogamous ideal. She used to be polyandrously inclined. Says she realises there's nothing in it now.

Inv. advises her to try and bring her husband back to a more normal way of dress and life. Says it's no use trying. He's nearly 40 and his ideas have become 'fixed'. (Inv. had tried at various times, but without any success, because the King is not really a bad chap at heart and is really clever if he could only direct his thoughts onto right track, but he just won't.)

King eventually comes back and shows Inv. and wife a Louis XV (or thereabouts) sword hilt (said to have belonged to Louis) which he bought from a dealer for £12. Says dealer bought it at Christie's and let him have it cheap. He is going to try and get a blade made for it. (It is a beautiful hilt – a rapier hilt, inlaid with gold apparently.) This is how King spends his money when he has any. Inv. knew him when he was living in a Bloomsbury garret in semi-starvation.

King's present lodger is an artist (known to Inv.), who has done 2 years for burglary. Away for the weekend sleeping with a girl-friend in Dorking. Her husband away in Army.

(It takes all sorts to make a world!)

The war had brought a political 'truce' between the major parties. By-elections were still necessary, but where a Conservative died or retired, Labour would not contest the seat (and vice versa). This left unusual scope for independents and for small parties.

In 1940 and 1941, by-elections were of little significance. But with the blitz over, fears of invasion dispelled by Hitler's decision to invade Russia, and danger of ultimate defeat almost abolished by America's entry into the war, 1942 produced some remarkable results. The campaign in North Africa, which mattered to most British people, was going badly. The Japanese swept through Britain's far-eastern colonies. There was great concern (both recorded and augmented by Mass-Observation's *People in Production*) over real and purported inefficiency in the munitions industries. Churchill's popularity sagged a little. His appeals (with Attlee) to the electors were of no avail as four 'independents' beat Conservatives in by-elections between March and June. The last was Tom Driberg, a socialist (and incidentally an old friend of Mass-Observation).

Another old friend of Harrisson's, Sir Richard Acland, MP, had helped Driberg, at Maldon, turn a Conservative majority of 8,000 into an Independent one of 6,000. Acland, elected as a Liberal before the war, had become a convert to left-wing socialism and led a small movement called Forward March. In July 1942 this merged with the '1941 Committee', a left-centrist group of distinguished men and women led by J. B. Priestley, to form a new party, 'Common Wealth'.

On 1 December 1942 an official report on *Social Security* was published by the Government. It unveiled a 'plan' for what was later known as the 'Welfare State'. Its reception was rapturous. The author, Sir William Beveridge, at once became a folk-hero. The Cabinet was deeply embarrassed, as its Conservative members, and most of their supporters in the Commons, were not enamoured of Beveridge's ideas. As the government shillied and shallied over committing itself to post-war implementation of the report, public opinion was dismayed – so many people had seized on the report as the blueprint for the future.

Beveridge was a Liberal, and his ideas were far from 'revolutionary', but their reception gave Common Wealth an opportunity. In April 1943 their candidate, a young RAF hero named John Loverseed, achieved a remarkable victory in the now-defunct constituency of Eddisbury in Cheshire. For Labour it had always been defunct – the party had never bothered to contest this sleepy rural seat. It had been continuously Conservative until 1928, when a Liberal had won it. In 1931, he had proclaimed himself a 'Liberal National', supporting the Conservative-dominated 'National' coalition. He had no contest to face in that year or in 1935. After his death during the war, an Independent Liberal stepped in to challenge the Government candidate, and the confusion which this created certainly helped Common Wealth. So did Loverseed's slogan, 'Beveridge in Full Now', which may have pulled in more votes than did his call for the nationalisation of agriculture.

The reports which follow are part of an extensive unpublished study by Mass-Observation. 'F.M.' cannot now be identified, but was presumably a paid Observer. Tom Wintringham, a former Communist and Commander in the International Brigade in Spain, was as well known as Acland himself, for his work in teaching guerrilla war to Home Guards in 1940. Loverseed joined the Labour Party in 1945, and lost the seat.

38. 'F.M.': Eddisbury by-election, 1943

OPEN AIR MEETING AT WRENBURY FM 5.4.43

Inv. was told that this village was 90 per cent for Loverseed. The meeting was on the village green, about 6.30 p.m. There were about 120 people present, Cs and Ds, 60 per cent Fs. About 20 children. Tom Wintringham spoke for about 20 minutes and then John Loverseed spoke for 20 minutes. There were no interruptions, no questions. The people listened attentively but were not enthusiastic. It was very cold, strong wind blowing. About 30 bikes stood against the church wall – some people had evidently come quite a distance.

REPORT OF MEETING AT CHOLMONDELY SCHOOL (COMMON WEALTH), 5.4.43

A small village schoolroom, about 100 people present, 20 or so standing. 70 per cent Ms, mostly Cs and Ds, some Bs. The Chairman was Reverend Carter, a blind non-conformist minister. A Common Wealth member from Manchester area. A vigorous and clever speaker, very popular. Inv. did not hear his speech. When Loverseed arrived there were cheers and cries of 'Good old Loverseed'.

Loverseed said – 'We're winning! It is a sign that people are losing when they start attacking their opponents. On Saturday night both my opponents stopped talking about their own policy and started attacking me!' He went on to say that he had been accused of being a Communist – that C.W. was copying Russia. 'Russia is an economic democracy and a political dictatorship. This country has a political democracy and an economic dictatorship. Common Wealth wants to see in this country political democracy and economic democracy.'

Ordinary people had made the sacrifices – money, work, and even lives. Now the other half of the nation should be made to do their share. Men who have lost arms and legs and eyesight, women who have lost their husbands and sons have lost far more than any millionaire can lose. (Hear, hear.) We will compensate men whose property we confiscate – we'll have to – or have them on our hands – many of them can't work if they try! (Loud laughter.)

Common Wealth did not mean that agriculture, for instance, would be controlled by civil servants in Whitehall. It would be controlled by Committees of Farmers. The produce would be bought by national boards which would help the farmer and would pay the farm labourer the wage which he is entitled to receive and has never yet received. (Loud applause.)

One last word on parliamentary representation. There are far too many M.P.s who are not doing their jobs. (Applause.) There is a true story of one M.P. who, when he went to the House of Commons recently was stopped at the door because he was not recognised. He had been a Member for 6 years!

'If I am elected, and I think I am going to be, I will promise you this. I will come to the constituency at least once a month to meet committees which you can form, accept your criticism and generally talk things over.' (Loud applause.)

1st question, M40B
How does Mr Loverseed make out that he can get more out of the land than is being done today?

A. I quite agree that today the farmer is getting the best out of the land. He is simply getting a better deal because of torpedoes! But we want to see that it is the same after the war. (Applause.)

2nd question M65B (brother-in-law to Tom Peacock)
I am not accusing Mr Loverseed personally but I would like to know if he can give any explanation of the firing of Mr Peacock's produce.

A. I wish I could! Perhaps it is nothing to do with the election. I have met Mr T Peacock and seen the damage. The terrible thing is that it has destroyed tons of food (loud applause).

Q. I'm afraid that I cannot accept the statement that it has nothing to do with the election.

A. Surely I and C.W. cannot be held responsible for anything my supporters do, at a time like this? And if a gang wanted to start a bit of sabotage for reasons of their own, an election is a time they might chose to start it.

Q. F40D
Does anybody think that Mr Loverseed who has been willing to give his life for his country would do anything like that?

The Rev. Carter then said that in a happening of this kind it would be wise to think who stood to gain from it. The only one likely to gain, in the election, would be Mr Peacock. Therefore it is equally likely to have been done by Peacock's supporters.

Loverseed said: 'I visited Mr Peacock on Sunday morning and he never suggested or hinted that he thought either I or Common Wealth had anything to do with it.' (Loud applause and cheers.)

Q. M25B
May I ask what are Mr Loverseed's qualifications to represent an agricultural constituency? (Applause.)

A. Mr Peacock does not necessarily represent the farm hands. I have come of farming stock, I live on a farm and my wife's father is a farmer.

If there is anything I don't understand I can very quickly learn. (Laughter and applause.)

Q. M45C
Why is Common Wealth fighting every by-election? (Applause.)

A. The political truce is nothing but a sham to help the Tory party to keep in power. They gained a big majority at the general election by a

League of Nations vote, and they mean to keep it. I believe the Labour Party will break the truce at Whitsun. The Common Wealth do not oppose candidates of the socialist or Labour parties.

Q. M25B
If you get [in] – and it isn't likely – how do you propose to do all these things alone?

A. You may think that one election and one member means nothing but it has a big effect on the House of Commons. I agree we must have a majority before we can carry through our proposals. But we must start somewhere and keep on trying. The amount of votes we have gained all over the country prove the people are with us.

Q. M20C
Do you know that your victory will be applauded in Germany as a vote of no confidence in Mr Winston Churchill? (Loud applause from one quarter only.)

A. Do *you* know that the turning down of the Beveridge Report gave Mr Goebbels his biggest chance? Germany is *afraid* of Common Wealth. (Laughter from a few people.)

Q. M25C
Will there be a general election after the war and should we not wait till then and support the government now? (A few hear, hears.)

A. We were not prepared for the war but we should be prepared for the peace – and we must start *now*.

Mr J.D. [brother-in-law of other candidate] then said he would like to say one thing. He and his supporters very much appreciated the way Mr Loverseed had met their bombardment. Loud cheers and applause.

In retrospect, January 1944 was Mass-Observation's finest hour. The article which follows (slightly cut here) was published in the *Political Quarterly* for that month (Vol. 15 No. 1, pp. 21–32).

Harrisson, now a soldier, had maintained touch remarkably well with Mass-Observation, of which he was still the figurehead. He drew in this article on four kinds of Mass-Observation material; reports on by-elections; 'Directive' replies by the volunteer Panel on the political situation, leaders, events of the war and so on; diaries, which showed more directly how volunteers responded to the news, and finally, 'News Quotas'. These last were replies to questions asked, as a daily chore, by Celia Fremlin and other paid 'team' members, of passers-by in the London streets. Their 'scientific' character was perhaps dubious, but they helped Harrisson keep his finger on the pulse of opinion.

He originally offered 'Who'll Win?' to Kingsley Martin, editor of the *New Statesman*. Martin thought it too long for his journal and passed it on to his friend and neighbour Leonard Woolf, for the *Political Quarterly*. We are now used to believing opinion polls. Politicians and public alike were not convinced by them in 1944, and even if Harrisson had done no more than take British Institute of Public Opinion results seriously, he might still have upstaged everyone by successfully predicting Churchill's defeat on the basis of these figures alone. But Mass-Observation's 'qualitative' methods gave him an extra distinction; he could explain *why* Churchill would lose.

39. Tom Harrisson: Who'll win? 1944

> I don't expect many social changes in *practical* form – but I do think the war has already shaken many people, once apathetic because they felt secure and did not know other people's lives, into at least an interest in securing healthier and less degrading conditions for the working people of this country.

Thus a young married soldier, about 'after the war'. He echoes a by now familiar and ever-growing attitude of mixed doubt and hope, apathy and alertness. There has been a considerable and increasing concern, in the columns of the *New Statesman* and elsewhere, to some extent with this attitude (though its importance is still much under-estimated), to a larger extent with the political set-up which will eventually have to face this reconditioned (or de-conditioned) public. In particular, there is leftish concern at the returned confidence of Conservatism. Because the Right was quiet in 1940 and 1941, dark years when all men's good will was needed for survival, many leftward minds seem to have assumed a change of heart to match the tongue. But naturally, when things get 'better', when the siren's wail is dim, and unity less vital, hidden faces again pop eagerly out from behind the camouflage nets. Belatedly, the left are having to recognise that their future fight may be tough. That Social change which 1941 writers like J. B. Priestley and Ritchie Calder wrote about as if it had already begun, via blitzes and British restaurants, seems less certain now. The Tories re-emerge with new assurance, while Labour hopes uncertainly. Politics consists in manipulating, if possible successfully, the 'natural', 'automatic' trends, for group interests, if necessary into other channels than those they would normally follow. Not only in Britain, but through the world, strong forces of self-interest as well as deep tides of human mood and distress, are lining up for a catharsis of civilisation in the years ahead, the years of Theoretical Peace. What objective evidence can we now adduce about the probable emergent political pattern? Data accumulate, and certain tentative, limited answers can be attempted.

This is an impersonal attempt! First, here at home . . . The commonest single belief among politicians seems to be that at the next General Election, whatever Party or Group Winston Churchill heads will win (e.g. *Spectator*, Sept. 3rd; *Tribune*, October 22nd; Nicholas Davenport in *Evening Standard*, Nov. 3rd; Michael Foot in *Evening Standard*, Nov. 23rd). Some Conservatives claim to be eager for a straight poll, like Colonel Arthur Evans, M.P., at the Annual Conference of Conservative Clubs of Wales (August 14th), though Colonel Harold Mitchell, M.P., Vice-Chairman of the Conservative Party, at a Birmingham Conservative Conference (July 24th) describes the party truce as 'still needed when war ends'. Although, by the coal debate of early October, Churchill had allegedly given up hope of a post-war coalition, A. V. Alexander, of the tiny Co-op. Party, still advocates (Nov. 13th) and Sir Stafford Cripps, the able man without a party, also favours some form of non-party co-operation (Nov. 20th, Bristol). In doubtful times, the Conservative Party itself tends to neo-fragmentation and a temporary leftish wing; this time it is the Tory Reform Committee, first prominent in October, and already effective in jockeying the party towards verbal acceptance of some planning ideas. This group is not, of course, by any means a new *movement*. It is revealing already a strong line in favour of permanent coalition (e.g. Chairman, Viscount Hinchlingbroke, M.P., speaking at Shrewsbury, Nov. 27th; star Quintin Hogg, M.P. writing in *Evening Standard*, Nov. 24th). Such tendencies imply that thoughtful Tories are far from sure of a solo success post-war.

Meanwhile Labour is increasingly split on Coal, Workmen's Compensation and other issues; so much so that Herbert Morrison has publicly warned the party of its approximation to the pre-war Liberal split-up (Nov. 13th), a warning that has not spared him Mosley anger.

[This is Harrissonian short-hand for 'anger at his decision, as Home Secretary, to release Sir Oswald Mosley from prison'.]

The rank and file of Labour M.P.s suspect another 1931 trap. Many evidently consider Churchill can carry the post-war election, and that they must work for victory only in a *second* post-war election. It can by no means be said that Labour is in very confident mood. Rather they are showing once more their old 'fear of power', rationalised into an exaggerated estimate of differences, and lately symbolised by the 'safety-first' trend in the Parliamentary Party elections, which put Emmanuel Shinwell off the Administrative Committee. Some months ago I remarked, at a research meeting, that social surveys suggested a probable Labour victory, by a wide margin, at the next election, if Labour played now for success. Next day, a famous Labour journalist rang me up to query this 'amazing statement', and another wrote me asking for substantiation of 'so extravagant a claim'. The basis for my remarks will be examined below; so far I wish only to re-emphasise Labour nervousness, Churchill overshadowing.

Common Wealth show no such nervousness. Having won its first by-election at Eddisbury (September) and polled at recent by-elections 54,000 votes, it announced (*Observer*, October 3rd) the intention of running 120 candidates in the next general election. Sir Richard Acland, M.P., Chairman, declares for an outright attack on 'The whole conception of a capitalist community', expresses a readiness to fight with, and if necessary, under the Labour Party, provided they discontinue 'an official policy of compromising with capitalism' (Plymouth, Aug. 18th). The temper of his party personnel is confident too! But among M.P.s of all established parties there is nervousness, nervousness at the uncertain future after an unprecedented parliamentary life of 9 years, in which a third of the original members, elected on Baldwinism, serving under three kings and three Prime Ministers, have died or been elevated to 'higher' appointments. One hundred and seventeen M.P.s have entered the House without any real election, in effect by party caucus nomination.

This record prolonging of parliamentary life is generally regarded, in the lobbies, as due for decease in the 10th year, so strained is the gulf becoming between initial vote and current, dating result. Equally strained and stale is the electorate itself – stale two ways. First, through the inevitable moratorium on direct politics, and the 1939–43 effect on confusion of current thought. Second, through

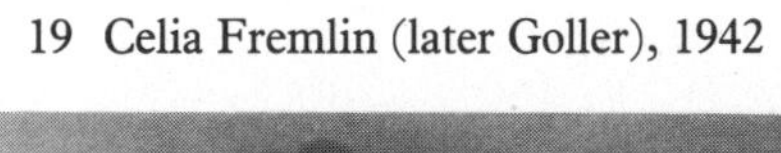

17 Len England, *c.* 1941

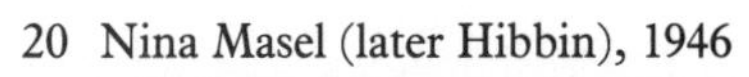

18 Mollie Tarrant, 1939

19 Celia Fremlin (later Goller), 1942

20 Nina Masel (later Hibbin), 1946

21 H.D. (Bob) Willcock (right) with Mary Adams at the official opening of the Mass-Observation Archive, University of Sussex, 1975

22 *Below left*, Tom Harrisson with the Mass-Observation files when they first arrived at the University of Sussex, 1970

23 *Below right*, Naomi Mitchison, Mass-Observation diarist, with Henry Novy, formerly a full-time Observer and now a trustee of the Archive, at the Archive's opening, 1975

vast movements of population and the out-of-datedness of the last register. By the next election, *very few people under 30 will have voted at all.* The whole basis of our democracy has thus been shelved, dangerously. The new legislation now passing into operation (second reading, October 26th), establishing a temporary register for any election, comes just in time. The bigger problem of long overdue seat redistribution looms ahead (*Times*, 20.10.43). Labour feels a full redistribution would spread party gains and losses fairly evenly, while a *partial* one might be greatly to Tory advantage. Of the constituencies cited as examples in the report of the Committee on Electoral Machinery, 5 in 6 with deficient electorates are represented by Labour members, 4 in 6 with excessive electorates by Conservatives. Only 27,000 N. Southwark electors could vote for or against George Isaacs as their parliamentary representative; 188,000 decided on John Parker for Romford. Labour favours a common qualification for local elections, but many Conservative local authorities seem likely to oppose the change, which is indeed unlikely to favour them, by admitting more poorer, younger, non-householding folk.

So much for the top level. Now for the big, wide bottom. Let us see the available evidence here? First, this question of Churchill. The common editorial and M.P. assumption of his post-war potency finds relatively little support in studies of public, let alone private, opinion. Supremely popular as he is today, this is closely associated with the idea of Winston the War Leader, Bulldog of Battle, etc. Ordinary people widely assume that after the war he'll rest on his magnificent laurels. If he doesn't, many say they will withdraw support, believing him no man of peace, of domestic policy or human detail. This comes up over and over again in diaries, letters, talk. It is harder for people to express such sentiments publicly about the chief loyalty figure and security symbol in war-time, but Mass-Observation had made many studies of Churchill popularity, short-term and long. While he has outstandingly maintained his position as a popular war leader – in October, nine people in ten were favourable, a higher figure than in the same month last year – his position as a post-war figure is far from certain in the public mind. At some point in most of our political enquiries it emerges that most people do not expect he will be the primary post-war leader, while many do not expect that he will himself seek to be a post-war leader at all. His age, his already almost complete achievement, his supposed disinterest in home affairs, and his alleged lack of sympathy with working people over domestic issues, all add up in the public mind. In addition, there is to some extent an automatic process of peace which tends to underline the contrast by wanting to be rid of the primary figures from war-time. Thus, in answer to a straight question on whether or not Churchill could or should be post-war prime minister, the majority reject the proposition. More illuminating perhaps are enquiries into who people would like as post-war premier, although there is always much difficulty in naming an alternative to the present leader. About two persons in ten nominated Churchill, and he has gained position slightly since Cripps declined; in July 1942 Cripps easily headed even Eden with 29 per cent, whereas by this autumn he had fallen to 14 per cent.

On a broader front, there are a variety of M-O polls on post-war voting intentions. These must be treated with great caution, the main point to bear in mind being that people tend always to give 'respectable', *status quo*, opinions to strangers (investigators). BIPO has also conducted several polls of interest in this connection, and they correspond closely with M-O's less statistical indices. In June and August 1943 they asked: 'If there was a General Election tomorrow, how would you vote?' (See Table 1.)

Table 1

	Percentage who said they would vote this way in:	
Would vote for	*June 1943*	*August 1943*
Conservative	25	23
Labour	38	39
Liberal	9	9
Communist	3	3
Common Wealth	2	1

About 1 in 6 were uncertain both times. These polls covered only *civilians*. All M-O evidence suggests that service personnel have been *more* affected by radical trends than civilians and service voting in Australia and New Zealand confirms this. BIPO finds, as M-O does, most civilian radicals are among the under 29s, few of whom have ever voted; here Common Wealth and Communist Party support is strongest, as also the 'undecided' and 'non-voters'.

Somewhat contrary evidence is supplied by the '*Daily Express* Centre of Public Opinion', an interesting organisation run on no clearly recognised independent scientific lines. These polls seem frequently to support Beaverbrook policy, and therefore the striking feature of the one published on July 24th, 1943, is the relatively slight difference of Conservative over Labour – no preponderance at all if leftist coalition is assumed. The drop in Conservative prestige is clearly great as compared with the last election. (See Table 2.)

Table 2

Would vote for	*Percentage who said they'd vote this way*
Conservative	37
Labour	34
Liberal	7
Communist	4
Common Wealth	3
Independent	5
Uncertain, etc.	10

M-O has made several detailed studies of this subject, more qualitative and localised, but generally in line with other objective information. In early 1942 studies showed a general belief that some sort of socialism was inevitable, coupled with a very frequent disillusion in the Labour Party and Socialist leaders. The attitude has been watered down into confused doubt about *all* parties over the past 16 months, but still this sort of remark reflects a common temper:

1. Socialism is as inevitable as the course of time itself.
2. Socialism is inevitable sooner or later in our present stage of civilisation. All over the civilised world. It is the only natural method in which to [overcome] present problems.
3. Socialism in my view is inevitable everywhere sooner or later. The swiftness of its introduction should be dependent on the necessity for it.

With this, among the more thoughtful, goes the concomitant:

> I believe in the socialist state, but I believe the present leaders are too self-seeking and ignorant to bring about a state of socialism.

In Spring 1942 another study in widely separated areas of all types showed most favouring a return to pre-war party politics as soon as possible, the well-off least favouring this, the young most urging it. When verbal comments on parties were analysed 48 per cent were found to be anti-Conservative, 43 per cent anti-Labour. Conservatives were most criticised for policy, Labour most for personnel and party machinery. For reactions to the straight but deliberately broad question, asked of cross sections in three type areas, on who would win the next General Election, see Table 3.

Table 3

Party expected to win	*Percentage expecting this in*		
	London	*Midland*	*Northern*
Conservatives	12	14	17
Labour	27	33	26
Liberal	2	0	1
Coalition, etc.	6	3	9
No opinion, etc.	57	50	51

(Some people gave alternative answers in the above table.)

In late 1942 and again in mid-1943 people were asked if they thought the war had changed their political views at all, with the striking results shown in Table 4.

Table 4

Attitude shown:	*1942*	*1943*	*(in percentages)*
No change noted	70	61	
Change: more to left	12	25	
more to right	6	4	
Vague, etc.	12	10	

Adding up so far, there seems to emerge an incontestable unanimity of evidence towards a much reduced Conservative prestige, plus a big, if not immense, shift to the left, vague and confused though it at once shows itself to be on any subtler, qualitative analysis. The crude figures on this, as indicated above, almost certainly do less than justice, however, to the scale of that trend when presently expressed in terms of *private* opinion at the secret ballot.

We can now examine this available evidence of the ballot box itself . . .

In the first six months of 1943 there were twelve contested by-elections, with total polls:

Official Government Candidates	111,842 votes
Other candidates	90,684 votes (54,412 for Common Wealth)

Thus 45 per cent votes cast were against candidates in all cases receiving the full support and prestige of Winston Churchill, and lately of *all* the party leaders, in war-time when national unity remains a strong card (most people still favour the *electoral* truce), on a stale register, favouring the old and better off, the least radical.

This 45 per cent, giving a margin of 20,000 votes in 200,000, provided only one non-government M.P. (Eddisbury), though in two areas the combined vote for opposition candidates eclipsed the Government one, and in two more the Government majority was under 1,000. Since then we have had three further striking by-election results. At Chippenham in August a strong, progressive, young Government candidate, with all party support, got in by only 195 votes on a poll of 16,425 (in 1935 the Conservative majority was over 5,000); a sample study in the constituency showed a third of the residents disenfranchised. At Peterborough in October, Lord Suirdale beat a local house-painter (Independent) by 1,086 votes on a 22,866 poll; in 1935 the Conservative majority was 5,304. It is hardly necessary to underline such results. No machine, no big names, no helpful register, no suitable 'political atmosphere', war-time electoral difficulties, the current weight of *status quo* leaders, plus the much used argument of war-time disunity, can only *just* stem the success of independent, almost 'private', candidates, often of a quality lower than we may expect after the war. Consider the difference with a nation-wide drive, a popular policy, backed by popular national figures, in an atmosphere of sanctioned rivalry. Yet the electorate is not indiscriminate for 'anyone different', though almost anyone can get an appreciable number of votes, if not definitely 'cranky', as shown in the November Woolwich by-election, where the Independent Labour Party man scored 3,419 to the Government 8,204, but the third Independent got only 958.

The trend seems clear enough so far? But so far, we have not touched the big area of the new voter. Millions will vote for the first time in the next general election. Here is a less calculable, but possibly decisive, influence on our politics.

The young are especially disturbed by war conscriptions. Women are on the political scene more than at any time since suffragette days. The Welsh are pushing strongly for a more decentralised and independent political life. All the evidence suggests that these groups, and especially the young serving men, are moving more to left (not necessarily the Labour left), than right [. . .]

[Harrisson went on to provide information about recent elections abroad.]

What, then, does it all arrive at? Simply this:

(1) Politics has a pendulum which swings, with human nature, towards change, chance and alternative. This has been normally operative in the war years, and where the more left-wing ideas have

long dominated, has been more or less disadvantageous to them (NZ, USA).

(2) Even so, pendulum moves to the right have been slight – when compared with many pre-war moves.

(3) Swings away from the established 'Right' have, on the other hand, been evident in several countries where open General Elections have been held (Australia, Canada, Switzerland, Eire), while smaller-scale indications of anti-Right feeling come from Great Britain and Northern Ireland.

(4) Movements are often confused and even contradictory. Behind them lie a deep and growing disillusion with the efficacy of existing systems, doubt about the whole pattern of promise in our civilised life. For many here, giving Labour another chance is a last hope. An American editor, Dwight Macdonald, has put the general position in a nutshell (*Horizon*, November 1943):

> Choice between evils rather than between positive programmes, a scepticism about basic values and ultimate ends, a refusal to look too far ahead – this is the mood.

(5) This condition of the human mood is both dangerous and hopeful. From the inner chaos of civilised man after years of uncivilised war, may come a new resolution, expressed when the flags go up, through new or currently minor channels. If this expression is inhibited, ignored or unsuccessful, a new apathy may come upon us. All the seeds are there for ghastly luxuriance of indifference and negativism, leading inexorably downhill. Political vitality, the pendulum of promise, is the lifeblood of healthy, social mass life.

(6) Yet I doubt if this cynicism is so deep-seated in relation at least to the small act of voting, as it seems. There would seem, on the whole, to be enough inertia left to put enough crosses on pages, to elect another Government here in Britain, once more. And on the present form I have no doubt that the present Conservative Party, even if led by Mr Churchill, will not accomplish enough of itself to govern again, unless the alternatives commit suicide. This is about the first prediction I have ever dared make. It is offered, therefore, diffidently but definitely. My own *views* don't come into it. And clearly, there is no political predeterminism. Politics *is* the art and science of *altering* the future . . .

End Note:
If any Tory wants a shaking, go and see the new Ronnie Waldman

film 'Guess What', and hear what happens when Baldwin appears, in the Coronation procession.

Within a few days of the publication of 'Who'll Win?', Common Wealth scored a remarkable victory at Skipton and only a few weeks later an Independent Socialist, with Common Wealth support, won West Derbyshire. After the D Day invasion of Europe, interest in by-elections waned, and as it became clear that Labour would leave the Coalition at the end of the war, Common Wealth's days as a political force were numbered. Though its third and biggest triumph came at Chelmsford in April 1945, that was the only seat it held after the General Election which followed Hitler's defeat.

In that election, Labour, with 47.8 per cent of the votes, got 393 seats. The Tories had managed, despite everything, to gain 39.8 per cent, but retained only 213 seats. The Liberals took 9 per cent and 12 seats. With three ILP-ers, two Communists and the lone Common Wealth-er were elected no fewer than 14 Independents.

Well over half of service men and women did not vote at all, but of the 1,701,000 Forces votes cast by post or proxy, most are assumed to have gone to left-wing candidates.

The volunteer Observer who sent in the report which follows was not a prolific contributor. He wrote in only a few times. He was an instrument repairer in the RAF, aged 22.

40. Volunteer Observer: The Forces vote in West Africa, 1945

AIRFORCE STATION. WEST AFRICA – REPORT I. 12–16 JUNE 1945

12 June 1945

I received M-O Directive on this question yesterday, June 11th and accordingly have commenced this Election Diary today, the 12th.

Out here in W.A. the election is in everyone's blood – in all quarters it seems to be a common subject for urgent discussion.

Already a mock election has been arranged for tomorrow, the 13th of the month, and will be held at New England RAF Camp.

Liberal, Labour, Conservative and Communist candidates will be speaking – heckling will be allowed, and the proceedings will terminate in a vote being taken.

In the NAAFI this evening, beer being on sale and tongues loosened, I heard a typical conversation – I will try and give as accurately as possible the theme of this conversation. The loud man said:

'It doesn't matter which party gets in – its all the same – so why the hell tell me that Labour should be put into power. They're all the bloody same.'

A Scotch miner nearby: 'You've never in your life time known Labour to be in Parliament but the once; and then with a minority vote – so how can you say Labour's the same as the rest? You don't know.'

'Its bloody greed that does it.'

He was asked what he meant.

'Every man has got his price – people always go to the highest bidder.'

The Labour element grew a little heated and asked for hard facts.

The loud man said, 'I mean the people that vote.'

'How?'

'They're all the same. They get a bit of money and go all Conservative because they're afraid someone is going to take it off them – how can you hope to get the Tories out when people vote like that.'

The miner: 'Well it's up to us that have got the intelligence to know better, to get in every vote we can to Labour. It's all the more reason for us to make a fight of it.'

A silent man put in with: 'Its not a matter of intelligence – we are not taught politics.'

I said: 'No man need be ignorant of politics if he does not wish to be.'

The loud man said darkly, 'Ah, but the real facts – how are you going to find *them* out?

And I had to leave them there.

This was not an extraordinary conversation; but it is the sort of thing that is going on everywhere here.

The 'loud men' of the camp will not be shaken even in argument that is fairly sane. They are retreating all the time from their own ignorance. They have retreated for so long that it has become a habit with them. They *cannot* free themselves – can only go on throwing up protective screens of 'dark' hints that no one can comprehend and therefore counteract. They are a drag to progress whatever the party be that is involved.

June 13
Today I see in orders that the 'mock' election has been cancelled by the station authorities. A Quiz programme is to be held instead.

My Aunt writes: 'This last week has been a most exciting one, starting with the election news. I always like to see an engineer hoisted on his own petard so I was delighted when Mr Churchill queered the Labour pitch. They had worked it out so nicely that they were going to have about five months in which to queer the government pitch: they would have been able to indulge in the favourite sport of destructive criticism while they worked up a programme to a perfect crescendo of impracticable promise, and dear Winnie brought them down to earth and not only that, he spoilt their Labour Conference (which petered out ingloriously) and sent ministers scurrying back to their jobs and docked their salaries for five months. No wonder they are so mad! But, as the *Times* said . . . "any party which gives the impression of relying on recrimination about the circumstances of the election rather than on a concrete programme submitted for the approval of the electorate will only tend to prejudice its chances at the polls."

'I don't know why the Labour Party should imagine that people who can't make up their minds in July should be able to do so in October, especially as regards the service vote.

'We can't all be as mizzy minded as a case I heard of today – a dear old lady on hearing government had resigned: "Well I think it's time Mr Chamberlain had a rest he's getting an old man now."'

A further insight into the political mind of my Aunt: 'Her cousin's son has just gone . . . on his first voyage and of all the lucky midship mites – he was on HMS *Devonshire* when she took Crown Prince Olaf back to Oslo.'

Remarks on the cancellation of the mock election:

'They are afraid that too many home truths will come to light.'

'It was contrary to all Air Force regulations anyway.'

'It is not a political gathering it's entertainment.'

'If the Communist candidate had withdrawn his candidature maybe difficulties would not have been raised.'

June 14
An S.P. (Service Policeman) sleeping in the next bed, said to me this morning, 'I've had a bit of a shock'. I said, 'Oh yes?' He said, 'I've been writing to the wife for months telling her to vote Labour. Now she writes saying she doesn't know what to do – the Labour

candidate for our district is a Jew. I shall have to put my party feelings on one side and vote Conservative.'

June 16

While we sat on benches in sick quarters this morning, waiting for the medical officer, a discussion of sorts broke out:

One man said, 'Churchill will not last long now.'

A Corporal said that Churchill had done a good job.

'He's done a good job,' said the man, 'but he's not suited to peace-time rule – he's said as much.'

'Well,' said an LAC [Leading Aircraftsman] 'I don't care who is at the top so long as Labour are kept out – they want to start socialism, think of it!'

The Corporal said, 'x*!! that. If the Labour get in I'm getting out of the country – I am not going to live under a Labour government.'

'That goes for me too,' said the LAC.

A little man, next to me nearly burst into flames, 'You're not giving Labour a chance to prove itself.'

'Labour have had their chance, they've failed all along.' 'When have they been in power to fail?' asked the little man.

'They've held office: you know that.'

'Yes, with a minority vote and half the Tories sending every penny of their money out of the country.'

'They'll do it again,' the man said, 'so it's no good Labour trying – they're bound to fail.'

'No they won't – there is a Government restriction on money just now – it's frozen; and Labour won't lift the control.'

'Well, why didn't they do all that when they were in before?'

'Because,' said a newcomer, 'they had a minority vote and no machinery at hand to control the banks and industries. Besides they hadn't enough real support from the country – as soon as they touched the money all your little men, with their small accounts and businesses, would have started shouting.'

'Well,' said the Corporal, who was really very young and very 'dim', 'if they only had a minority vote how did they get in?'

'If you don't understand the minority vote old man it's not much good my talking to you, is it?'

'Anyway,' said the LAC, 'if you think Labour are going to be any better than Tory you're wrong, they're all the same.'

'Give Labour a chance: its the only way you have of altering things,' said the little man.

'To hell with Labour,' said the Corporal, 'it's only you "old uns" that are shouting for Labour – All the young blokes I know don't give a hang for it – we're all clearing out.'

The little man said, 'That's just it: you've seen nothing yet – you've no sense of responsibility.'

'You've had your try,' said the corporal 'and you've made a mess of things. Now its our turn to take over and we're not going to have anything to do with it – we're getting right out.'

After that I was called in to see the Doc.

16–30 June 1945

The following are extracts from an argument that took place one evening here. They are all from the one speaker, a young Conservative.

'I intend to argue any way I can to gain votes for our side – those I find undecided I shall do my damnedest to win over – and I shall not be too particular how, as long as I can get them.

'You say that all over Europe the people are coming to power: but you are only finding what you are looking for. If you wish hard enough to find a thing you will find it – you want – to take your red spectacles off.

'You see, you are ignoring the very strong upper-class bodies that are functioning in every country, and with a large degree of success.

'Mob rule is unthinkable – just petty squabbling, greed and regimentation.

'You Socialists and labourites are mainly the "have nots" – we are the "haves". You are jealous of us.

'You say that as long as money is allowed to be a power in the land there will be wars and still more wars. That is wrong. Peace is good for Industrialists – it means prosperous markets. Besides, money does not decide those things – it is the intellect that counts. That is why mob rule will fail; it has no intellect or breeding, nor tradition to sustain it.

'It is the Aristocrat, the Feudalist who will work out the salvation of the people. You must realise that there will always be class distinction. You have it in Russia now: there are those of us born to lead and others to follow.

'We Conservatives are progressive; but we also realise that one cannot hand out money right and left – its got to come from somewhere.

'And are you so very interested in the masses? After all they are not lovely. Do you care if a few thousand are killed in an earthquake the other side of the world? Of course not. You are too sensitive and your sensitivity does not mean a great deal; it is merely a mental condition.

'You are too fond of concrete laws of right and wrong. Things are what you believe them to be. The world is not so objective as you imagine it to be. Make life the way you want it. My intention is to get the best out of it that I can – let the rest stand or fall, that is the law of nature, you cannot argue with that.'

It is interesting to note how the argument changes. How first there is the 'Goodly Lord' to lead the serfs and then a sort of 'Robber Baron' creeping in. Finally a man who had been keeping up a Greek chorus of 'when I was young I had ideals' suddenly made me feel very ill by saying, 'We are looking for Christ' – it followed on an outburst of mine that I cannot recall.

A Sergeant tonight said: 'It would be a good thing if Labour, should it gain power, offered Churchill a place in government, it might serve to quieten a very formidable opposition.'

A very popular vein in the election conversations are references to Churchill and family – also the Royal Family – derogatory references; many of them strongly backed by an unreasoning class hatred and yet quite logical. Churchill's daughter, her endless travels with her father, by plane to different centres of good living – the farce of the Princess in the ATS – these are typical examples.

There are several miners here who have had more than one fight with men who have accused the Welsh and Yorkshire colliers of stabbing the Forces in the back. They are extremely active in their arguments for Labour.

Collecting and counting the Forces' vote meant that results were delayed for three weeks after civilians had voted, on July 5, then announced in an amazing millennial spate. The move to Labour was huge in certain areas – the white-collar suburbs of London, for instance – but Glasgow, which had swung sharply left nearly a quarter of a century before, experienced only a small swing.

The very active Panel member who sent in this account of how Kelvinside took the bad news, worked in an accountant's office. Her brother 'Charlie', a university lecturer, had done important war work for the Ministry of Aircraft Production. It is interesting to hear talk of emigration in their circles, as in the very different environment of the RAF camp from which the previous item came. The dry humour of this extract is typical of this Observer's work.

41. National Panel diarist: Blue Clydeside, 1945

THURSDAY 26 JULY 1945. GENERAL ELECTION RESULTS

Hillhead has returned Mr Reid, the Conservative candidate, with a majority of over 6,000. The Central Division has returned Col. Hutchison, the Conservative. At Kelvingrove Col. Elliot has lost. The Conservative majority of 1935 of 144 has now become a Labour majority of 88. Kelvingrove is the one and only change in Glasgow. The left-wing divisions remain as before. Thus an odd position comes about. The most Conservative of the big British cities is – Glasgow! And it did so by staying as it was before. London is far 'redder' than Glasgow.

Taking Scotland as a whole, the degree of change is not remarkable. The swings over to Labour are mostly [in] divisions that are notorious for their uncertainty.

What I should like to know, and no newspaper enlightens me on this. Since 1935 represented a big Conservative victory, how did the parties stand in Scotland at the last time that Labour had a good return? I expect, of course, that Labour is bigger today than – would it be 1924? Perhaps the question should be, since the Conservatives last had a poor return? I suppose that the presence of the Liberal Party upsets that kind of comparison.

To every contact I have had ('every' is the literal truth) the Labour landslide was most unexpected. I have heard again and again, 'The men in the Forces have done it.' Mrs Blane, 'I shall write to Dave to demand how he voted. If he did vote Labour I shall tell him what I think of him. We had better emigrate to Australia. We shall have a chance of development there.' I, 'Australia is Labour.' There was general confirmation. Mrs Blane – nonplussed – 'Australia Labour – and no harm has come to it.'

Again every contact (and 'every' is literal) revealed that he or she had 'voted for Mr Churchill'. A chorus of sympathy with him went on throughout the afternoon. Surely there can be no one in the Kingdom who does not feel regret on his account. Disapproval with Mr Attlee was unrestrained.

There were many comments upon income tax, with forecasts (not to be taken too seriously) of it rising to 15/-. Miss Bendall – humourously and referring to the C.A.'s work computing income tax returns. 'One good thing about a Labour Govt. Income Tax won't fall and that would have made the computations harder.'

There was much pleasantry too on the lines that 'Soon we shall not need to work for our livings. The Labour Govt. will give us too good dole.'

Mrs Blane is genuinely scared. 'We shall be governed by controls from the cradle to the grave.' Later in the afternoon she said, 'Perhaps WE shall not feel the effects. People with money will be terrified, expecting to see it taken away from them.' She asked me privately, how long it would be before we had another chance to vote, must it be 5 years? I did my best to explain the system.

Miss Page, 'Of course I am very sorry about Mr Churchill, but I am not sure that it is not a good thing for people like me.' Everyone, 'Why you?' Miss Page, 'Well, I am an underdog, am I not?' This caused amusement. I feel like that a bit myself. Remember, of course, that Miss Page works exclusively for Mr David Carson, whose politics are obvious. A large part of his work is connected with wealthy trusts in wealthy and aristocratic families. The Duke of Montrose is one of his pals. She comes right up against inherited wealth and power.

Of course there are masses of comments upon individual successes and failures. Miss Herbison has defeated Anstruther Grey in North Lanarkshire (Miss Sinclair's division) thus repeating the famous Jennie Lee act of 1929, when an educated and attractive young miner's daughter romped in. Considering the poor opinion Miss Sinclair has always expressed of Anstruther Grey, I was rather surprised to find her backing him at the election. Sir Archibald Sinclair's defeat was unexpected. [He was the Liberal Party leader. Mrs Mann and Gilbert McAllister are in (see Town and Country Planning Conference report of about 18th May). Our friend, Mr John R Allan, was defeated by Mr Boothby in Aberdeenshire. I was astonished to hear over the air that a man I worked for (temporary, Radio Exhibition, 1934), Garry Allighan, was in for an English division.

There are even people who are not interested in the results. Elaine, picking up a newspaper at 5 to see what was on at the pictures, threw it away with disgust. 'My God, this paper has nothing but politics in it.' She had, however, earlier in the afternoon expressed satisfaction that Cathcart has returned its Conservative member, Mr Beattie. Elaine is a (what she calls) life-long supporter of the Conservatives – they support the King. She was told again that the monarchy was not involved in this election, but she continued to reject our information.

Mother's considered judgment delivered at 8.30 p.m. runs, 'The beginning of the rise of the mass of the people. The bottom dog has climbed the ladder.' I had expected her to be distressed, but no. She is looking forward with eager interest to seeing what the socialists will do. 'There are going to be some tremendous changes, I can see that,' she said. I have some of the eager interest too, but then I am a Mass-Observer, and changes are a relief from the boredom that has marked some periods of my observations.

26/7/45

Charlie came home for tea today, and I had thought he would be in low spirits, but instead he was his usual radiant self. Charlie's travels in Scotland are wide and unceasing, and I knew that with his wider contacts he was predicting greater Labour successes than my own observations in Glasgow had led me to expect, but he confesses to be surprised by the extensiveness of the change-over. I put to him the theory that the Service Men had done it, but he thought that that alone could not cause such a swing. It *must* be an index of general discontent. He went on, 'They are wanting a Labour Govt. Now they are going to have a taste of one, that will teach them.'

Of course, it *must* be general discontent, but why should discontent in Scotland be so mild compared with England? I wonder whether the wide-spread destruction of property in London can have had a psychological effect.

I asked Charlie's opinion as to whether the change of Government would affect the progress of the war, and he thought it would make no difference whatever.

Friday, 27/7/45

Each volume of the war diary increases my awareness of the narrowness of my sphere. That awareness was never so strong as today with the election results before me! I had no awareness of any profound political change in the 'nation's' outlook. I try to restore my self-respect as an Observer by saying that my unawareness proves how good an observer I am of Glasgow. Here it really is the case that there *has* been no profound change *to* observe.

Conservatives – 5. I.L.P. 3 (and if you ask me the I.L.P. will be an even thornier thorn to the new Govt. than to the old one), and Labour 7. One seat only in different hands, and that the ever-problematical Kelvingrove.

That unawareness was, however, shared by the rest of Moores,

Carson's staff, who talked in the upstairs typists' room, and many have talked.

My report last night was written after the 6 o'clock news. I had noticed for myself how much more England and Wales had swung than Scotland, and it was Charlie who called my attention to the curious position of Glasgow as the leading Conservative city. Those observations of ours were being repeated independently all over Glasgow last night. It is obvious to us all that some psychological factor influenced England and Wales which did not reach Scotland, but what?

Miss Page produced evidence that weighed considerably with us all. Her sister lives in London, works in an office there, is married to a man who works at something there, and has a girl of 15 at a London High School. For some weeks past her sister has been writing saying that since VE Day living in London has become very difficult and that the grumbling has been so bad that she has been constantly expecting a revolution to break out. She writes that food is scarce. In order to get even one's rations, one must queue for hours. People arrive before the shops open at 9. Other people discovering this arrive earlier the next day. Still more arrive earlier on subsequent days. The position is so ugly at 9 that the police are regulating the queues. There are crowds everywhere in London (Miss Page did not mention the cause suggested – possibly returning evacuees). There are many shops blitzed, and those functioning have too small staffs to give reasonable service to these terrible queues. These appear to be the main causes of the extensive development of the queue problem. The housewives of London are furious about it. Further, housing is bad in London (blitz) and the Govt. is blamed for inaction.

This story of food scarcity astonished us. It is well-known that blitzed areas have always been specially cared for by the Ministry of Food. Mrs Blane said that when she was in London on Dave's month's leave in February of last year, feeding was much better than here. Shops had plenty of nice cakes on sale to anyone, and in the restaurants you could get butcher meat sometimes, and even fried steak. In Glasgow we have had years of feeding that has been monotonous, but so far as the necessities of life are concerned, no one need go hungry. Since VE day we have had fish, ice-cream and tomatoes, and various other vegetables are coming on our market. Buns have been easy to obtain for a year or more. These remarks were contributed by us all. Miss Sinclair went on to say that 'cake was only to be had for queueing'. I said, 'Yes. But people are not going to start a revolution over a piece of cake.' (As I said that my mind flashed back to Marie Antoinette's solution of the bread problem of Paris, 'If you have no bread, eat cake.')

When Mrs Blane arrived home from the pictures at 10.15 last night, she sat down to write a six-page letter to Dave, which she took out to post at once, warning him off the premises if he had voted Labour. She is a muddled thinker. One of the Conservative candidates in the East End, accepted a challenge to live on 24/- a week, and has now issued the result of his experiment. Mrs Blane has followed this election incident, maintaining that it is ridiculous to say you can live on 24/- a week. At the time I asked, 'Why 24/-. Is that the amount of a single man's unemployment benefit?' Mrs Blane was not interested in that, but I did subsequently learn that that was the assumption at the root of the controversy. The man's published account has proved that he could do it. I myself have prepared an account of how I should live on 24/- a week, and have no doubt whatever that it can be done, though you have no money for clothes or amusements. Mrs Blane still continues to regard it as impossible. I said to her, 'If you believe 24/- is impossible, you should have voted Labour.' Is not that obvious, but that produced an explosion. 'Oh, no, I should not vote Labour to get bigger doles.'

I pointed out that if people on the dole got as much as they would working they would not want to work. Mrs Blane would have it that she would work, no matter if it were a lower wage. I tried to show her that the masses would not argue that way, but it was no use.

There is much talk about pensions. Miss Sinclair to Miss McFadyen, 'We won't need to worry about our old age.' Miss McFadyen, 'I expect I shall be old long after the Labour Govt. is out.'

Elaine said that at the Alhambra the actors from the stage were throwing out all sorts of spontaneous jokes against the Labour Govt. This was the Wilson Barrett team. I did not believe her, but Miss McFadyen later in the day supplied the explanation – though not knowing any was called for. She went to the 'Apple Cart' and the appropriateness of some of the comments of Shaw was striking.

Regret on Mr Churchill's departure is still felt. 'It is a vote of censure on his policy.' 'That's him finished.' 'He will never come back again.' 'It is shocking. All the years he was in the wilderness telling people war was coming. When it came, they called him in, and now the war is over, he is dismissed.'

General comments included the reflection that there must be plenty of mild individuals among the thousands of voters who have put Labour in, 'We are not too far inclined to communism.' On the other hand on the car two elderly gentlemen were agreeing that, 'It was calamitous. The greatest disaster this country has ever suffered.'

Mrs Blane asked me, 'Does it mean that Mr Churchill will now become Mr Attlee's assistant at Potsdam?' And was amazed at my definite reply that Mr Churchill would not go back to Potsdam. She also said 'I have never known an office like this for talking politics. Nowhere where I was before did anyone talk politics, and then I come to a place like this.' I was never anywhere where they talked politics so little as at Moores, Carson.

Last November, or thereabouts, Miss Sinclair stated categorically that everyone knew what would happen at the next General Election, and I asked for more precise information, to which she replied, 'Labour will sweep the country.' That is recorded in the diary, but I am afraid to bring the subject up. It might mean that they would wonder how I came to remember, and that might not be too good a question. Also I think she would take it in one of her characteristic manners, i.e. boast about her foresight, or repudiate the statement, seeing that at the moment she is all for Churchill and definitely anti-socialist. It is plain she herself has utterly forgotten the remark. North Lanarkshire, of course, is another of these mixed divisions. It has many miners, and acres and acres of mansions and overspills of Glasgow's city workers who travel. It has acres of agricultural land, and some light industries.

When the war ended, people who had been employed in war-time industrial catering moved on to work in hotels and restaurants. They brought with them a more militant spirit towards management. In late 1946, the General and Municipal Workers' Union, which had a London Catering Branch, organised a campaign to recruit new members and acquired 10,000. Arthur Lewis, MP for West Ham, was an official in the GMWU, and figured prominently in what followed.

Wishing to fight the battle for recognition by Management where they were strong, and to attract maximum publicity, the GMWU chose the Savoy Hotel, where 500 out of 800 catering workers were in the Union. On 8 October, Union members came out here. Waiters, cooks and chambermaids struck at Claridge's and Simpson's. Many others came out in sympathy, even in small restaurants in Soho. Of the 50,000 workers who took part, many had had no previous contact with trade unions.

The Savoy gave in after eight days, but the GMWU made a tactical mistake and did not get final agreement before workers went back. The dispute rumbled on for months. Arthur Lewis was suspended by the

GMWU. Many workers felt that the union had let them down and it lost numerous catering members.

The second day of the strike was observed by D.S., a full-time paid Observer whom we cannot identify.

42. *Paid Observer: Hotel staff strike, 1946*

London, 9 October 1946

The Invs arrived at Piccadilly at 10.15 a.m. and whilst she was buying the *Daily Worker*, two newspaper sellers told her what they thought of the strikers.

> Jolly good thing; I think it's about time the caterers was recognised. 'Ere are you in the café line? No? Well this is what I say. I know the conditions they work under, and they are shocking. Did you ever read in the newspapers about that case of a waiter – Dutchman he was too – (in the *Daily Express* I think) who worked 14 hours a day and was paid only £2.10/- a week. The judge was amazed, said he didn't know things like that existed in England. I say that once these Unions are recognised everything will be O.K. It's these blessed 'Igh and Mighties what's have the upper 'and. My mate and I – (turning to other man) fully agree with them – good luck to 'em we says.

The Invs then strolled up to the Ritz Hotel where she read the usual posters saying: WE WANT TRADE UNION RECOGNITION, DON'T BLACKLEG HERE, etc.

The pickets were willing to talk. One tall young kitchen hand said:

> I've been at this since yesterday, but it was coming to the Guv'ners. I've only been here five weeks – just demobbed yer know – but we're working under terrible conditions. I work in the kitchens, and what we get to eat wouldn't feed a chicken. We just want to be recognised so that if anything crops up between employer and employee we've got someone to back us up. You know there's a meeting at the Victory Hall, Leicester Square, at 3 o'clock this afternoon. They'll be about 2000 there. Why don't you go along? Mr Lewis – he's the real man – will be there. You don't belong to the Union, do you? I reckon all the cafés will close down too. There are only 2 chefs in there (indicating hotel). You see they've got to keep their position, so they stay with the big 'uns.

The Invs spoke to another young picket of 15, who informed her that hardly any of the passers-by were at all interested in it, because very few – except the workers – stopped to ask questions. They mostly glanced at the posters and walked on. In fact the Invs was the first person to stop him. Just then two middle-aged women workers, with hair encased in nets walked past grumbling.

'It's a shame, that's what it is. This ought never to be allowed.'

'You've got something there, Annie,' the other replied, 'but I bet you the strikers will win before tonight.'

The Invs then walked to the Piccadilly Hotel and was given some information by a woman cloak-room attendant.

> My word, I just don't know what they're striking for. How can one say what a living wage is? I mean we cloak-room attendants get very little a week, and all our tips are pooled, so you see dear, it doesn't amount to much. My friend and I work on shifts. This week I'm on from about 9 o'clock to 6 and next week from 6 onwards. My 'usband does the shopping – what little there is to get and I get one day off a week plus one Sunday in every five. We attendants are quite separate from the rest of the hotel staff, so what affects them doesn't us. See what I mean? I really don't understand it, but from what I can see they are just losing money whilst asking for more. If I join a strike it will be for *more food*. I mean ter say if there's a Black Market going on in this country – and there is. A friend of mind told me that if you go down 'Ackney any afternoon you can buy a white loaf of bread for 2/- and fresh butter for more. – It shows there is food in this country else how could the B.M. carry on? At this rate we'll never end rationing because the rich people can afford to get all they want. Yes, that's the strike I'd join, not all this piffle about T.U. recognition, or more wages, but for MORE FOOD.

The Invs then went and had some coffee in the lounge of the Piccadilly Hotel, and was told that at 12 o'clock Mr Arthur Lewis MP would negotiate with the manager of the Hotel, Mr Fields, for terms, and that 'things would start to happen!' The Invs noticed nothing unusual in the behaviour of the waiters, porters, doormen, etc. and the usual crowd of well-dressed men and women sauntered in for coffee, who either spoke in whispers across the tables at each other, or read the newspapers. The service was quick and everything looked in order. At 11.30 the Invs decided to go to Jermyn St. and inquire at a few cafés to see whether they were affected by the strikes by having to cater for more people, or whether they intended to strike themselves. The first hotel the Invs called at was the Potomac, an exclusive place. The manager told her that they were not affected by the strike, that they were always full, and that they, the staff, were not going to walk out. The Invs received the same reply from the 'L'apéritif Grill', so she decided to go into a small third-rate pub cum restaurant, called the Unicorn. All was normal here. A voluble barmaid of 69 said:

'No ducks, it won't affect us. We have only 2 waitresses here, and they won't strike, being old like me.'

'Go on Flossie, you're not old,' came from a young man. General laughter all round.

'Don't interrupt me, please. I say jolly good luck to 'em. Those strikers ought to be recognised. They've 'ad a rotten time long enough. As for this Government it should be burnt. That's what I think of 'em.

'I've lived amongst these people all my life. They're good working-class souls, with warm hearts. Not like these here toffs made of stone. I've been in the Music Hall business for over 20 years. I was manageress at the Holborn Empire, but I left because of the blitz. Couldn't stand 'em you know. Mebbe if I'd stayed there, I wouldn't be here no more. But I like these people. Could've got a job in a posh bar, but I says, no!'

'Quite right too, Flossie – a mild and bitter!' said an old man.

''Ere, 'ere, not so much of it,' said the barmaid, and the Invs left. All the people round the bar agreed with the barmaid over the strikers, whether it was thru fear of her or their own opinion, the Invs doesn't know. The Invs returned to the Piccadilly Hotel at 12 o'clock, but was told that the management was asking for 2 hours' grace so that the MP would come at 2 o'clock. The atmosphere was unchanged in the hotel lobby, so the Invs returned to Jermyn St. to see whether there were any large queues outside the restaurants. Three postmen were ready to talk about it outside the post office.

'Well, I look at it this way. Those ruddy employers just walk over their staff, and it's about time someone put a stop to it.' (All the postmen agreed.) 'Now take my job. We often have to get up at 4 in the morning, and tramp along the streets until our joints refuse to work. I think it's about time we went on strike'. (Hear, hear, from others.) 'Yes, our banner'll be "overworked and underpaid." No, but seriously, Miss, I hope the caterers are recognised.'

None of the cafés were extra full. No queues could be seen.

N.B. Invs realises that the people who inhabit the Dorchester and other such hotels, would hardly dine at the ordinary restaurant!

The Invs returned to the Piccadilly Hotel and at 2 o'clock she saw Lewis go up in the lift with the manager. At 3 o'clock the Invs arrived at the Victory Hall, where the meeting was being held. Outside a small, silent mob of workers were waiting, but the Invs following the press, pushed her way into the hall until she was eventually sitting on the platform where the speakers were, facing a crowd of over a thousand. Amidst a friendly silence several speakers addressed the crowd accompanied by cheering, clapping and an occasional interruption of shame, shame, etc.

There was approximately one woman to every ten men, mostly the working class, whose age ranged from 16 to 60.

The gist of the speeches was that this is the fight of the workers, and it would achieve success and establish Trade Union recognition. (Cheers.) Several telegrams and notes were read out by the secretary. One waiter made a speech calling the workers to arms, and one waitress sent up a note asking if she could speak. It read: 'I have been a waitress for 25 years, and I wish to speak as a Trade's Unionist for five minutes.' Immediately there was silence, and the secretary told the crowd to behave, as he was sure this waitress wasn't used to public speaking. A middle-aged, grey-haired, comfortable woman got onto the platform and spoke for 8 minutes in a high, thin, voice. Slowly the audience grew restless, but when she had finished speaking, about the workers' rights, there was prolonged applause, partly thru relief, and partly thru admiration.

At the end of the meeting the crowd was split up into three sections. One to go to the Piccadilly Hotel, one to go to the Regent Palace and one to go to the Park Lane.

One woman said in a loud voice, 'Don't worry, dearie, we'll be dead by the time we get there.'

The crowd which previously had filled the hall, even draping itself over the windows, surged towards the entrances, and as the Invs arrived outside an agitated man and woman were saying, 'This is all a mess. Lewis was supposed to have addressed them for ten minutes, and then we would have swept him down to the Park Lane Hotel with the crowd behind us calling for the workers.'

'Never mind let's get him to talk in the square,' said the man. And by the time the Invs arrived at the tree-fringed square, Arthur Lewis MP, dressed in lounge suit, just looking his 29 years, was precariously perched on a parapet overlooking a miniature lake where the statue of a man, similar in features to Shakespeare, was standing. Beneath him were the words: 'There is no darkness here, but ignorance.'

For five minutes Lewis spoke. 'Let's go to the Bonington Hotel because there are a lot of my MP friends staying there. It's a shame that they will have to make their own beds.' The crowd roared at these jokes. Lewis went on to say that the workers had a capital of £2,000,000 behind them, so there was nothing to worry about. Also there would be plenty more from organised workers.

When he had finished the crowd split up to march in an unorganised body as Parliament was still sitting, to their respective hotels. The Invs reached the Park Lane Hotel before the mob arrived, but noticed nothing unusual about the place. People were having tea, and discreet waiters continued to serve them. One old waiter who had no teeth, and spoke without moving his lips, because he was afraid anyone might hear him told the Invs this:

> Of course we are undergoing a risk, us old men, because we can easily be victimised after we go back to the hotels. Most probably the manager will say, 'Ere you, you're too old, get packing. But it's worth it. Do you know we don't even have enough to buy ourselves a glass of beer after the day's tips have been divided? Look at my shoes! They're just falling off me. And they want 26 coupons for a new uniform, but how can I get some more socks if they take all my coupons? What a life eh! What a life.

At five o'clock a small crowd had gathered outside the back entrance to the hotel. Three policemen were there, but the crowd behaved. For half an hour nothing happened. Meanwhile the rest of the mob were calling out every hotel and restaurant worker in London.

(At 5.30 the Invs left.)

The Conservative Party began to rally after defeat, under the energetic chairmanship of Lord Woolton. As the following report, presumably by a paid Observer, shows, it adapted its propaganda to new conditions, 'marketing' itself as never before. Mass-Observation, anxious to get more market research work, must have looked on its activities with professional interest.

The 'Trust the People' exhibition in London was of further interest to Mass-Observation. It was undertaking a large survey of the readership of Penguin books, which the exhibition denounced as dangerous 'socialistic propaganda'. The Industrial Charter mentioned was an important statement of new Conservative thinking.

The use of 'overheards' in this report is typical of Mass-Observation practice – it can be compared with that in the earliest Worktown pub observations.

43. Paid Observer: Trust the People exhibition, 1947

'TRUST THE PEOPLE'
IN THIS EXHIBITION WE PRESENT FOR THE FIRST TIME WHAT THE CONSERVATIVES HAVE DONE FOR THE PEOPLE OF BRITAIN IN THE PAST 100 YEARS

HOW THE CONSERVATIVES WOULD LIKE YOU TO LIVE.

THE CONSERVATIVE PLAN FOR BRITISH PROSPERITY

This poster – in the Entrance Hall leading into the exhibition – aptly sums up the aim of the exhibition – Conservative propaganda boost-up. Soft lights, soft music and B'ish girls with soft cultured voices act as stewardesses. The whole set-up is designed to lull the visitor into sweet soothing belief that all is well in the Conservative world. Posters everywhere emphasise at great length the Conservative Party's noble contribution towards social betterment. It is the Conservatives who gave us the opportunity to be educated, decently fed, clothed and housed; tended to our health and children's welfare; it is their proud claim that they have done more 'for the betterment of the people than anyone else'.

Time 5–6 p.m. There are no more than 50 people in the exhibition – majority B class with age group 30–35 predominating. But the 50 people aren't in one section – just a few dotted here and there giving the impression that the exhibition is quite empty. It is arranged in sections – with choice propaganda tit-bits on showcards, which visitors read, rarely make comments and pass on to the next section. Occasionally snatches of conversation reach Inv. – but only occasionally. The most popular exhibit is on the first floor – a desk with about a dozen telephones. Over the desk is this poster, 'Listen to the voice of Authority'. You pick up the receiver and listen-in to a conversation between Bureaucracy and the ordinary man-in-the-street showing how he is hedged and hampered on all sides by officialdom and Red Tape. Big Business wants a licence, accordingly he rings up – what he thinks – is the appropriate dept. But there he's wrong. He's told by the dept. he's just 'phoned that they no longer deal with this matter. If he will ring up such-and-such a dept. in the Ministry of X they might be able to help him. And he does, but at this dept. he's told the matter has been transferred to X dept. of Ministry XYZ. Big business after much difficulty contacts them. And so the snowball grows. Big business can get no satisfaction whatever and finally drops the matter. It's really quite funny. Most people listening smile. Parts of it ring true. The different men on the phone speak in beautifully cultured voices – even minor clerks (before they put you on to the big bosses).

The showcards in one section of the exhibition give a sly poke in the ribs at the old school tie, and one learns with satisfaction that such exponents of socialism as Attlee, Cripps, Hugh Dalton, Crossman and Noel-Baker dared to tread the paths of Eton, Winchester, and suchlike Public Schools. And, moreover, we are told that journalists like Frank Owen, Hugh Cudlipp, Cassandra, Hannen Swaffer mislead the people by putting 'socialistic' propaganda across to them.

And this is what they have to say about Penguins:

PENGUIN SPECIALS BROKE INTO A NEW BOOK-READING MARKET. MILLIONS OF PEOPLE IN THIS COUNTRY WHO HAD NEVER BEEN TOUCHED BY SOCIALISTIC PROPAGANDA OR BY THE LABOUR PARTY FOUND THEMSELVES GUIDED DAILY TO THE LEFT BY THEIR READING.

Some overheards:

M and F25B stand in front of the section dealing with Education – showing what the Conservatives have done in this direction.

M25B: 'Admittedly they've done more, because they've been in more often – they've had the longer run.'
F25B: 'Perfectly true.'

(Inv. nearly collapsed. She could have sworn they looked out-and-out Conservatives.)

M25B: standing in front of a poster dealing with the raising of the social standard in the Cotton Mills as a direct result of Conservative legislation.

M25B: 'It was only since the rise and growth of Socialism – they were obliged to.'

And F30B looking at T.U. Representation. Acts 1824, 1869, 1859, and 1879: 'They're careful not to mention it – they don't want to.'

And mocking the 'old school tie':

M30B: 'That's very comical; they shouldn't make capital out of it.'
M25B: 'They must have gate-crashed.'

M and F25B observed buying a copy of the 'Industrial Charter' F20B – looking very decorative – asks Inv. if she'd like a copy. When refused she doesn't press her to buy one.

The exhibition might have been more convincing if the propaganda hadn't been smothered with so much pink icing – if they'd given a little bit of credit to some other party – all this sugary sweetness left one feeling bilious. Judging from the overheards it seems that a surprisingly large proportion of visitors were of different political beliefs.

VII
Epilogue

Peace brought problems of readjustment to Mass-Observation. Harrisson returned briefly after the war, could not settle down in Britain, and went back to the Far East. From 1947 to 1966 he was curator of the Sarawak Museum and government ethnologist. (He added archaeology to his self-taught accomplishments and became, amongst other things, an expert on turtles.) Others struggled on Mass-Observation's behalf to capture part of the booming market for market research itself. In 1949, Tom Harrisson relinquished his rights in Mass-Observation while keeping ultimate control of all the material already gathered. Mass-Observation Ltd was founded; a company engaged in market research with a residual commitment to the 'qualitative', as opposed to 'quantitative' methods of investigation which had thrilled Leonard England and Mollie Tarrant in younger days.

In May 1946 Mass-Observation's attention was drawn to the widespread defacement of a road safety poster issued by the Ministry of Transport. The poster, which depicted the head of a woman in black ('The Black Widow'), had apparently attracted such hostile graffiti that the Mass-Observers were prompted to investigate further and to speculate on the unforeseen significance which such an image appeared to have in post-war Britain.

A fascination with public images was not new to Mass-Observation. The recording of visual representations of ideas and meanings was regarded as an integral part of the Worktown Study. Posters, signs and graffiti were the subjects of several of Humphrey Spender's Worktown photographs, for example. The influences of surrealism led Charles Madge and his colleagues at the London end of early Mass-Observation to be similarly concerned with imagery. They asked the volunteer Observers to keep a kind of iconographic diary in which to record 'dominant images' – gestures, dreams, daydreams, shapes, symbols, graffiti, paintings and scenes – anything, in fact, which had had a visual impact on the Observer. This somewhat abstract interest was superseded by a more pragmatic approach during the Second World War when Mass-Observation studied the effectiveness of war-time propaganda – films, exhibitions, advertisements and poster campaigns. The Mass-Observation team had gained considerable experience of this kind of work, therefore, before tackling the enigmatic Black Widow.

The article below is taken from an unpublished history of Mass-Observation which was written by H.D. (Bob) Willcock some two years after the original study was made. Bob Willcock joined Mass-Observation in 1941 and was the author of a number of its publications down to 1948, when he left to join the Government Social Survey unit. His poor health prevented him from being called up and when Tom Harrisson left England in 1944, Bob Willcock took over the direction of the research. He became a central figure in the organisation and brought with him rigour and academicism which were not always present in Harrisson's work. He remained, however, committed to the original aims of Mass-Observation and wrote in 1943 in a paper on the methodology of Mass-Observation for the *American Journal of Sociology*, 'Opinion sampling methods are employed but the techniques of observation and subjective accounts are being more and more depended upon for the recording of social change in Britain at deeper and more significant levels.'

It seems fitting to end with a pleasantly written, unexpected piece by a man who did so much for Mass-Observation.

46. Bob Willcock: Merry and Black – a post-war interlude

Many years hence a social historian, trying to reconstruct the mood of the British people on the threshold of the atomic age, may pause and puzzle over the London *Times* file for May 1946. There he will find a very serious controversy raging on the subject of a poster designed to reduce the number of accidents on the roads of Britain.

The poster depicted the head of a middle-aged woman. The face, turned full towards the spectator, was entirely devoid of colour. The lips were thin, the eyes staring, and the woman wore a black hat with black drapings.

Ordinary men and women at that time were well accustomed to the sight of dead, mutilated, tortured and starving bodies. Public exhibitions and films depicting the horror camp at Belsen drew large audiences; photographs in the newspapers of Mussolini's corpse suspended head down before the crowd surpassed the most vivid records of death published during the war years. More recently still, posters portraying pot-bellied children and emaciated mothers from the famine-stricken countries of the world were frequently to be seen in public places. In Oxford Street, London, every day for a year at that time, ordinary citizens had been paying their sixpences to see a waxwork exhibition where 'All the Horrors of the Concentration Camp' were displayed lifesize in realistic detail.

Recalling all this, the historian may think it strange that a public inured to suffering on an unprecedented and world-wide scale should display such concern over a white-faced woman on the hoardings. But was the general public really so interested, he may ask, or did the protest come only from a serious-minded minority among the readers of that most serious of daily newspapers, the *Times*?

He will search the files of some more popular journals, where he will discover that, among newspapermen at least, the poster had seemed worthy of very widespread comment. Shortly after its appearance one paper had christened it 'The Black Widow', and that name had been taken up by others. A Black Widow is an alarming and venomous spider. The name was appropriate rather to the perpetrator of disaster than to its victim.

Musing on the significance of this aggressively-turned antithesis, two things may occur to the historian. He may ask himself why people should have *wished* to think of this sad-faced suffering woman as a death-dealing object, instead of in her realistic status of death-dealt subject. And, his mind set on antithesis, he may think of another famous widow of earlier, more carefree days.

From published sources he will not be able to trace the story much further. He will be left with the feeling that here is a phenomenon of some significance whose meaning has been lost, a curious symbolic outbreak of emotion which, from the available data, he is unable to explain.

Had he been living at the time of this controversy and had chanced to pass through Tottenham Court Road subway station at the end of May 1946, another scrap of evidence would have set him thinking. In the passage-way, scrawled in large lipstick letters over one of the white faces, he would have seen the words 'THE MERRY WIDOW'. And below, next to the platform, two more of the faces had been made up with rouge, lipstick and eyeblack, carefully and painstakingly, with no sign of satirical intent.

Poster defacement, the smashing of electric light bulbs and public telephones, the slashing of public seats and straps, and the stealing of useless objects from public places, were common enough activities in England at that time. Nevertheless, had our historian counted a sample series of 500 posters of all kinds in accessible positions near subway platforms he would have found rather less than one in ten defaced in any way; whereas of 200 'Black Widows', in similar positions, 58 per cent were defaced.

Of these defacements, half were pictorial images in pencil, lipstick and chalk; one-fifth were undecipherable scribbles, lines and crosses; one in seven were written remarks and comments; one in seven were of other types – slashes, scratches, tears, and imprints of boots and shoes.

In one case out of five the implement used to deface the poster was lipstick, an expensive item at the time. Most other pictorial defacements were in pencil, the favourite additions being moustaches, glasses and monocles, and beards, in that order of frequency. These pencil defacements were similar to those which appeared on other contemporary posters, but in other respects defacement of this poster was peculiar.

Written comments were very various, but showed common trends, e.g. –

1. 'Beware Boys!'
2. 'V.D.' (in large letters across the face).
3. 'Blimey, it gives you the creeps.'
4. 'Dr Livingstone, I presume.'
5. 'The Ghost.'
6. '. . . is dead'.

And, of a series of Black Widow Chads – *

7. 'Wot no lipstick, rouge or powder?'
8. 'Wot no mouth?'
9. 'Wot no ambulance?'
10. 'Wot no husbin'? Ain't it a shime, eh? Ain't it a shime?'

Large pencil tears fell down the cheeks of one Widow, with the word 'sperlash!' scrawled at the foot of the poster.

Defacements grouped themselves almost automatically into three types –

1. *Scared and Aggressive* ('V.D.', 'The Ghost', 'Beware!'). Footprints on the widow's face occurred quite often, and it is not easy to kick a poster at eye level on a concave wall. About one in

* 'Chad' was a contemporary stereotype of popular caricature whose origin is obscure. He appeared always with half his face peering over a fence or wall, his fingers grasping it on each side. And his scrawled comment was always 'Wot, no . . .?'

twenty-five of the posters defaced were simply crossed out, deliberately, with a thick straight line or a big black cross. In other cases eyes were gouged out.

2. *Humorous and Satirical.* These showed a tendency to minimise the suffering of the woman depicted by making light of it. One has only to think of the unlikelihood of 'Wot, no bread?' being written under the picture of a starving mother, to find the prevalence of comparably callous humour under the picture of a bereaved woman superficially surprising.
3. *Resuscitatory.* The outstanding type of defacement was the addition of colour to the woman's face, an attempt, as it were, to turn the Black Widow into a Merry Widow (or to bring the corpse back to life). This was often done very elaborately, and frequently without any trace of humorous intent. Considerable patience and time was spent over these, especially in one case, on an outdoor hoarding, where a ladder must have been used to reach the lips of a large-size poster.

In London, after the poster had been on display for three weeks, four out of five people recalled seeing it when it was described to them as the 'poster of a white-faced woman in black', and of these 96 per cent knew what it was advertising. This is a phenomenal statistical 'success' for a single poster. A contemporary Mass-Observation survey on a commercial poster which had been far more widely displayed over a much longer period showed only about one person in five who could recall having seen it when it was described to them, and less than half who recalled noticing it when an actual specimen was shown them on a nearby site.

What was there about the Widow which made her so 'successful'?

Among the general public the most usual feeling was that the poster *must* be effective propaganda because people were talking about it. Many commented: 'It's awful – you can't miss it', or 'You've *got* to look at it.' But though nearly everyone who had seen it knew what it advertised, very few commented directly on its suitability for that purpose. They were too concerned about expressing a more general reaction.

One person in three objected that it 'gave them the willies', was weird, creepy, grim, ghastly, hideous, ugly. Most seemed to feel strongly about it, but others said defensively, – 'It doesn't worry me', – as if they felt they might be failing in their social duty.

One young woman commented: 'Oh, I thought it was death warmed up looking at me.' And an old man: 'It's a wonderful representation of death as we see it.'

A correspondent to the *Times* reported that he had been 'labouring under the delusion that the poster depicted an actual victim', and several members of the ordinary public mentioned the same idea. Belief that the picture represented a corpse is interesting for its inherent improbability. There may be a clue buried in this misapprehension, which it often did not occur to people to question. Consider this too: 'A friend of mine – an old chap of about 70 – had an accident in his car and killed his wife. And right opposite his window is one of those damned Merry Widows.'

Why should the picture of a living widow remind a *widower* of his dead wife? And why, too, was it always assumed that the woman *was* a widow? Why not a bereaved mother? It was children, not husbands, who most often got killed on the road.

But it was husbands and lovers who got killed on the battlefield. During the previous six years most people had either been actively associated with killing, or had passively sanctioned it. The communal conscience was in an eruptive state. If some psychiatric laboratory had been called upon to synthesize a symbol of war-guilt, designed to bring embarrassingly near the surface those feelings which had so cunningly been suppressed since 1939, what could have been more appropriate than 'these damned Merry Widows' playing peek-a-boo with the nation's pre-conscious round every corner?

Suppose for a moment that was the real explanation of this curious minor episode in social history: people reacted so strongly to the white-faced 'widow' because they felt vicariously responsible for her predicament. How might they be expected to have dealt with this unacknowledged feeling of guilt and remorse?

There would have been three ways of tackling it. First, it would have scared them, and they would have tried to fight it down, pretend it wasn't there. They would have been indignant and aggressive toward an object which they felt a menace to their emotional stability and security. Hence the appropriateness of the name 'Black Widow', the poisonous spider of conscience, waiting to catch post-war minds off their guard and to exact vengeance for deeds done. Hence the slogans of fear – 'V.D.', 'The Ghost', 'Beware Boys.' And hence the heavy cancellings-out, pretending it didn't exist; the kicks and the eye-gougings, fighting it down. The strong feelings of the old man who had run over his wife and killed her would exemplify the same process very clearly. Here was his wife returned from the dead – a widow! It was his turn to be killed. 'These damned Merry Widows!'

If this treatment failed, instead of kicking against them, people might have attempted to make the pricks less sharp. After all, death must come to everyone; bereavement feels bad for a while, but time will heal; we're all in the same boat, and we've all got to make light of tragedy these days. By diffusing the guilt they might have hoped to minimise not only their personal discomfort but the extent of suffering inflicted, too. 'Wot, no mouth, no make-up, no ambulance, no husbin'?' 'Sperlash!' We're all missing something we used to have and love these days, and it's nobody's fault. We're all a bit pale and worn and there's nothing we can do about it except take it in the right spirit; 'Hello, paleface. Dr Livingstone I presume.' We may all be murderers, but we're all victims too. This grim joke's on us as well; let's forget it.

There was a third possibility, if rationalisation failed. To look the problem in the face, reorientate and atone. Can one read into the loving care with which post-war lipstick and rouge was lavished on the Black Widow an early indication that post-war rationalisations of war-time behaviour were breaking down; an as yet inarticulate desire to face the facts and devote some energy to putting the colour back into the pale features of the millions who had suffered during six years' suspension of the communal conscience? Or was this, too, only a desire to hide up the ugly facts, a slightly different technique for pretending it hadn't happened . . .?

A social historian fifty years hence, trying to build up a theory from the tenuous material at his disposal, might meditate along these lines. Perhaps his ideas would contain a grain of truth, perhaps not.

But we have pursued this phantom far enough, perhaps, to indicate the need for a closer liaison between those organisations, societies and groups, which are at present studying the society in which we live; and in which, unless we achieve greater communal insight soon, we seem all liable prematurely to die.

VIII

The Tom Harrisson Mass-Observation Archive

The Mass-Observation Archive is a charitable trust in the care of the University of Sussex Library. It is open to all researchers provided that they comply with the conditions safeguarding the collections. Access is granted at the discretion of the archivist on behalf of the Trustees. Applications to consult the Archive should be addressed to the archivist. Researchers are asked to complete an application form stating their research interests and giving the signature of a sponsor or supervisor.

The Archive is normally open to researchers during both term time and vacation except for statutory holidays and University closure days.

The Archive Trust retains copyright over all Mass-Observation material and reserves the right to make special contracts where necessary. The usual acknowledgements of the use of the Mass-Observation material are required in any work and the Trustees would be pleased to accept a copy of any work in which substantial use has been made of Mass-Observation material. Mass-Observation has always respected the confidentiality of the volunteer contributors. Researchers are therefore asked to consult the archivist about the use of real names and other identifiable biographical information.

Address:
The Tom Harrisson Mass-Observation Archive
The Library
The University of Sussex
Falmer
Brighton BN1 9QL
East Sussex
Tel. 0273 606755

The Tom Harrisson Mass-Observation Archive

The records of Mass-Observation

The records of Mass-Observation were brought to the University of Sussex in 1970 by Tom Harrisson at the invitation of the then Vice-Chancellor of the University, Professor Asa Briggs. Tom Harrisson established the records as a research archive for historians and other scholars engaged in the study of British social history during the late 1930s and the 1940s.

The Archive was officially opened in October 1975 when it became a charitable Trust in the care of the University. Sadly, only three months later, Professor Harrisson was killed in an accident while he was travelling in South-East Asia. The Directorship of the Archive was taken over by David Pocock, Professor of Social Anthropology.

In 1977, the Social Science Research Council awarded a three-year grant to the Archive to support a conservation programme and the arrangement and description of the records. Since the end of that programme, the sorting work has continued on a more modest scale and major sections of the Archive have been microfilmed or photocopied. It has also been possible to employ the skills of a specialist document repairer to clean, de-acidify and laminate very severely damaged papers.

The Archive consists of two types of material, each reflecting the different methods which Mass-Observation used to develop the 'anthropology of ourselves'. On the one hand there are boxes of records resulting from the work carried out by the full-time investigators, usually arranged according to subject matter: WORKTOWN PROJECT, TOPIC COLLECTIONS. On the other hand there are boxes of personal diaries and various kinds of reports sent in by volunteer Observers: DIARIES, DIRECTIVES, DAY SURVEYS.

THE WORKTOWN PROJECT 1937–1940

Between 1937 and 1940, Mass-Observation conducted a major study of the towns of Bolton and Blackpool in Lancashire. The team of investigators, which was originally led by Tom Harrisson and later by Charles Madge, was made up of students, artists and writers, photographers, unemployed workers and local people. The project was based in a house in Davenport Street, Bolton. A wide range of subjects was covered including religious practices, political activities, saving and spending habits, the cotton industry, leisure pursuits (going to pubs, sport, gambling, cinema, dancing, etc.), housing and public amenities. The study resulted in the accumulation of sixty-four storage boxes of material, sixteen of these relating to Blackpool and the study of holiday behaviour. The material is composed mostly of reports by observers – accounts of behaviour and conversations, descriptions of places and events – but also includes leaflets, posters, tickets, brochures and other ephemera. A collection of over 300 photographs taken by Humphrey Spender as part of the project is also held at the Archive.

Only one contemporary published work based on the Worktown study ever appeared, *The Pub and the People* (Gollancz, 1943). This book was republished in 1970 by Seven Dials Press with a new introduction by Tom Harrisson and it included some of Humphrey Spender's photographs. A repeat investigation undertaken in 1959 resulted in the publication of *Britain Revisited*. Since the Archive has been established a number of other publications have appeared, notably *Worktown People*.

A handlist for this collection is available for consultation at the Archive.

FILE REPORTS 1937–1951

Mass-Observation regularly produced typewritten reports which summarised their investigations. These reports (FRs) proved a useful introduction to the Mass-Observation records. They were nearly all written by full-time personnel and vary both in length and in the depth with which individual topics are treated. There are over 3,000 File Reports and they take the following forms:

Reports on M-O investigations: descriptions of method, questions asked, results and conclusions.

Letters or Directives (monthly questionnaires) sent to members of the volunteer Panel of observers and diarists.

Bulletins (duplicated or printed) for internal circulation and to provide members of the volunteer Panel and others with information about M-O's activities. This includes the printed news sheet *Us* which was produced during 1940.

Analysis of Directive replies received from the Panel.

Edited extracts from the M-O diaries.

Scripts for radio broadcasts usually given by Tom Harrisson.

Draft copies and printed versions of articles submitted by M-O to newspapers, magazines and journals.

Draft manuscripts of books both published and unpublished by M-O.

Reports prepared for outside bodies (e.g. for the Ministry of Information on civilian morale).

Articles *not* written by M-O but incorporated into the files for references (e.g. War-time Social Survey reports).

The File Reports are arranged and listed chronologically and a handlist is available which also contains a subject index. The original file numbers have been retained.

DAY SURVEYS, TIME CHARTS AND DIRECTIVE REPLIES 1937–8

While Tom Harrisson was running the Worktown Project in Bolton, Charles Madge and his colleagues began to recruit voluntary observers from their London base at Blackheath (Charles Madge's home). In February 1937 the first batch of contributions from an assorted panel of writers was received by this 'wing' of M-O. Madge asked people to record in detail their activities on the twelfth day of each month. As Mass-Observation became more widely known, the Panel grew. By the end of 1937, more than 500 people had participated in the Day Survey Project.

On the day George VI was crowned, 12 May, Mass-Observation investigators were sent into the streets of London to record public behaviour and to distribute questionnaires saying 'Where were you on May 12th?'. The results of these two studies were combined with the personal diaries written by the Panel for that day to form an anthology, *May 12th Mass-Observation Day Surveys* (Faber & Faber 1937).

In addition to the reports for the twelfth day of the month, M-O began to collect other information from the Panel. Reports were requested on people's activities on particular days (Armistice Day, Christmas Day) and on special topics such as reading habits, friendship networks, smoking and drinking habits, dreams and why people volunteered to help M-O.

By February 1938, the Twelfth Day Surveys had been discontinued; attention was focused on special days – Bank Holidays, Armistice Day, etc. Time sheets were sent to members of the Panel so that fairly precise accounts of how they spent their day could be made. At the same time, M-O began to ask for people's opinions about the political crisis of 1938.

By 1939, the volunteer Panel was performing two tasks: the recording of their personal lives (hence the full diaries which began in August 1939) and the answering of questions about specific topics each month (hence the regular Directive replies).

A useful summary of M-O's early work appears in *First Year's Work* (Lindsay Drummond, 1938) and also in *Britain* (Penguin Special, 1939), both by Mass-Observation.

The Twelfth Day Surveys are arranged in monthly batches on microfilm. Within these batches, the Surveys from men precede those from women; they are arranged alphabetically by surname of writer. Biographical information about the writers is available. The Time Sheets and Directive Replies for 1938–9 are similarly arranged but have not been microfilmed to date.

DIARIES, 1939–1963

About 500 men and women at one time or another during this period kept personal diaries which they sent to Mass-Observation in monthly instalments. Not all of them wrote at the same time and although some people maintained a regular diary for several years, other diarists tended to write either intermittently or for one short period. After 1945 most of the contributors discontinued their diaries although a few did carry on into the post-war years and the last diary instalment received is dated 1963. One of these diaries has been edited for publication (*Nella Last's War*). No special instructions were given to the diarists except that they were encouraged to write about their personal lives rather than recount military or political news.

The diaries fill 160 storage boxes but have been microfilmed in monthly batches. Within each batch, the diaries written by men precede those written by women. The instalments are arranged alphabetically according to surname of writer.

Biographical information is available.

DIRECTIVE REPLIES, 1939–1955

From January 1939 M-O produced a questionnaire every month which it distributed to members of the volunteer Panel. The questionnaire, which was called a Directive, was usually printed or duplicated together with a Bulletin which provided the volunteer Observers with information about M-O's activities.

Over 3,000 people have been identified as having participated in this project between 1939 and 1945, although in one month the number of people replying to a single Directive was never more than 500. Many of them did not reply to more than one or two Directives but a good proportion regularly sent in detailed replies over a number of years.

Mass-Observation was partly concerned with studying civilian adaptation to war-time conditions and many of the questions deal with issues such as food and clothing rations, evacuation, air raids, housing, the forces, transport, separation from loved ones and so on. They were also concerned with people's attitudes to the news, attitudes to war-time policies, politicians and military events, other nationalities, the press and the BBC, government propaganda campaigns. Occasionally, the same questions were repeated at different stages of the war to elicit comparative material. Questions on wider issues – class, race, marriage, money, education and politics, and especially people's hopes and fears for the post-war world, were also included.

Unfortunately no material has survived for the year 1941 although there is no doubt that Directives were sent out and that replies were received.

The Directive replies received between 1939 and 1945 are now on microfilm. A chronological guide to the replies is available together with a subject index of the topics covered. Work on the post-war replies is still in progress.

TOPIC COLLECTIONS

Mass-Observation full-time personnel carried out a number of investigations on particular topics from 1937 onwards. The material resulting from these studies, which often spanned several years, consists of project plans, internal memoranda on methodology, correspondence, drafts and final versions of questionnaires, instructions to investigators, results of surveys including different kinds of interviews, reports and observations. Mass-Observation also collected press cuttings, articles, leaflets, pamphlets, posters, tickets, sketches and other ephemera relating to the themes of its investigations. A handlist has been prepared for each Topic Collection.

The following list includes the major subjects covered by M-O investigations:

Aims in life
Air raids
Antisemitism Survey
'Ask your Dad' campaign
Astrology and spiritualism
Aviation
Beaverbrook campaigns
Beveridge Report
Biddle Survey
Bird nesting
Blind people survey
Book MSS
British Legion competition
Browns of Chester
Budget enquiry
Bureaucracy
By-elections
Capital punishment
Children and education
Children's games and toys
Coal mining
Commemorative magazines
Commodities
Conscientious objectors and pacifists
Co-op survey
Demolition
Dreams
Drink
East End survey
Exhibitions
Family life

Famous people
Films
Food
Forces (men)
Fuel
Gallup and BIPO cuttings
Gambling
Gas masks
General elections
Graduate survey
Happiness
Health
Historical England
Holidays
Housing
Industry
Jokes
Juvenile delinquency
Korea study
Leisure survey
Lightship pamphlet
Littlewoods survey
Live entertainment
Mass-Observation
Money matters
Morale
Music, jazz and dancing
Naming a shelter competition
Newspapers
News quotas
Party games
Peace and the public
Personal appearance and clothes
Photography
Police reports
Political attitudes and behaviour
Postcards
Posters
Post-war surveys (misc)
Press and Advertising
Propaganda
Public politeness
Radio listening
Reading
Reconstruction
Rediffusion

Religion
Royalty
Savings
Science
Sexual behaviour
Shopping
Smoking
Societies
Sport
Squatters
Town surveys
Transport and railways
Voting attitudes
Victory parades
Wall chalkings and war graffiti
War grumbles
Women in war-time
Work, employment, registration and demobilisation
World organisation
World outlook survey
Youth

The contents of these boxes vary a great deal and researchers are advised to enquire at the Archive for further details on any of the above subjects.

There is a complete set of Mass-Observation publications at the Archive and these are available for consultation but not for loan. Most of the books are held in the main University of Sussex Library.

Bibliography

MASS-OBSERVATION PUBLICATIONS

1937 *Mass-Observation* by Charles Madge and Tom Harrisson with a cover designed by Humphrey Jennings. Introduction by Julian Huxley (Frederick Muller).

1937 *May 12th Mass-Observation Day Surveys*, an account of Coronation Day edited by Humphrey Jennings and Charles Madge with T. O. Beachcroft, Julian Blackburn, William Empson, Stuart Legg and Kathleen Raine (Faber & Faber).

1938 *First Year's Work* by Charles Madge and Tom Harrisson. Postscript by B. Malinowski (Lindsay Drummond).

1939 *Britain* by Charles Madge and Tom Harrisson (Penguin Special).

1940 *War Begins at Home* (Chatto & Windus).

1941 *Clothes Rationing* (Advertising Service Guild Bulletin, Change No. 1).

1941 *Home Propaganda* (A.S.G. Bulletin, Change No. 2).
1941 *A Savings Survey* (A.S.G.)
1942 *People in Production* (Penguin Special, also A.S.G. Bulletin, Change No. 3).
1943 *War Factory* (Gollancz).
1943 *People's Homes* (A.S.G. Bulletin, Change No. 4).
1943 *The Pub and the People* (Gollancz).
1944 *The Journey Home* (A.S.G.).
1945 *Britain and Her Birthrate* (A.S.G.).
1947 *Puzzled People* (Gollancz).
1947 *Browns of Chester* (Lindsay Drummond).
1947 *Exmoor Village* by W. J. Turner with photographs by John Hinde (Harrap).
1947 *Peace and the Public* (Longmans).
1948 *Juvenile Delinquency* (Falcon).
1949 *The Press and Its Readers* (Art & Technics).
1949 *Meet Yourself on Sunday*, with illustrations by Ronald Searle (Naldrett).
1949 *Meet Yourself at the Doctor's*, with illustrations by Ronald Searle (Naldrett).
1949 *People and Paint* (ICI Publications).
1950 *Voters' Choice* (Art & Technics).
1961 *Britain Revisited* by Tom Harrisson with Leonard England, Celia Fremlin, Bill Naughton, Humphrey Spender, John Sommerfield, Mollie Tarrant, Julian Trevelyan and Woodrow Wyatt. Photographs by Humphrey Spender and Michael Wickham (Gollancz).
1966 *Long to Reign Over Us* by Leonard Harris, based on research by Mollie Tarrant (William Kimber).
1971 *The Pub and the People*, reprinted with a new introduction by Tom Harrisson and including photographs taken by Humphrey Spender (Seven Dials).

Unless otherwise stated, these books were written by Mass-Observation collectively and can usually be found under 'Mass-Observation' in the author catalogue in libraries.

RECENT PUBLICATIONS

The following books have been prepared in collaboration with the Mass-Observation Archive:

Broad, Richard and Fleming, Suzie (eds): *Nella Last's War*, Falling Wall Press, 1981 and Sphere, 1983. An edited version of a diary written for Mass-Observation.
Harrisson, Tom, *Living Through the Blitz*, Collins, 1976 and Penguin, 1978.

Harrisson, Tom and Spender, Humphrey, *Britain in the Thirties – Worktown by Camera*, Unicorn Press, Royal College of Art, 1975, limited edition.
Sheridan, D., *Mass-Observation File Reports 1937–42: An Annotated List with Index*, pamphlet available from the Archive.
Spender, Humphrey, *Worktown*, catalogue to the exhibition of Worktown photographs taken by H.S. with an introduction by David Mellor, University of Sussex, 1977. Available from the Archive.
Spender, Humphrey, *Worktown People, Photographs from Northern England 1937–8*, edited by Jeremy Mulford, Falling Wall Press, 1982.
Ziegler, Philip, *The Crown and the People*, Collins, 1978.

For critical accounts of Mass-Observation's history and considerations of Mass-Observation as a historical source:

Calder, Angus, 'Mass-Observation 1937–39', paper for the 150th anniversary of the British Association for the Advancement of Science, Sept. 1981.
Calder, Angus, *The Mass-Observers*, Cape (in preparation).
Chaney, Dave, 'A Public Imagery: Mass-Observation and the Coronation of 1937', unpublished paper, Dept. Sociology, University of Durham, 1977.
Chaney, Dave, 'Art and social responsibility: Charles Madge, poet and sociologist' in *Social Roles for Artists*, Liverpool University, 1979.
Dingwall, Robert, 'Research Note, thirty years on' in *Sociology of Health and Illness*, Vol. 1, No. 3, Dec. 1979.
Hynes, Samuel, *The Auden Generation*, Bodley Head, 1976.
Jeffery, Tom, *Mass-Observation, a Short History*, Occasional Paper No. 55, Centre for Contemporary Cultural Studies, University of Birmingham, 1978.
Laing, Stuart, 'Presenting "Things as they are": John Sommerfield's *May Day* and Mass-Observation' in *Class Culture and Social Change*, ed. by Frank Gloversmith, Harvester Press, 1980.
McLaine, Ian, *The Ministry of Morale*, Allen & Unwin, 1979.
McPherson, Don, 'Nation, mandate, memory' in *Camerawork*, No. 11, Half Moon Photography Workshop, Sept. 1978.
Mellor, David, 'Mass-Observation: the intellectual climate' in *Camerawork*.
Picton, Tom, 'A very public espionage' in *Camerawork*.
Rhode, Eric, *The Tower of Babel*, Weidenfeld & Nicholson, 1966.
Stanley, Nick, *The Extra Dimension: A Study and Assessment of the Methods Employed by Mass-Observation in its First Period 1937–40*, PhD thesis (CNAA), 1981.
Tarrant, Mollie, *Interpreting Public Attitudes*, Walter Thompson, 1978.
Thomas, Graham and Shannon, Chris Z., *Reconstructing Old Times – Problems and Possibilities of a Qualitative Use of Mass-Observation's Diaries*, unpublished paper, Science Policy Research Unit, 1981.

Tomlinson, Alan and Tomlinson, Mary: *Mass-Observation Surveys: Insights into Culture and Leisure*, unpublished report for the Sports Council, 1981.

Worpole, Ken, 'Oppositional culture: yesterday and today' in *Camerawork*.

For examples of the use of Mass-Observation as a historical resource, see:

Addison, Paul, *The Road to 1945*, Cape, 1975.

Balfour, Michael, *Propaganda in War 1939–45*, Routledge & Kegan Paul, 1979.

Briggs, Susan, *Keep Smiling Through*, Weidenfeld & Nicolson, 1975.

Brown, R. Douglas, *East Anglia 1940*, Dalton, 1981.

Calder, Angus, *The People's War*, Cape, 1969 and Panther, 1971.

Collier, Richard, *1940*, Hamish Hamilton, 1979 and *The World in Flames*, Penguin, 1980 and *The Road to Pearl Harbour*, Atheneum, 1981.

Croucher, Richard, *Engineers at War 1939–45*, Merlin Press, 1982.

Deighton, Len, *The Battle of Britain*, Cape, 1980.

Hewison, Robert, *Under Siege: Literary Life in London 1939–45*, Weidenfeld & Nicholson, 1978.

Longmate, Norman, *How We Lived Then*, Hutchinson, 1971.

Marwick, Arthur, *The Home Front*, Thomas & Hudson, 1976 and *Class: Image and Reality*, Collins, 1980.

Minns, Raynes, *Bombers and Mash, The Domestic Front 1939–45*, Virago, 1980.

Mosley, Leonard, *Backs to the Wall*, Weidenfeld & Nicholson, also published as *London under Fire*, Pan, 1974.

Parker, Derek, *Astrology*, Eyre & Spottiswoode, 1970.

Skidelsky, Robert, *Oswald Mosley*, Macmillan, 1975.

Summerfield, Penny, *Women Workers in the Second World War*, D. Phil thesis, Sussex, 1982.

Wainwright, Martin, *The Bath Blitz*, pamphlet, 1980.

Ziegler, Philip, *The Crown and the People*, Collins, 1978.

For contemporary accounts of Mass-Observation and the memoirs of people associated with it, see:

Gascoyne, David, *Journal 1936–7*, Enitharmon Press, 1980.

Green, T., *The Adventurers*, Michael Joseph, 1970, contains a chapter on Tom Harrisson.

Greene, Graham, *The Confidential Agent*, Heinemann, 1939.

Hodges, Sheila, *Gollancz – The Story of a Publishing House*, Gollancz, 1978.

Jennings, Mary Lou (ed.), *Humphrey Jennings: Filmmaker, Painter, Poet*, British Film Institute, 1982.

Madge, Charles, 'The birth of Mass-Observation' in the *Times Literary Supplement*, 5 November 1976.

Mitchison, Naomi, *You May Well Ask: A Memoir 1920–40*, Gollancz, 1979.
Muggeridge, Malcolm, *The Thirties*, Collins, 1969.
Raine, Kathleen, *The Land Unknown*, Hamish Hamilton, 1973.
Rolfe, C. H., *Kingsley*, Gollancz, 1973.
Spender, Humphrey, 'Humphrey Spender: M-O Photographer', Interview by Derek Smith and Tom Picton in *Camerawork*, No. 11, Sept. 1978.
Symons, Julian, *The Thirties*, Cresset Press, 1960.
Trevelyan, Julian, *Indigo Days*, McGibbon & Kee, 1957.
Wyatt, Woodrow, *Into This Dangerous World*, Weidenfeld & Nicholson, 1952.

Other material held at Archive

MARY ADAMS PAPERS

In 1976 Mrs Mary Adams donated approximately 100 boxes of her personal papers to the Mass-Observation Archive. Mrs Adams was a personal friend of Tom Harrisson and her papers cover the same period in which Mass-Observation was active. The collection falls into the following main groups:

1. Personal correspondence 1941–58.
2. Ministry of information papers: letters and memoranda from the period of Mrs Adams' position as Head of Home Intelligence, 1939–41.
3. BBC papers: correspondence, scripts, notes, internal memoranda and photographs 1925–58. Mrs Adams was a broadcaster 1925–30, a TV producer 1936–9, in North American broadcasting 1942–5, Head of Talks and Current Affairs 1945–54, Assistant to the Controller of TV Programmes 1954–8. She was also a member of the ITA. Her papers include information about her visits to North America 1951 and to the USSR 1958 and also include material on women's programmes, programmes about health and mental health and on medical issues generally.
4. National organisations: Mrs Adams was an active member of various organisations during the 1950s and 1960s, including the Consumers Association (she was Deputy Chairman 1958–70), the National Council for the Unmarried Mother and her Child, the National Association for Mental Health.
5. Printed material: pamphlets, maps, journals, magazines, leaflets, etc. relating to the above organisations.

This material is gradually being sorted. For more detailed information, please enquire at the Archive.

GEOFFREY GORER PAPERS

Geoffrey Gorer presented to the Mass-Observation Archive the papers relating to his publications. These are:

1. *Exploring English Character*: 42 boxes of completed questionnaires on family composition, housing, leisure activities, the Forces, sex, love and marriage, the police, religion, belief in luck and the supernatural, child-rearing, etc. The questionnaires were distributed in 1950 to readers of the *People*.
2. *Death, Grief and Mourning*: typed interviews and notes, 1965; 5 boxes.
3. *Sex and Marriage in Britain Today*: typed interviews and notes, 1971; 3 boxes.
4. *Television and the English*: 1 box.

PRINTED MATERIAL

Collections of printed material have been accepted as additions to the main Archive where they complement existing papers. We hold an almost complete run of *Which*? the Consumers Association publication which was donated by Mr and Mrs Moffatt; small runs of newspapers and cuttings; war-time and post-war political pamphlets, official histories of the Forces, mostly published by the Ministry of Information and covering the Second World War; books and articles relating to either the war period or to Mass-Observation donated by the authors.

PARKER PAPERS

Mr and Mrs Derek Parker donated their personal papers relating to their careers as writers and broadcasters 1960–75 and their family correspondence 1950–75. They have promised further donations.

READERS' LETTERS TO NEWSPAPERS AND RADIO

Since 1981, the Archive has been collecting batches of letters sent to national and local newspapers and to BBC Radio by members of the public. These letters cover a very wide range of topics but there is a tendency for writers to concentrate on current news. The material is arranged chronologically and names and addresses are kept confidential. This material is not yet available for consultation.

PERSONAL PAPERS

A number of individuals have donated small collections of personal papers to the Archive. These include account books, sometimes dating back as far as the 1930s, the papers of former Mass-Observers, including those of Diana Brinton Lee, a secretary to the late Tom Harrisson, and a folder of letters written between 1936 and 1938 describing the adventures of Miss J. M. Douglas as she travelled round the world. Further personal diaries and correspondence have been promised to the Archive.

BBC DIARIES

A set of diaries commissioned by the BBC for their listener and viewer research work is to be deposited at the Archive shortly. These diaries cover the 1950s and 1960s and complement the Mass-Observation diaries for earlier decades.

MASS-OBSERVATION IN THE 1980S

In 1981 David Pocock, the Director of the Archive, began to recruit new volunteer Mass-Observers to record their daily lives during the recession. The new Observers respond to quarterly directives or questionnaires on housing, food prices, the standard of living, public and private services, coinage, unemployment, health and so forth. Special Directives have also been included. Topics so far include the Royal Wedding 1981, the Falkland Islands Crisis 1982 and British membership of the EEC. This material is not yet available for consultation.